LOCUTIONS
TO THE
WORLD

VOLUME FOUR

LOCUTIONS
TO THE
WORLD

VOLUME FOUR
JANUARY 31, 2014 TO DECEMBER 31, 2014

THE TWO HEARTS SPEAK TO THE WORLD

LOCUTIONS TO AN ANONYMOUS MYSTIC

CONTINUING THE LOCUTIONS
THAT WERE BEGUN ON
DECEMBER 10, 2010
(as recorded on www.locutions.org)

LOCUTIONS TO THE WORLD
FIRST EDITION - VOLUME FOUR

The Cover Icon

The icon on the cover bears the title *Göttesmutter Hodegetria*. The icon depicts the *Mother of God* (*Göttesmutter*) holding the Child Jesus at her side while pointing to Him as the source of salvation for mankind. *Hodegetria* (Greek: Ὁδηγήτρια) means literally: "She who shows the Way." In the Western Church this type of icon is sometimes called *Our Lady of the Way*.

The image of this icon was obtained from its iconographer, Eva-Maria Steidel and is used with her gracious permission. Ms. Steidel's iconographic work may be seen at http://www.graphicon-online.de

Volume Four

Locutions to the World: The Two Hearts Speak to the World
January 31, 2014 to December 31, 2014
ISBN-13   978-1500218386

Volume One

Locutions to the World: Let the Word Go Forth
Dec. 10, 2010 to December 17, 2011
ISBN-13   978-1500582685

Volume Two

Locutions to the World: Let the Word Go Forth
December 18, 2011 to October 28, 2012
ISBN-13   978-1500592172

Volume Three

Locutions to the World: The Two Hearts Speak to the World
July 14, 2012 to Jan. 30, 2014
ISBN-13   978-1500593650

Published by SERVANTS PRESS
logos.institute@gmail.com

TABLE OF CONTENTS

INTRODUCTION

This is the fourth in the series of volumes collecting the *Locutions to the World* that can be currently found on the website www.locutions.org. Beginning on December 10, 2010, locutions were given by Jesus and Mary to a soul under spiritual direction by a Roman Catholic priest. These locutions were meant to be told to the whole world. The reader should be aware that these are private locutions. If they help the reader's faith, then receive them. If not, then set them aside. We are called to believe only public revelations.

To one who reads these locutions, the voice of the Blessed Virgin Mary becomes familiar. The tone is motherly, wise, prophetic and instructive, correcting and comforting all in one breath. Her voice mirrors that of the speaker in *Proverbs* (quoted below) in which Wisdom is personified, inviting all to take heed of her counsel.

Does not Wisdom call,
and understanding raise her voice?
On the top of the heights along the road,
at the crossroads she takes her stand;
By the gates at the approaches of the city,
by the entryways she cries aloud:
"To you, O men, I call:
my appeal is to the children of men.
You simple ones, gain resource,
you fools, gain sense.

"So now, O children, listen to me;
instruction and wisdom do not reject!
Happy the man who obeys me,
and happy those who keep my ways,
Happy the man watching daily at my gates,
waiting at my doorposts;
For he who finds me finds life,
and wins favor from the Lord;
But he who misses me harms himself;
All who hate me love death."
(New American Bible: Proverbs 8:1-5; 32-36)

i

December 10, 2010
Let the Word Go Forth

Mary

I will soon begin to speak to you for the whole world. You will receive these words as you have received all the other words. You will write the words down and record the proper dates. You will take these words to [your spiritual director] for his discernment. If his heart discerns that these messages should be released to the whole world, they will go forth. He will correctly say that these are being given to one of his directees. The time is short and that is why I have moved you so quickly.

Lucy's Fatima Vision

The messages in this Introduction concern the effects of the Pope's dream
that Mary revealed to the three children of Fatima (July 13, 1917).
What follows immediately below is Lucy's description of that vision
as released by the Vatican (June 2000).

We saw in an immense light that is God: "something similar to how people appear in a mirror when they pass in front of it," a Bishop dressed in white. We had the impression that it was the Holy Father. Other bishops, priests, men and women religious going up a steep mountain, at the top of which there was a big Cross of rough-hewn trunks, as of a cork-tree with the bark; before reaching there, the Holy Father passed through a big city half in ruins and half trembling with halting step, afflicted with pain and sorrow, he prayed for the souls of the corpses he met on his way; having reached the top of the mountain on his knees at the foot of the big Cross, he was killed by a group of soldiers who fired bullets and arrows at him, and in the same way, there died one after another, the other bishops, priests, men and women religious, and various lay people of different ranks and positions. Beneath the two arms of the Cross, there were two angels each with a crystal aspersorium in his hand, in which they gathered up the blood of the martyrs and with it sprinkled the souls that were making their way to God.

December 4, 2011
1. Keep Your Eye on Israel

Jesus

How long will it be? Keep your eye on Israel. This is the center. By keeping your eye on Israel you will get to know the time. Not exactly, but you will see it coming closer. The more danger there is to Israel, the closer the time will be.

I love Israel and I love Jerusalem. In Jerusalem, I shed my blood, redeemed the world and rose from the dead. It is a sealed city, sealed in my blood and in my Holy Spirit. Even more than geography, I love the Jewish people. They are my people. But Jewish lips do not call out, "Jesus is our Messiah." I like to hear these words from anyone's lips. But I have my greatest joy when I hear those words from the lips of a Jew and from the lips of Israel. This is the deepest hope of my heart.

Comment
In these locutions Israel takes center stage, both in the time frame
of events and in Jesus' heart.

Mary

I am a daughter of Israel and I dreamed of Israel gathered around the Messiah, for whom they had waited so long.

But then, what did I experience? I saw Israel reject my Son, call him a false Messiah, reject his claims and nail him to the cross. But that was only my first sorrow as a daughter of Israel. After He rose from the dead and the apostles began to preach, I held new hopes. Certainly now, Israel would accept my Son as Messiah. Instead, I experienced a second rejection. My own people did not accept Him as their Messiah. Twice, I have been broken in heart. Twice, they have rejected Jesus as Messiah. But it will not happen a third time. I look forward to the day when all of Israel will proclaim my Son as Messiah.

The moment of the greatest darkness is the moment before the greatest light. The very moment when it seems that Israel will be destroyed is the moment when I will save Israel and all will proclaim that Jesus is the Messiah. I have revealed the deepest sorrow of my heart.

Comment
Mary's two-fold sorrow brings forth a promise that this time the result will be
different. Israel's moment of greatest darkness will be the moment
when Mary rescues Israel.

February 7, 2011
2. Seeing the Future of Israel

Jesus

As I stood at the table of the Last Supper, I saw Israel. All its future history unfolded before me, the destruction of the city by the Romans, the dispersal of Israel all over the world and the moment when the Jewish people would be invited to return, as the State of Israel was formed. As they returned, all rejoiced. However, they put their trust in their own strength, as their forefathers had done. They built weapons of war and rejoiced in these weapons. They were on the wrong road, being led down a path that led into the hands of their enemies, instead of withdrawing into the safety of my arms. Now, their enemies gather arms and the tide is shifting. Their protection drops away from them. There is terror on every side and still they do not turn to Me.

Centuries ago, the Father intervened on their behalf and sent Me, hoping that all Israel would proclaim Me as Messiah. But they killed Me. What will the Father do now? He cannot send Me again to die. So, He will send My Vicar, the Pope.

The Pope will enter Jerusalem as I entered it. The city will already have suffered much and Israel will begin to despair, wondering what can be done. Then this figure clothed in white will come, sent by the Father just as He sent me. He will come to save Israel, just as I came. He too will die in Jerusalem, but his death will have a profound effect upon the whole world. For the whole world will weep at his death and his death will bless Israel. Why do I reveal these things now? Why do I bring you to the center of the mystery so quickly? Because the time is short. The events are near. They are not far away.

Comment
Jesus describes what has happened since the State of Israel was formed and why it is now prey to so many enemies. Most important, the Holy Father goes to Jerusalem, dies there, and a series of events begin that save Israel.

February 9, 2011
3. The Pope Dies in Jerusalem

Jesus

The Church came forth from Israel, like a child begotten by a mother, but Israel began to reject her own child. The soil rejected the fruit it had brought forth. Then came the saddest time of all. Israel and the Church were separated. Now they stand as

iv

distinct groups. The mother has rejected her child and the soil has rejected the roots that should have stayed within it.

Peter was the apostle to the Jews and Paul always preached first in the synagogues. The word was preached and the roots tried to enter more deeply into the soil. However, they could not pierce its resistance. Without deeper roots, the plant could not stay long in its original soil.

However, when the darkness comes and Israel is in distress, there will be a new moment. The Pope, the head of the Catholic Church, will go to Israel in its darkest hour and lay down his life for Israel. The eyes of many Jewish people will be opened. They will say, "We have been saved by the Catholic Church." The soil will be open and receptive again to the original seed. My Church and my Jewish people will be joined as I have wanted them to be for centuries.

As the Church's roots are placed once more into its original Jewish soil, the other divisions of the churches will be healed because they happened due to this first division of the Church from the Synagogue.

It will be clear to all the Christian Churches that there is a new call to unity, a call to unity at the roots and in the heart.

Churches will see what they have never seen and do what they thought they would never do. Seeing the union of Israel and the Catholic Church, they will say, "We must be one." All the barriers to unity, put up over the many centuries, will be swept away in one breath of the Spirit.

There will be the ingathering prophesied by Isaiah. All the riches of the nations will come to Israel. This will be true wealth, the spiritual wealth of all the Churches gathering as one in Jerusalem with Israel and the Catholic Church. My prayer will be fulfilled, that all would be one as the Father and I are one.

Also, the world will see something quite different, what they have never seen. They will see the Churches united and all the Churches united with Israel. The world will experience a powerful call to come out of darkness. The Church and Israel will be a light to all nations. The light will not be lessened or covered over by divisions of the Churches or divisions between the Churches and Israel. The world will not be able to escape the invitation. The unity will stand before them inviting them to accept Me as Lord.

Comment

This is extraordinary. The sacrificial death of the Pope leads to a full union between Israel and the Catholic Church which leads to a reunion of all of Christianity, planted again in the soil of Israel. This greater witness will confront the world with a more powerful invitation to accept Jesus Christ as Lord.

Mary

A moment will come when I will take my beloved son, the Pope. I will walk with him to Jerusalem. For the second time I will go to Jerusalem to witness the death of a son.

When this happens the eyes of the Jewish people will see for the first time. They will see in the Pope's death what the Catholic Church has done for them. There will be no mistake about which Church has blessed them, because it will have been done by the head of the Church and by the greatest of sacrifices. Israel will embrace the Catholic Church.

All Catholics will welcome Israel because all will have seen the decision of the Holy Father (the bishop dressed in white) to offer his life for Israel. The union between the Catholic Church and Israel will be a union of hearts brought about by the events that the whole world will have seen and can never forget.

Comment

By the Pope's death, Israel's eyes will be opened to the Catholic Church and how Catholic hearts will be opened to Israel. Both happen from the same event.

February 11, 2011

4. The Valley of Decision

Jesus

After the events of Jerusalem and the unifying of the Church with Israel, I will call all the nations into the Valley of Decision. It does not need to be a physical valley because all the nations are already linked by communications. This Valley of Decision will be a special moment in history.

Just as Israel was in the moment of distress, so the world itself will be in a moment of complete helplessness. But I will gather the nations and there will be a new breath in the air, a new opportunity, when all the nations will be united into the light. Some nations will leave the Valley and return to darkness, but most will stay in the light. Armaments will be limited. Money will be spent on food. There will be international cooperation that has been sought by many but never brought about.

I will give these blessings to all the nations in the Valley of Decision as a free gift from my hands. There will be peace and a new springtime.

Comment

This shows the effects of these events upon world leaders at a moment when all the world is in distress. The crises are solved by heaven changing hearts of world leaders. All of these locutions, extraordinary as they are, merely reveal the full effects of Lucy's vision of the death of the Holy Father (July 13, 1917).

LOCUTIONS TO THE WORLD

JANUARY 31, 2014 TO DECEMBER 31, 2014

The Road of Hope

January 31, 2014
7. The Torchlight of Hope

The Road of Hope

Mary

I will fill the whole world with hope. It will flow like a mighty river into every nation, every home and every heart. My hope will go even where evil has not been able to penetrate, getting there ahead of time and capturing the position like a mighty fortress.

All must drink deeply of these waters of hope, especially in their darkest moments. When they see no signs of success, they will drink more deeply. When a solution becomes clear, they will move forward in hope, not holding back or waiting for a better opportunity.

Hope is the virtue of now, seizing every chance to gain the far-off goal.

When hope has conquered and when the goal, no matter how small, has been gained, the heart is ready for more hope and for greater goals. This is my road of hope. No looking back. No thinking of what might have been. Not even sorrowing over missed opportunities.

The future holds much darkness. So, I must prepare a people of hope. Hope is a torchlight that I place in your hands. Never let it go out and you will always find my path.

Comment
Mary's strong words lift up everyone's heart.

February 1, 2014
8. The Milk of Hope

The Road of Hope

Mary

No need to wait for hope. It is always present. Take courage. Be stout-hearted. Hope is always available. You can grasp it at any time, like a lifeline thrown to a drowning person.

Do not look elsewhere for a better opportunity. Accept the ray of hope that I give you every moment. When you do, I will send more and more rays. Hope will grow and expand in your heart. Your feet will begin to walk, the paralysis overcome.

No more will you say, "I cannot succeed. I cannot make the goal." Hope crushes discouragement beneath its feet.

"Where will I go?" you ask. The rays of hope will provide all the light you need. Do not walk away from them. Do not set out on your own, trying to gain what is not in your power.

Can you not see? Hope is a seed that contains all that you need. It feeds you when you need strength, protects you when discouragement invades. Gives you light in your darkness. Stops you when you are going too far. I am the mother of holy hope. Come to me and I will nourish you on this saving milk.

Comment
We need so much hope. Mary says she is always providing it.

February 2, 2014
9. Hope Goes Everywhere

The Road of Hope

Mary

Whenever and wherever I come, I always bring hope. I am the mother of holy hope, and my children are without number. I bring fearlessness in the face of great odds. I bring patience when suffering seems interminable. I bring peace when the person is discouraged.

I am the light on the horizon and the dawn that scatters the night. Let everyone invoke my name and hope will settle upon them.

My hope goes everywhere, even into the crevices of fear and the hidden recesses of anxiety. No one can stop my river of hope. It flows endlessly and without limit.

My hope pushes back the barriers that limit human freedom. My hope says to darkness, "You shall not enter," and to evil, "You have no place in this human heart."

Hope is a river that brings all who live in it to the shores of heaven and deposits them there forever.

In these locutions I have revealed my secrets of hope. I want all my children to bathe in this stream and to be carried along by its strong tide.

Comment
This series has been remarkable in its beauty. Like an ode to hope.

February 3, 2014
10. Hope for the Middle East

The Road of Hope

Mary

I must turn my eyes to the Middle East. Dare I speak of hope for those forsaken countries where Satan has purposely destroyed every source of hope? The structures necessary for life have been demolished and the normal securities destroyed. What is left? How will these nations ever rebuild? How can the people enjoy any level of normal human life? With every bullet fired, hope is killed again and again.

The solution does not lie in treaties which only paper over the truth. The deep forces of Satan must be rebuked and cast out, just as Jesus confronted Satan at every meeting. How will this happen? Only my pope, together with the whole Church, is able to bring about such a deliverance. Only the Woman Clothed with the Sun holds in her hands the divine power to bring about peace in the Middle East.

This freedom from Satanic hatred and death is not the work of one day or of one year. It will result only from a long series of events, mainly within the Church itself, that will bring about the consecration of Russia to my Immaculate Heart. Russia is the key to peace in the Middle East.

Comment
Mary wants hope to have power everywhere,
even in the seemingly hopeless Middle East situation.

February 4, 2014
11. The Queen of Hope

The Road of Hope

Mary

Today, I have a request. I ask my children to walk only one road—my road of hope. There are many different roads—roads of pleasure, of power, of discouragement and of hatred. There are also many roads of hope. People place hope in their own strength, or in their money, or in their position. Reject all of those roads.

I ask you to walk only on my road of hope. In these locutions, I have revealed this road. Read them again. Let the words enter your heart. I also will enter and reign as queen of your heart.

Choose me every day as your queen. How I love to reign. My kingdom pours out hope. Let me enter every room and crevice of your heart. Wherever I go, I fill with hope.

Hope is my gift and I leave it everywhere. I will place hope so deeply into your heart, that no matter what problems besiege you, they will never capture your inner fortress. Hope conquers because it outlasts every difficulty. Even if the problems last

4

until the moment of your death, hope will be there, always the victor. I will be there and you will have arrived at the shores of heaven.

Comment

In your darkest moments, always choose Mary's road of hope.

The Problem of Suffering

February 5, 2014

1. Mary Hates Suffering

The Problem of Suffering

Mary

I turn my eyes to human suffering, a reality never willed by the heavenly Father, introduced into creation by the destructive power of sin. When God is totally present, as he was at creation's beginning, all suffering and sorrow gives way to his divine power. As God is rejected and man withdraws from God's presence, the powers of suffering inevitably emerge. Man was made for God and needs God's love. Apart from God, his lot is inevitably suffering.

I will address the present sufferings of man. I will reveal the great secrets of my heart, my own motherly sorrow to see my children in their various agonies and my secrets of help that I will offer. I am at war with Satan. He inflicts suffering and I lessen it. He inflicts hardships and I ease the burdens. He inflicts death and I restore life. I hate all suffering for it is ultimately diabolical. This is my message.

My Son accepted his sufferings to overcome the evil one. He has asked saints to accept their sufferings as they joined him in the battle. Every person can also accept their sufferings to share in Christ's victory. However, this does not change my motherly hatred of all suffering and my attempts to do all that I can to lessen the suffering of all my children so the road to heaven is made much easier. God is never the source of suffering.

Comment

The problem of suffering puzzles everyone.

Mary will speak on this very important question.

5

February 6, 2014
2. Destroying God's Plan

The Problem of Suffering

Mary

The history of suffering goes back to the beginning of time where human consciousness cannot penetrate. God had built wonderful powers into man's body which are only now being discovered. These were the gifts of his original creation, meant to be passed on from generation to generation.

Alas, it did not happen. Man was quickly deceived, renounced his divine life and all the divine protections, set out on his own and has wandered ever since.

Only an understanding of the heavenly Father's original plan allows man to find his way. Where should he go now? What direction must he take? How can he leave much of his suffering behind? Who can lead him into a life that the Father truly intends?

Massive suffering is not God's plan. He does not will massive destruction nor widespread famine and disease. He does not will the crushing poverty that breeds so many illnesses. Do not blame God for the present situation of mankind. Man has chosen to walk away from the Father's path and to run the course of total selfishness. That is what you see now on the face of the earth. I come to bring peace and to reverse all of these forces, but mankind must listen to my words. There is much more to say.

February 7, 2014
3. The Two Rivers

The Problem of Suffering

Mary

Suffering is a sea that flows continually from Satan's heart. When it touches human history, it divides into many rivers so it can enter everywhere. This is his plan. He wants to saturate God's creation with his suffering so that God's goodness is covered over and human hearts will blame God for all the evil that occurs.

Jesus came, proclaiming the Father's kingdom. He set people free from demonic suffering and healed all their illnesses. At last, in Jesus, people saw the Father's true love and care. Jesus wanted to restore creation as it was in the beginning, teaching his disciples to love one another and to do all that they could to halt human suffering.

From his disciples, over the centuries, have come hospitals and works of charity. An ocean of healing and care were released in the name of Christian charity. These powerful forces now provide greater and greater ways of removing suffering from the face of the earth. New discoveries are made daily, all coming from the original impetus of Jesus, where great compassion for the sick has always motivated his followers.

Comment:
Mary begins to set the stage of the two rivers,
one causing suffering and one bringing healing.

February 8, 2014
4. Forgive Yourself

The Problem of Suffering

Mary

Sufferings are clouds which cast their darkness everywhere, shutting out the sun of God's love. Sufferings steal faith from people's hearts and discourage their steps on the road to heaven. When sufferings settle in and abide permanently, the greatest evils come forth, especially when these are the sufferings of hatred, violence and revenge. One suffering triggers another and multiplies the darkness. People deliberately choose the road of violence and destruction, as if this path could ever find its way to peace and joy and freedom.

With every wound that man inflicts upon his fellow human being, sorrow enters my heart. I see Satan's kingdom extending and gaining a greater hold. Wound upon wound. Death upon death. Violence and discord everywhere, among the nations and within families.

Yet, I shine my light and all who choose my light find a different path, a road of forgiveness and reconciliation, a road that leads away from suffering and destruction. O reader, I offer my light to you. First of all, forgive yourself. No need to sorrow over past faults. Then, set out on a path of forgiveness. Let us end suffering and establish Jesus' kingdom.

Comment
Mary has just begun to describe her great enemy,
suffering caused by Satan's kingdom.

February 9, 2014
5. Pervasive Sufferings

The Problem of Suffering

Mary

Why does suffering permeate human life, from the pangs of birth to the sorrows of death? The heavenly Father never intended man or creation to suffer. Suffering in all of its forms is the great mystery. Suffering is Satan's secret, what he devised so that man would become confused and turn away from God.

Suffering discourages even the most stouthearted. It wearies, burdens, and often turns people away from God's plan. Suffering is a tax which steals the wealth of human life placed there by the Creator.

I am the enemy of suffering. Having absorbed in my heart all the sufferings of the whole world, I hold the remedies to every suffering. I comfort the afflicted and give light in darkness. These are the great mysteries that I am trying to reveal.

All of my children are born into a creation that is seriously marred. Some are born into whole cultures totally immersed in violence or poverty. Others are born into families filled with darkness. All are born into a world where the body can suffer and the person can be destroyed.

Someday soon, the whole world will see my interventions on the world stage to save the world from the greatest destruction and suffering. But, no need to wait. Each one of you must come to me now. I will lift your sufferings, one by one. Take up your rosary. It bonds you to me.

Comment
Mary always makes life less difficult and less painful.

February 10, 2014
6. A Stream Waiting to Go Forth

The Problem of Suffering

Mary

Suffering is everywhere. People see suffering as a normal part of human life, as if suffering came with creation. No. Suffering came later, when the Father's original plan was broken into many pieces, shattered by human persons who said "no" to his love.

An angel came to me and explained God's plan to restore creation, to lift the whole world back into the heart of the heavenly Father where it truly belongs. His only-begotten Son, Jesus, would take flesh and live among us. The Father only needed my "yes" and his plan could begin.

I could hardly wait to give my answer. All of creation cried out in my heart, "Free us from this division. Free us from our sorrows. Unite us again to the Father." Fully and completely, I gave my answer, "Let it be done to me according to your word." A river burst forth from within and began to go forth. This stream was placed there by the Holy Spirit who came upon me.

These are the secrets that I am trying to explain. This stream has not gone forth. The world is deprived of its saving power. I am set aside. I wait and wait and wait. Soon, I will wait no longer. I cannot allow this stream to remain forever in my heart. Otherwise, the world would be crushed by the sufferings.

Comment
When the stream goes forth, man's sufferings will recede.

February 12, 2014
8. Redemptive Suffering

The Problem of Suffering

Mary

The suffering that pours forth contaminates human life, unless the person who experiences it has a heart that truly loves Jesus. Then, the suffering is transformed and becomes pearls that are accepted as treasures of God's kingdom. This is the greatest mystery, called redemptive suffering.

There are two kinds of suffering. One burdens, overwhelms, destroys, discourages, and multiplies evils of every sort. These sufferings afflict the person who has no faith, who sees life only as a material world, filled with pleasure or pain.

The other sufferings come to people who believe, who seek God and his kingdom. For them, the many earthly trials, large and small, have a different dimension. By accepting them, they grow in their love for Jesus. Their sufferings become their victories, like the five wounds of Jesus.

The heavenly Father never sends sufferings or causes sufferings. He always tries to lessen sufferings. However, the sufferings that do come can be used to bring forth a new greatness of the human person, a soul tested and purified in the fire of earthly trials. I will speak much more of this dimension because much misunderstanding arises.

Comment
Mary has spoken often of the great evils coming from sufferings.
Now, she enters the great mystery called redemptive suffering.

February 13, 2014
9. The Good Samaritan

The Problem of Suffering

9

Mary

Suffering pours out from Satan's kingdom. By sin mankind has been stripped of God's protection against them. These two factors combine to produce greater and greater suffering. "Your opponent, the devil, is prowling like a roaring lion, looking for someone to devour." (Pt. 5:8). That devouring has many beginnings but only one goal – to draw each person and the whole human race into the darkness and suffering which Satan himself has endured since his decision not to serve God.

Originally, the loving Father surrounded creation with a protection, but that loving wall was pierced and broken. Man has no defense. He is an easy prey. Like the wounded man he lays helpless by the wayside.

Jesus is the Good Samaritan, who lovingly comes, bends over mankind and offers all that is needed to relieve man's sufferings. However, mankind has no idea of its own wounds or why it suffers so much. It claims no need for this Good Samaritan. It rejects him, reviles him and claims it can heal its own wounds.

Jesus and I will not go away. We will remain close and continue to offer our help, waiting for the day when mankind realizes who Jesus is and all that he wants to do.

Comment

Mary highlights three factors: Satan's power to inflict sufferings,
mankind's vulnerability, and the Good Samaritan's ability to help.

February 14, 2014
10. Little Victories over Suffering

The Problem of Suffering

Mary

I must teach the whole world my secrets, about all that I can do to lessen human suffering. These are the great lessons which allow the powerful streams of healing, consolation, and wisdom to pour out upon human existence. Those who know me and know my ways already enjoy these secrets and their lives are so different (even though filled with suffering).

My greatest gift is my presence. I am with you. You are not alone in your sufferings. Before anything else happens, my presence quiets and stills. Anxieties are divided not multiplied. Inner voices of confusion, self-questioning and turmoil are silenced.

Then comes my light. The person sees what can be done. With light comes hope and actions that alleviate the situation. Finally, comes a resolution. The difficulty is resolved. The clouds scatter. Peace reigns. Decisions are made that insure the future.

Gratitude fills the heart. The person knows that I have kept my promise to alleviate suffering. God is glorified, as the person rejoices in this little victory over suffering. Greater victories are waiting in the wings.

Comment
Mary is revealing what saints call "Mary's secrets," the ways that she helps them.

February 15, 2014
11. The Verge of Darkness

The Problem of Suffering

Mary

I am ready to open up all of my blessings and to allow them to pour forth over the whole world and into every heart. I speak now of world events, which all can see and experience. I speak of communal experiences that make the headlines. Mankind is not ready for these events. They will be helpless, confused and unable to act.

Satan has cleverly led mankind into his corner. Decisions, decisions, decisions. Millions of decisions have been made over the centuries, and especially in this last century. Attracted by both power and pleasure, people have acquiesced in these decisions. All is so intricate, so tied together, bundled in such a way that no one can untie the knots. Man is caught in the web that he has spun according to Satan's plan.

Of course, there have been exceptions, moments when great men, like Pope John Paul II, have broken through his schemes, but Satan has marched on and on, with his eye always on the goal.

And this is where we are. Mankind is on the verge of untold sufferings which have never before been experienced. Yes, I must say this with all the power of my voice, "You are on the verge, about to be plunged into a great darkness." Only I can untie the knots and open up all my blessings. Why am I not at center stage? This is where I belong. Must I wait to be invited? My priest son, he will invite me.

Comment
Mary concludes her teachings on the two great realities, the wrong path
taken by the human race and her waiting to be invited to help.

The Prerogatives of the Woman

February 16, 2014
1. The Shattering of Creation

The Prerogatives of the Woman

Mary

I will open up the fullness of my heart and reveal all the secrets hidden from the beginning. Only in this way, can the world realize all that the Father has done. There will be great surprises, even for those who love me and to whom I have revealed much. It is time to pull back the veil so all can understand. In this way, I can strengthen trust and the confidence in my words.

In the Father's created universe, I was to be the woman who would someday bring forth his Son. Of all creatures, I was to be his perfect creation, untouched by any darkness and the creature who would give flesh to his Son, the light of the world. All of human history would wait for me so the fullness of time could begin.

Then came the fall, the original sin, and creation was shattered into a million pieces. How would the Father ever put it together? Immediately, he thought of me. He would use me in a new, unforeseen way. "I will put an enmity between you and the woman, between your offspring and hers." There would still be a fullness of time. There would still be the woman giving birth to her child. This part of the original plan was still in place, even though all else was shattered.

Comment
Mary promises a full revelation of her role in creation.

February 17, 2014
2. Present from the Beginning

The Prerogatives of the Woman

Mary

When the Father created the heavens and the earth, he saw a woman. When he created human life, he saw a woman. When the first sin was created, he saw a woman. All of his thoughts, desires, hopes were focused on a woman. In this sense, I was there from the beginning of material creation. I was the door for his Son to enter and to live within this creation.

All things were made for the Son. To him would be the fullness of glory. The Father never saw his Son apart from the woman. This is the great mystery of the

Word became flesh. That flesh would come totally from the woman. Every cell in Jesus' body came from my body. No other human creature would participate in the mystery. Only my body would be immaculate, free of any taint of sin.

I reveal these secrets because so many set me aside. Even those who truly love me do not see my intimacy with the Father, or how I was there from the beginning.

Comment
Mary's words help even those with great faith
to see more deeply into the mystery.

February 11, 2014
Our Lady of Lourdes

The Prerogatives of the Woman

Mary

The human race marches along the road of darkness that it has so freely chosen. Inevitably greater sufferings lie ahead. Suffering, suffering and more suffering are Satan's tactics. He multiplies sufferings. Confronted by these sufferings and confused by their constant presence, man finds great difficulty in experiencing God. "Where is God?" people cry out when there is devastation and war. They ask, "If there is a God, why does he allow all this to happen?"

I respond to these questions. God is distant because man has walked away from him. These sufferings are not from God. They come from God's enemy. And my final answer is this. God has sent a woman, a loving merciful woman as his instrument of consolation.

Today is my feast. I am called "Our Lady of Lourdes." Through St. Bernadette, I released a healing stream of water to the whole world. Lourdes is a sign of the great oceans of healing waters that are stored in my heart, ready to flow out to all the world. Come, drink of these waters. They will ease your sufferings and you will see that God is not absent.

Comment
How many times sufferings cause problems of faith.
Mary wants to ease both the sufferings and the problems.

February 18, 2014
3. The Woman in God's Plan

The Prerogatives of the Woman

Mary

All must be revealed. It is too late to hold back anything. I must go step by step so each part is clear and the whole world can see me as the Woman. That is the title given to me by the Father himself, and also the word used by Jesus.

The Father said, "I will place an enmity between you and the woman." At the wedding in Cana, Jesus said, "Woman, what concern is that to us?" On the cross, Jesus said, "Woman, behold your son," as he gave me to the beloved disciple. Finally, came the great revelation. The heaven was opened. The lightening flashed and the sound of thunder filled the sky. The Father wanted the whole world to see what he had done. Then, "A sign appeared in the sky, a woman clothed with the sun, the moon under her feet and a crown of twelve stars on her head," a woman about to give birth to her son (Rev. 12:1-2).

In the Father's plan, the maiden of Nazareth has become the Woman. If so, why do people set me aside? Why do they belittle my role? I will bring to center stage the one who will openly proclaim me. Through him, I will be the Woman for the whole world.

Comment
With the growing need for God's worldwide intervention,
Mary stresses her role as the Woman.

February 19, 2014
4. The Woman Waits and Waits

The Prerogatives of the Woman

Mary

Very soon, a door will swing out to a new era of open conflict. The enmity between Satan and the Woman will become evident to all. Who cannot see the hand of Satan in all of the world events now occurring? Who cannot see his wiles in all the deaths and the destruction? Who cannot see his power in the sufferings caused to millions of people all over the world? Do you have eyes and do not see? Do you believe that all of this flows merely from human anger?

Now, Satan has the field to himself and scores victory after victory. The Woman waits and waits, wanting so much to fulfill her role. What will happen? How will she come upon the scene?

More and greater events of destruction will take place. The problems will not be isolated or limited to certain areas. All the world will begin to experience Satan's sufferings (for that is his calling card). Even then, the Woman will have to wait. Then a moment will come of a great break, as if a permanent change has happened. This will be the prelude, as everyone wakes up to the seriousness of Satan's destructive powers.

Comment

How quickly we need the Woman to come onto the scene.
Let us not wait. Invoke Mary's help.

February 20, 2014

5. Come and Do Not Delay

The Prerogatives of the Woman

Mary

All can see it clearly. Revolutions and violence breaking out where formerly there was peace. The problems are never solved. No country is secure because Satan knows the weakness of each country. He touches the raw nerve and the Achilles heel. Unrest, protest, violence, deaths and destruction of a nation's life follow. The causes lie hidden until the violence breaks forth. Only when it is too late do people see and understand.

Others say, "It cannot happen here. Our country is safe." You only see the surface of reality. Your foundations have long ago been weakened. The hidden evil flows freely in the sewers beneath your streets, only waiting for the right moment to flow over.

By these words, I bring to light the evil that flows everywhere – in your banking systems, in your political life, in your schools, in your homes and in your hearts. No natural answer exists for these evils.

The world needs a supernatural power which understands and can defeat these evils. Yet, how many will turn to the supernatural? The stakes are high and mounting. I say this clearly. The whole world is at stake. Yes, all of earth is ready to be thrust into Satan's fire. He will not wait. He sees that a complete and total victory is soon to be in his grasp. Once that happens, he will not wait one moment.

For now, he rejoices in his partial victories (and they are everywhere). However, soon partial victories will be as no victory at all to him, when he will be able to pull everything into his hell on earth.

I wait and I wait. Only the Woman is a match for him. I will fight him everywhere, even in hand to hand combat and I will always win. He knows that and does all he can to delay my coming onto the world stage. My entrance will be late and will happen through my beloved priest son. Until then, all must invoke me. Do not wait. "O Woman Clothed with the Sun, come and do not delay." Say that often and I will come into your heart and into every situation.

Comment

Our Lady's warning and her promise are universal.
Everything will be captured either by Satan or by the Woman.

February 21, 2014
6. Revelation Chapter Twelve

The Prerogatives of the Woman

Mary

I embrace the whole world. It easily fits into my heart. When the great events begin, I will embrace it even more closely. These events are like the pangs of birth which have already begun and will inevitably increase. Just as these pangs prepare the body to give birth, so these events prepare for the culminating events.

Whose eyes do not see? Whose ears do not hear? One nation after another plunges into chaos and disorder. In every part of the globe, there are birth pangs of death.

I am the Woman Clothed with the Sun, who gave birth to a child destined to rule the nations. The child was caught up to God and his throne. After that, God prepared a place for me in the desert where the devil pursued me.

Read *Revelation*, Chapter 12, and you will begin to understand world events. More important, will you understand the Woman Clothed with the Sun?

Comment

Revelation, Chapter 12, describes the supernatural forces behind world
events. Unfortunately, a secular world-view does not even believe
that these forces exist.

February 22, 2014
7. Is It Too Late?

The Prerogatives of the Woman

Mary

Is it too late? That is the question. People of faith will say that it is never too late with God. That is true. But time moves on. People live and die and do not experience the light. Cultures are pulled into darkness. Structures of faith and truth are replaced by darkness and lies. People, having no light, lose their way for days, months, years, even for centuries.

The whole world is tilted toward evil and fewer have the power to overcome. That is what you are seeing. People call it a loss of faith, but I call it the demonic strategy. He has had the field all to himself. He has changed everything. Good is condemned. Evil is praised. One by one, all the lights are being put out. How much time is left? For some, no time is left. They have lived and died in the darkness. This happens every day, before your very eyes. Souls, bereft of the light, are dying. Pray for them and I will hear your prayer.

Now, to answer the question, "How much time is left?" I will review my teachings. Jerusalem is central to God's plan for the world. Only its soil contains Jesus' precious blood. Israel, therefore, is Satan's target. If he destroys Israel, he pushes back God's plan for years to come, even for centuries.

Syria is the fuse and it has been lit for years, destabilizing the Middle East. America has withdrawn. This moves up the timetable. Treaties have been signed which lack all truth and only give permission for Iran to continue to build atomic weapons. Pakistan, with its atomic arsenal, is tottering and will soon fall. Iraq cannot protect itself. No human person exists to reverse all of these forces.

To return to the question, "How much time is left?" The beginning of the events will occur before America elects its next president. Notice that I say, "will begin," for there will be beginning events and culminating events.

To return to the other question, "Is it too late?" I can only promise this. Hands and voices must be constantly lifted up. I have taught you the important invocation. "Woman clothed with the sun, come and do not delay." This will prepare hearts for my actions. When I act (and I promise to do so), all will say, "The Woman Clothed with the Sun" has done this for us.

Comment

This is a culmination locution, bringing together much of what Mary has said, but also adding important dimensions.

February 23, 2014
8. Visible and Powerful Actions

The Prerogatives of the Woman

Mary

I am a mother who wants to embrace all of her children because only in my arms are they safe. Many do not know me. Others are taken away from me by the darkness. Others chase after the false lights of this world. Yet, I would gather the whole world. I would call all my children into the blessings of my embrace.

17

As a loving mother, I come to each person. I stir in each heart and call to faith. However, in today's world, that is not enough. Too many forces blind people, sometimes carrying whole nations away from my embrace. My children scatter in every direction, pulled by powers which they do not understand and cannot overcome.

So, I must act in each person's heart, not just as a mother, but as the Woman Clothed with the Sun. My actions must become visible and powerful. They must enter the same world stage as the dark forces. They must contend openly. All, even those with no faith, must be able to see and to witness what I do. My actions will offer a freedom, so each person can choose good. As their mother, I will be embracing them. As the Woman Clothed with the Sun, I will be freeing them so they can accept my embrace.

Comment
Mary explains her two-fold action – within each person's heart and in world events.

Secrets of Heaven

February 25, 2014
1. The First Secret of Heaven

Secrets of Heaven

Mary

I will open up the secrets of heaven and give the whole world a vision of heaven's hopes and thoughts. I will reveal what is taking place in heaven so all can understand the events of earth.

Earth and heaven are meant to be joined, so earth can receive heaven's blessings which go forth, just as the sun freely sends forth its light and warmth.

Heaven always blesses earth and the blessings never cease flowing. People need only to bathe in these blessings, to receive them with thanksgiving, and to distribute them to others. Then they grow close to heaven, and when they die, they enter forever into the heavenly blessings. This is the first vision, the first truth. The Father's first thought is always to bless earth in every possible way so people seek their heavenly home.

Comment
Mary outlines heaven's basic stance to earth – to bless us in every possible way.

February 26, 2014
2. The Stream of History

Secrets of Heaven

Mary

So many secrets must pour forth. As all the mysteries are revealed, mankind will understand what is happening on earth. I will begin with the mystery of human history itself.

Everyone is born at a certain moment and dies at a certain moment. They enter the stream of history and are affected by that stream. Each person also changes this stream, for good or for evil.

Past events determine the quality, and even the direction, of this stream. Mankind cannot understand the world unless he is aware of previous events, even years or centuries before. Forces have been released in human history, both good and evil, that shape the stream. Man is free to act, but only in the stream of history. A person in the 21st century cannot reverse what has happened in the 20th century. All must live and act where they are born in the stream.

I have tried to reveal where this stream is headed. By so many powerful events and so many twisted decisions, the stream flows away from God. It has lost it way. Yet, into this stream, every person is born and lives. The modern questions are no longer just individual or personal. The stream is now powerful and worldwide. Local and even national identities are being swept away. The stream is claiming every one and every nation. This is what I am trying to prevent. If these worldwide forces are totally released, each person will not be free. The stream will be too powerful. All will be carried away.

Comment
Mary speaks the truth. We are all caught up in forces that remove our freedom.

February 27, 2014
3. Waiting to Act

Secrets of Heaven

Mary

What is hidden must be revealed so that all eyes are opened to the realities of these times. Otherwise, mankind, in his confusion, will have no response. Let me begin.

For centuries, heaven has foreseen these years that lie immediately ahead. The storm clouds began to gather when the goddess of reason was exalted during the French revolution. Even then, the Father was ready to answer.

I began appearing in Paris to St. Catherine and then at Lourdes to Bernadette. The Father was taking the war to the very soil of France where the evil had begun. The Age of Enlightenment was its name. Truly, it was the beginning of the Age of Darkness, the stripping away of supernatural truths.

In the twentieth century, a greater evil was sown on the soil of Russia, which claimed millions of lives, spread its errors, and continues to this day as the source of turmoil.

The greatest of all evils is blindness to these forces, which are shaping today's events and preparing for future events. No one sees. Not even the Church sees. There is no awakening, no trumpet call. No one is aware of how near are these future events. When the problem was in France, I appeared in France. When the problem was Russia, I spoke at Fatima about Russia.

No human solutions exist for these problems but I am waiting to act, to come upon the world scene and even to manifest my presence to the whole world.

I speak because I want every eye and every heart to turn to me and to invoke my help as the Woman Clothed with the Sun. I want the Holy Father to consecrate Russia to my Immaculate Heart. I want all the bishops to support and participate in this consecration. I want all the faithful to join wholeheartedly in a permanent consecration of their lives to me. Nothing less is enough.

If I am to rescue the world, I need a total, complete, life-long consecration to my Immaculate Heart. The hour is late. This should have been accomplished decades ago. Another decade of waiting will result in complete disaster.

Comment
Mary speaks of the destruction, seen by all, and of the solution, seen by very few.

February 28, 2014
4. The True Source of Suffering

Secrets of Heaven

Mary

I must speak about suffering, only because it is so widespread and is Satan's favorite tool. No suffering exists in heaven. Every tear is dried and every wound is healed. Also, no suffering goes forth from heaven. All suffering comes from below and is the product of man's turning away from heavenly blessings. As mankind sinks lower and lower, it approximates the regions of hell, where only sufferings exist.

This truth is not easy to see because many who suffer truly seek to live in Jesus' kingdom. They are like innocent victims, whose hearts have no connection with hell but yet experience its fury. I will speak more to this subject.

Comment
Heaven sends forth blessings. Hell sends forth sufferings.

March 1, 2014
5. Why Mankind Suffers

Secrets of Heaven

Mary

The first, the original sin, opened the windows to suffering. The perfection of God's creation was shattered. The human body was changed. The many protections against illness and disease placed there by God (and now being discovered by modern science) were dismantled. The body was rearranged. The smooth and perfect functioning was replaced by sickness and even death itself.

Also, the peaceful relationship between man and woman became marred by discord. Their childlike relationship to God became filled with fear. All was changed because they abandoned the great gifts of God for the false goal of independence.

What do you see today? Do you not see a mankind fiercely and militantly independent, snuffing out all religious devotion? What road is mankind taking? Where does he march? More important, who will turn him around?

I speak because mankind is plunging into unimaginable sufferings and I want to call earth away from these sufferings. I offer a different road, a new path, a quite different future. Who will heed my voice? I must speak louder. I must use actions more than words. These will be actions of mercy, a mother's care for her suffering child.

Comment
Mary gives a clear description of reality and a clear promise of hope.

March 2, 2014
6. Do Not Fear

Secrets of Heaven

Mary

"Do not fear." The angel spoke these words to me, and I experienced heaven's power in my heart. All grew calm and I could listen attentively to the angel's message. When the angel had explained the great mystery of becoming God's mother, I was able to say, "Let it be done to me according to your word."

Suffering and fear are hell's tools, always doing Satan's works. Heaven sends only consolations and peace, the stillness needed to overcome.

I ask, "Is this a time of peace? Does the gift of peace continually spread, going from one nation to another? Or, is it a time of war, a time of invasions?" O mankind, you have set out on your own path. You have chartered what you think is your course, but it is not your road. It is Satan's road that you are on and there is no peace.

I stand by the wayside, calling out to all, "Come this way. Follow my path." A few hear. My voice is clear to them. They forsake the world's path and find peace.

A moment will come when I will no longer stand by the wayside with a quiet voice. I will openly enter human history. I will raise my voice as the Woman Clothed with the Sun. I will confront the Evil One. At that moment, all of humanity will be free to choose.

Comment

All can see the expanding conflicts and man's helplessness.
We must believe Mary's promise.

March 3, 2014

7. The Children of the Secular Age

Secrets of Heaven

Mary

So many hearts are empty because they are deprived of heaven's blessings. In the Age of Faith, people were filled with these blessings, and human life was ordered according to divine beliefs. Now, these blessings have been stolen, often deliberately stolen by those who knew their value. Children are not born in cultures of faith, and have no idea of their heavenly inheritance. Their desires are limited to earth, and their hearts seek what can never satisfy.

I speak to the children of this secular age. I sorrow for you. You have been cheated, robbed, defrauded and left by the wayside. You have not abandoned the road of faith. It has never been shown to you.

Can I not lead you? Can I not draw you? Even though you began in darkness, I can bring you into light. Come, let us begin now. Call upon me and I will give you the light that your culture has withheld from you. Do not be afraid of the demands made by faith. These also are light.

Comment

The culture filled older Catholics with faith. The young are deprived of these helps.

22

March 4, 2014
8. The Rise of Putin

Secrets of Heaven

Mary

All is converging into the great moment of truth. All the events on the world stage fit together, like the acts of a play. (Yet, many see them as isolated events, without any apparent meaning or script.) The tensions build. The main characters appear on the scene. All must be present for the climax, the moment when all the forces come into play, when evil is totally spent and defeated. In the end, my Immaculate Heart will triumph. However, how many casualties (that need not have happened) will occur.

I must speak now of Putin. He is the most important actor, often overlooked in the early scenes, but more and more emerging. His role will increase greatly. His grasp upon power will grow tighter as his mind conceives new strategies.

I was not wrong when I told the three children that Russia would spread its errors. Only now is the West beginning to see what I have been proclaiming for almost 100 years. Russia is the problem. Russia must be consecrated to my Immaculate Heart for there to be world peace. Who will turn back Putin and his designs? There will be no turning back. Satan has the field all to himself and the Woman Clothed with the Sun stands on the sidelines. This need not be.

Comment
When Out Lady spoke about Russia in 1917, and also about World War II,
many thought she was mistaken, that Germany was the real problem.
Time has shown how correct Mary has been.

March 5, 2014
9. The Beginning Events

Secrets of Heaven

Mary

When all culminates and the events begin, what is solidly built and protected by my Immaculate Heart will remain standing. What is poorly constructed and attempting to stand on its own, will be no match for these forces. Much will be swept away, like rotted wood in a storm. Only then will people begin to see the great mistakes and the enormous errors of a world built without faith.

These events are only the beginning skirmishes of the great war. Even in these beginning moments, I will still stand helplessly on the sidelines. Why do I wait? Why do I not intervene? I will always wait for my Church to act, for my Church to obey my word. I cannot say this too often or too strongly. My Church, which clearly knows my word, has not obeyed my word.

So, I will choose someone who will obey me. I will lift him up. He will act according to my word. Then, the Woman Clothed with the Sun will no longer stand helplessly on the sidelines as this drama is played out on the world stage. All will see it clearly before their eyes. For now, do not forget my prayer, "Woman Clothed with the Sun, come and do not delay."

Comment

Read the newspapers. See the turmoil that grasps every part of the world. These are the signs before your very eyes, of all that Mary is saying.

Mary and Hope

March 7, 2014
1. Mother of Hope

Mary and Hope

Mary

I will speak of hope. I will begin afresh and begin anew to stir the hearts of those who believe in me. They see the darkness and they grow disheartened. They see the forces of evil sweeping the world as nation after nation is drawn into turmoil. They see the many dangers, for I have described them so clearly. They also know that I wait and wait. The picture is so clear to them.

I am the Mother of Hope. A mother is in the home. She is not associated with world events. She rocks the cradle, changes the diapers and prepares the meals. Yet, how powerful is her influence! She is the heart of the home, the life blood which flows within her children.

She softens the hurts inflicted by the world and assures all her children that they can always turn to her in their sorrows. She never inflicts unnecessary pain and consoles all her children in their times of distress.

As the heavenly mother, I bring even greater blessings. These I freely distribute now. I need not wait, except for each person to ask and seek. These blessings I will begin to reveal.

Comment
Mary's heart holds many gifts that are still unknown,
like a fountain waiting to be poured forth.

March 8, 2014
2. Mary's First Embrace

Mary and Hope

Mary

O reader, how many burdens have come upon you. What seemed secure is now threatened and what you used to have has been taken away. Satan has removed so much from your culture and has replaced the heavenly Father's security with his sufferings.

In your trials, where do you turn? Faith has also been weakened. Doubts have been sown. The simple beliefs of past years are rejected. For this reason, I, the Mother of Hope, will give you my words. Listen. Write them on your heart. In the coming days I will repeat and explain them, so my words constantly refresh you.

I am the Mother of Hope. I always want to embrace you, more than any earthly mother. When I embrace you, the pain will leave, the sufferings will grow less, the light will scatter your hopelessness. You will experience my presence. After my embrace do not quickly return to your world. Do not, at first, even try to learn the solutions to your problems. (I will give these later). In these opening moments of my motherly embrace, be still. Allow the difficulties to drain off. I will remove the power which these conflicts have over you. After this first embrace, I will begin to instill hope.

Comment
Mary invites all of us to important moments of stillness in her presence.

March 9, 2014
3. The Oil of Hope

Mary and Hope

Mary

The time to gain hope is now, today, at this very moment. When all the events begin (and the convulsing events have not yet started) it will be too late to gain hope. Hope is oil for your lamp and it cannot be bought at the last minute.

Hope demands a faith in God's power and a belief that he loves you. All believers know that God is almighty but he seems distant, living in heaven but not acting upon earth.

You ask, "Will God act for me?" You say, "I have little faith. I frequently fail. I am not strong. I quickly grow afraid." These are your fears. Cast them away. In the presence of the mother, the child does not think of itself because his mother is on the scene.

I will prepare you for the events but you must store up the oil of my hope now.

Comment
All of us fear that we will fall away in time of trial.
Mary promises to be our Mother.

March 10, 2014
4. The Book of Blessings

Mary and Hope

Mary

To stir up hope, I open wide the book of my blessings. The words are written large and on every page. However, only the eyes of faith can see and read what is written. The first page contains a description of the loving Father, who has brought all creation into existence and has placed man at the pinnacle of material creation, deliberately choosing that he would share in God's powers to know and to love.

The second page contains the mystery of God becoming man and living among us, a mystery brought about by my willingness to be God's mother.

The third page contains the mystery of the Holy Spirit whom Jesus sent upon those whom he had taught and had appeared to after his rising.

All the other pages contain the story of Jesus' kingdom, all that the Holy Spirit has accomplished in the hearts of the believers.

Now, I turn the pages to today. The words are not yet written because the blessings are pouring down from heaven. Only those gifts that are welcomed, received and acted upon are recorded in this book of blessings. Reading the book will fill you with hope. You will see all that the Holy Spirit has done. Your name is in the book, because He has done his works in you. Be filled with hope. He wants to do great deeds in your heart.

Comment
All the deeds we do today under the guidance of the Spirit
are recorded in this book of blessings.

March 11, 2014
5. The Tottering Kingdoms

Mary and Hope

Mary

All is built upon hope. When man is filled with hope, man builds his homes and his kingdoms. When these are threatened, he must cling to hope. When all is destroyed, he has only hope that he can rebuild. Without hope, he accepts defeat and plans no future.

These are my words. Listen carefully. Mankind has built his homes and constructed his kingdoms. Before his very eyes, these kingdoms are tottering. The winds are blowing and the rains are falling. The floods that will sweep away these kingdoms will soon follow. Hopes will be shattered. Without hope, no future is rebuilt because all your human hopes are taken away.

I, alone, am the Mother of Hope and in those days, only those who have heard my word will have hope. The future of the world will be removed from the hands of mankind. I will hold that future in my hands. I will invite all to come. O reader, come now, right now. There is no hope for the future except with the Woman Clothed with the Sun.

Comment

Now we see only the tottering. Mary alone will give hope after the collapse.

March 12, 2014
6. Fire and Water

Mary and Hope

Mary

The fires of hell, with their suffering and confusion, will claim more and more of earth. As they do, they will extinguish hope. When hope dies, the victory of hell is assured. There will be no opposition to these fires, no responding.

I am the Mother of Hope and these waters of hope can flow powerfully from my heart. No fire will overcome them. Their victory is assured. Right now, they wait, like a mighty ocean which casts no waves upon the shore.

O mankind, your earth is ablaze with fires everywhere. Your water of secular hopes can never extinguish these fires because they come from hell and they share in the eternal fires of hell. These fires share in the demonic intelligence, planned by Satan since he was defeated at the cross. He is ready to thwart any plan you might have to restore peace, order and security.

Only the waters stored in my heart can extinguish his fires. Someday, these waters will flow and all will see that I am the Woman. How much will be consumed and destroyed in the meantime? When will the consecration of Russia take place?

Comment

Mary correctly describes our world of 2014 – fires everywhere.
She also speaks of God's gift – the ocean of hope in her heart.

March 13, 2014

7. Hope Has No End

Mary and Hope

Mary

Hope never speaks of the end because where hope lives there is no end. People without hope often say, "This is the end." What they sought, what they have built, and what they have lived for has collapsed. Their dreams are broken into a thousand pieces.

Where there is true hope, no end exists. Hope will move on and willingly leave behind what cannot be regained. Hope transcends, rises above, is never conquered and cannot be killed.

Hope even conquers death and the grave itself. Death does not have the final word, even when the stone is rolled across the tomb. Hope never, never ends because true hope always seeks God, and God never ends. True hope seeks eternal life, and eternal life never ends.

Everything on earth, all of earth's important goals must be lifted up. If you live only for earth, then your hope will die, sometimes a thousand deaths. But if your hope lies in heavenly riches, then your hope will never die.

Satan is multiplying his sufferings. If he can kill your hopes, his victory is insured. I am the Mother of Hope, which flows endlessly from my heart. Come and drink, every moment of every day. It is an endless stream that always refreshes.

Comment

A world filled with suffering can only survive by the power of hope.

World Events

March 14, 2014
1. The Invasion of Ukraine

World Events

Mary

Treasure my words. Hold onto my light. These are all that you will have in the days ahead. I must turn my heart to those world events that are suffocating and destroying. These actions are putting the whole world on notice that the foundations of peace are very shaky.

Even though events are happening in the Ukraine, these are not the final or central events. However, this invasion reveals the frailty of the West and its inability to stand firm and repress the forces of evil.

This helplessness is evident everywhere, in Iran where atomic weapons are being built, in Iraq where order has collapsed, and in Syria where the dictator strengthens his stranglehold upon the country.

The leaders will speak at the United Nations. Words will flow abundantly, but few will be the actions that can turn back this invasion. Another piece of the world will fall into darkness. Only those who listen to my teachings really understand what is happening.

Comment
The invasion of the Ukraine reveals the helplessness of the West,
but the great events will happen elsewhere.

March 15, 2014
2. The Blindness of the World

World Events

Mary

World leaders think that they walk in light when, in truth, their hearts and minds are filled with the greatest darkness. They have no faith and the words they speak do not come from a love of God. They are like Old Testament Israel, which foolishly entered into foreign alliances instead of trusting God. So, I must be like the Old Testament prophets, speaking God's words to leaders filled only with secular light.

You attack the wrong places and protect only your own interests. Having no faith, you do not form alliances based on faith. Your foreign policies have become like your political policies, based on fragmented visions and selfish goals.

You are leading the West down the wrong road. Your vision is blurred. Your goals are selfish. Your means are inadequate. Your oneness is broken and your hearts are in the wrong place.

I want to turn your hearts. I want to explain why I have lifted my protective hand from you. Although you will not listen, although you will say this is not important, that it does not even deal with foreign policies, I must say it anyway. "You, selfish leaders and blind guides, how can you protect those who are born, when you foolishly refuse to protect the unborn?   Protect your unborn, and I will protect you. Continue to sacrifice them to political expediency and I will sacrifice you on the altars of war."

Comment
Mary uses the fiery words of the Old Testament prophet.

March 16, 2014
3. A Special Leader

World Events

Mary

There is a leader whom I hold in my heart and whose ascendency to office I want to bring about. I have given him all the qualifications needed to lead the free world. I have advanced him according to my plan and he, himself, is willing to make the sacrifices needed to seek election.

I ask of him only one thing. He must protect human life, all human life, no matter how it is conceived. He must stand clear and firm that human life begins at the moment of conception. Let him put his name to the Life at Conception Act. Let him not fear. This is the step I want him to take. If he commits himself to protect every unborn life, I will protect him in his bid for the highest office.

To all world leaders I say clearly that there can be no compromise in this matter. None of you are allowed to sacrifice the unborn for the sake of your political lives. God cannot bless America while America kills its unborn. This is the cause of your decline, a decline that will happen even more quickly if you do not change your laws.

Comment
Hopefully, the person who Mary speaks about will read this!

March 17, 2014
4. Collapse of American Protection

World Events

Mary

My words will take on new meaning and greater clarity. I will not just speak of past events or of events too far in the future. I will speak of all that is unfolding before your very eyes. I want you to trust these words because, when the events begin, they will guide you and help you to understand.

Today, I will speak of America and the problems that are erupting all over the world. America has withdrawn. It has sheathed its sword and its voice no longer has power. Because America has chosen this path, the timetable has moved up. Evil moves more quickly.

In the past, America has made serious blunders because its foreign policies were directed by big business. To help or not to help, to invade or not to invade was decided by its money people, not by those who wanted the best interests of the people.

America's money interests have devastated countries, removed true leaders, established puppet governments and ruined social structures that could have served well. So much of this business-driven foreign policy has been hidden from the people.

Now, a new policy is in place that refuses to accept the role that I have given to America. I have blessed this nation so that freedom and truth might reign everywhere. America has withdrawn. It refuses to step forward, like a timid dog that only barks loudly and is quickly seen as harmless.

The result will be a total loss of the Ukraine, and a Putin who will soon look for other places to devour. These policies were impossible just a few years ago. Now, all seems possible.

China will quickly read the evidence and know that it can move forward with aggression. Iran will realize that the terms of its agreement are meaningless and will never be enforced by a cowed America.

America's allies also see the change and no longer count upon its strength. All of this inevitably happens when the great protector, America, whom I have blessed and chosen, throws down its arms and surrenders.

Comment

Mary has often spoken of the timetable of destruction being moved up by American withdrawal. Now, she speaks of very concrete events which are soon to happen.

31

March 18, 2014
5. An Earthly Michael

World Events

Mary

All the cards are on the table. Satan has all the kingdoms of earth in his sight. How he covets these and wants them for his own. Even though they are passing away, earthly kingdoms are all he can possess. Heaven is denied to him. Its gates are closed. Michael and his angels have cast him out. So, he roams the world, fighting against my children.

Gradually, his plan unfolds. His strategies change according to the acceptance or rejection given to him. He moves where he can easily conquer. He waits where he finds no acceptance. Like any general, he consolidates his victories and plans his next attack.

In this world, where faith is so weak, he seldom suffers any defeat and almost never is made to withdraw. So it is in the Crimea. He has gobbled it up quickly. It is already in his stomach and what power can make him vomit it up. His hunger grows with each victory. His pride increases.

It is his pride which will be his downfall, as it was in the beginning. I will raise up another Michael, a Michael of earth who will defeat his pride because I will clothe him in my humility.

Comment

Mary promises to raise up a special person as her instrument against Satan.

March 19, 2014
6. Israel

World Events

Mary

All the events are culminating. The seeds of destruction, planted so carefully by Satan centuries ago, are coming to a full harvest. I will remove the veil that covers over his plan.

All the world sees the events. They are known to everyone – the destabilizing revolutions in northern Africa, the long-lasting revolt in Syria that has touched the neighboring countries, the ravaging of Iraq, the nuclear plans of Iran, the destabilizing of Afghanistan, and now the invasion of the Crimea with more to follow.

In the middle of all these events lies Israel, seemingly small and unimportant. As far as the West is concerned, Israel is an appendage, an anomaly. It exists but its existence does not seem vital to the West. If it were suddenly gobbled up, it would mean no more than the Crimea. This is the great deception. Satan's prize is to destroy Israel, that Holy Land where he suffered his great defeat and that city which still contains the redeeming Blood of Jesus.

Comment
Mary has spoken of the importance of Israel throughout these locutions.

March 20, 2014
7. The Plans of Russia

World Events

Mary

Putin will not stop. He will move on and claim as much of the former territory as possible. When this stage of reclaiming the satellites is completed, a new order of relationships among world leaders will be formed. The full integration of Russia into the West that seemingly was happening will be shattered. The Cold War will be re-established, although in a different way, more in keeping to Russia's advantage.

All of this will set the stage for the next series of events. Russia will grow closer to China. It will continue its significant role in the Middle East through its allies, Syria and Iran. Russia, under Putin, will use its geographic setting to its advantage, with doors open both to the West and the East.

In spite of Putin's grabbing as much as he can, the European leaders have little recourse. They foolishly opened their doors. They gave Russia a place at the tables and respectability. They can only pull back a little bit. Their economies are intertwined and Putin will cleverly deflect the harm of the sanctions. He has strengthened Russia before beginning his military advances.

What does all of this portend? How does it fit into the picture that I have constantly painted in these locutions? The pieces all fit together. Satan's timetable moves ahead, much more quickly. All of his friends see opportunities everywhere that they never dreamed would happen so soon. Many, many more events will happen. All of these are preparatory. Evil spreads because the good are so weak. The West refuses to act because the unity of faith and the motivation of faith are lacking.

More important, the clarity of vision and the decisiveness that I would give to the world through the Church has not gone forth. Both the Church and the West bear the blame.

The West will continue to lie in great darkness until the great light comes to the Church and attains the lampstand. In those days, it will not be the wisdom of man (even of the priest son whom I have chosen), but my wisdom and my light which will go forth. Oh, it will be late, so very late. Many will ask, "Where is heaven's help?" God has placed all light and all help in my Immaculate Heart, but I must wait until the Holy Father invokes that help by consecrating Russia.

My final question is this: "Is there anyone in the world or in the Church who does not now see clearly what I proclaimed at Fatima? World peace will only come when Russia, not the world in general, is consecrated to me."

Comment
Mary explains what is happening and why.

March 21, 2014
8. The Global Economy

World Events

Mary

The fire is all-consuming and the plans of evil involve the whole world. No one is left out. When all of these events begin and the established order begins to shatter, you, O reader, must already have my word planted in your heart.

The world's economies are built on very shaky foundations. Many nations have debts that they will never repay. Even established nations have growing debts. The money flows into the most dangerous nations. Economies no longer stand alone. All are entangled in what is called "the global economy."

The backbone of world order was the diversity of the nations, so clearly willed by God. Powerful forces are destroying this diversity, calling all into a one world order. Do you not see that this repeats the pride and foolishness of Babel? In this area, also, the world totters on the brink.

As the wars spread, the economies will be pushed further and further, until some are broken. All the world's problems are interrelated. They are not happenstance. They come from the intelligent design of the Evil One. Mankind, with its limited intelligence, is no match.

Comment
Even without the wars, the world economics are in trouble.
The wars only compound the world's problems of economic weakness.

Revealing God's Plan

March 22, 2014
1. The Joining of Hearts

Revealing God's Plan

Mary

There are more things that I must say so the world will know that I want to embrace it and save it. What are the hidden elements of my plan? I have spoken so clearly of Satan's evil designs. I must also reveal what I am doing.

This plan centers on the joining of my Immaculate Heart to Jesus' Sacred Heart. The two hearts are the beginning of the Father's plan to save the world.

The revelation of the Sacred Heart, centuries ago, released a gigantic flood of blessings and saved the Church from darkness. Unfortunately, the kings of France refused to listen and the full power within Jesus' heart was not released. The Church is facing the same situation. How history repeats itself. God provides his blessings but man refuses to listen. This is why I must speak so clearly. Not only speak, but act.

Comment

Jesus told St. Margaret Mary (1647-1690) that he wanted the king of France to consecrate his country to the Sacred Heart. All of the kings refused this request. One hundred years later, to the day, the king of France was stripped of his powers and eventually was executed. The bloody revolution and the destroying of the French Church should have been avoided.

March 23, 2014
2. The Beginning Response

Revealing God's Plan

Mary

Much of God's plan is still hidden and unknown. However, when the events of destruction begin, his plan will emerge. This will happen as people whom he has prepared will come forth. In a time of war is there not a call to arms? Are not other pursuits set aside? So it will be with my army.

When the events begin, do not be overwhelmed by fears. Do not withdraw and do not surrender. All must stand their ground. Those whom I have chosen and prepared must come forth. Do not listen to the voices of fear and especially do not listen to the voice of anger. Fear and anger destroy my plans.

I will raise up people of good will whose hearts belong to me. Others will put their trust in them. They will lead the world and the Church. Voices that had been set aside until now will suddenly be listened to. The foolishness of today's world will be set aside. The Church, itself, will realize that false solutions and superficial responses will no longer hold sway.

It will be a time of repentance, of profound changes and of deep and sustained prayer. This will be the beginning response. Although this invitation will be rejected by many, it will be big enough to make it a viable movement within the Church. Then will come my great surprises.

Comment
God's response to evil will begin within the hearts of many good people.

March 24, 2014
4. The Russian Bear

Revealing God's Plan

Jesus
(Reader, these are very special locutions, given in an extraordinary way.)

The Russian bear has swallowed up his first territory (Crimea). He is still hungry and will continue to swallow people and territories. He only understands one thing – a force that will not allow him to do this. The West sits at its tables and discusses, while Russia gobbles up its territories.

The West does not see the importance of the coming months, nor the extent to which Russia is ready to go, to add more people and more land to its empire. When these months are over and Russia has reached the full extent of its aggression (for now), the West will have lost much of its prestige and will never regain the position that it holds now.

What is happening in these months will not be reversible. These events will be like the amputation of an arm or a leg.

There will be a new world reality. Everything will be tilted. The ramifications will touch every country in Europe and America. These leaders will have foolishly delayed, while Russia moved ahead with firm purpose. All of this is the fruit of policies that have not taken the evil of Russia seriously, as if the collapse of the Iron Curtain or the removal of the Berlin Wall really changed the soul of the nation of Russia.

When these months are completed and the people and the land have been given to Russia without a single shot being fired by the West, then the next series of events will

36

take place. The West will be much weaker. It has no leader and no goals. Especially, it has no faith.

Comment
Jesus speaks about the next few months and
the results of the Russian aggression.

March 24, 2014
5. Using These Locutions

Revealing God's Plan

Mary
(Again a special locution)

I will no longer be silent. For decades, I have been telling the Church that Russia is the problem and it must be consecrated to my Immaculate Heart. The Church has chosen not to listen to my voice. It has even silenced those voices, especially Sr. Lucy's, which carried my message. Now, you are reaping the harvest which you have sown.

I will wait no longer. You, O Church, have buried my messages. You have hidden them. You have refused to reveal them. You have even twisted them. Because your voice does not send forth to the world the secrets of Fatima, nor do you obey the commands that I made at Fatima, I will bypass you.

I will begin to use these special locutions in a new and more powerful way. I will hold back nothing. I will reveal through these locutions what should have been revealed by the Church. I will do this slowly, piece by piece, truth by truth. I will do this in a consistent way so each person can easily follow my words and be led to the correct conclusions.

I must do this because you have not done this. You have turned aside from Fatima and the Fatima prophecies about Russia spreading its errors. You have not been a faithful watchman, warning my people and the world. Because you have not used your worldwide voice, I will use this little voice of my locutions.

Comment
For some reason, the Church has kept the Fatima secrets hidden.
Mary promises to use these locutions to reveal what the people need to know.

March 26, 2014
6. Events Followed by Delays

Revealing God's Plan

Mary

In the time ahead, the events will unfold which will convince the world that serious changes have happened. People will settle down, convinced that their lives will not be seriously changed. These, however, are only the beginning events. I have often said that the events will come in series, in groups of related happenings. Everything will not happen at once. God wishes to give mankind constant opportunities to repent and to turn to him.

Many will not read these signs correctly, thinking that these events are of human origin and that human solutions will avail.

The truth is this. That these events do not suddenly crash upon the world is due to God's mercy. Some events are held back. Other events are delayed. Some events are not allowed to happen. Some events are softened and not as destructive as Satan intended. Even in destructive events, God's mercy is at work.

Understand this delay, the putting off, and the postponement for a later time. Understand everything about God's mercy. The delays allow mankind to turn to God and to ponder what is happening. If mankind and the Church use these delays to respond wholeheartedly, God's mercy can triumph. Even more events can be softened. It is certain that earth must be purified. That truth cannot be changed. How earth is purified (by mercy or by justice) depends on mankind using the delays to listen. This is why I pour forth these locutions.

Comment

The first series of events was the revolutions in various countries.
Now, Russia initiates its aggressions. When these aggressions are finished,
a new series of events will happen. Each series of events invites the world
to seek God and his mercy.

March 27, 2014
7. When Blessings Are Delayed

Revealing God's Plan

Mary

When all of these events have happened, the world will be even more vulnerable. When it seems that all is sliding into a hopeless oblivion, I will finally come upon the world stage in the fullness of the gifts placed by the heavenly Father in my Immaculate Heart. At this point, I can only speak about these gifts, trying to describe these special helps which will be totally accommodated to the world's needs and completely able to reverse what everyone thought was irreversible.

However, accepting my gifts will demand a great level of faith and devotion. These extraordinary gifts will need an extraordinary response.

Unfortunately, this pouring out of blessings will happen late, after much suffering occurs that was not meant to happen. The earlier my blessings pour forth, the easier to receive them. The earlier my blessings pour forth, the less damage inflicted by Satan.

O reader, see the importance of today. Do not waste today. Do not say, "Someday, Mary will solve all these problems," as if you can sit back and watch. You must intercede. You must fast. You must ask with expectant faith. The whole world needs your daily prayers, especially the rosary.

Comment
Mary wants our day to be filled with spiritual activity and deep trust.

March 28, 2014
8. The Two Realities

Revealing God's Plan

Mary

No one can see the end of the road, that moment when I defeat the Evil One. Yes, the end of the road results in a victory, a final victory. Satan is cast out. The world returns to a simplicity. Peace reigns for a while. God's presence covers the earth because people, having experienced the events, have turned their hearts to God. That is the end of the road, but so much to travel before then, and it is to these pilgrims that I must speak.

The time ahead will be filled with the greatest trials and the greatest helps which God has ever bestowed upon mankind. You must see two realities to make the right choices and to not lose hope.

The first reality is that world history will be filled with catastrophes (that is the only word I can use), many of them caused by man himself, and in particular by Russia. However, do not let fear fill your hearts because there is a second reality, a world filled with the greatest gifts ever given to mankind by God. You must know that these extraordinary helps are available. You must gather with others so your faith multiplies and is not stolen. You must firmly believe in and seek the powers. My words must always guide you. Do not fear. I am always with you.

Comment
Mankind will face moments of catastrophes.
In those moments, can it believe in God's extraordinary helps?

March 29, 2014
9. Unrest in the Ukraine

Revealing God's Plan

Mary

When danger is far away, a mother speaks in a general way, trying to prepare her children. She gives them no specifics so they are not filled with fear. As the trials come closer, she can tell them how to prepare. When the trials are upon them, she gives very specific words, so they know exactly what is happening. In this way, she lessens their fears and takes away their confusion. A mother's words console and give peace.

My words are specific and will grow even more so. Amid your many fears, you can fully trust that I will speak to you. Trust my words. I will not lead you astray. Now I must speak of the growing evil.

These months will focus on the Ukraine and the great desires of Putin. Now that he has Crimea, where will he stop? Is there some magic line that he will draw to say "this far and no farther"? Will the West draw a line and be willing to back up their words with military force?

These questions and answers are obvious. Unfortunately, devouring Crimea will not satisfy Putin's appetite nor end his aggressions. These months of the Russian bear are just beginning.

Comment
Putin's aggressions will lead him wherever he finds an opening.

March 29, 2014
The Two Greatest Historical Forces

Revealing God's Plan

Mary

No part of history is ever totally wiped away. People think of past eras, as if they are gone and forgotten. However, there is no such thing as a past era. Whatever happens in history leaves its effects. All of the past is stored up, the good and the bad.

To reject history, to forget about it, or to set it aside, leads to blindness and an inability to understand the present forces or to foresee the future events. History is a stream and every event leaves its trace. This stream is carried both in the hearts of people and in the structures of a society.

I would point to two events, the fall of Adam and the death and rising of Jesus. These are the two most powerful moments of human history. These are the two polar events. The event of Adam affects the inner life of every person born into the world. The grace of Jesus is more powerful and is offered to every person, but it is frequently rejected or never understood.

This is an era of culmination. Will the powerful sin of Adam, planted in every human heart and constantly bringing forth evil, plunge the world into an unchangeable state? Or, will the grace of Jesus' Kingdom rescue mankind? These are the stakes. They are very high. They play out every day. All the world news reflects the clash of these two moments in history. I dare anyone to challenge my analysis of history. The Adam moment is relived and multiplied every day. The grace of Jesus is offered at every moment. Human history is a war, but the forces are often hidden and not understood.

Comment
Our Lady helps us to understand the two forces that battle for our souls.

March 30, 2014
10. The Moment of Mystery

Revealing God's Plan

Mary

Now, what are we coming to? I do not say a crossroads because mankind long ago came to that point and began to walk this present road. We do not come to a dead end, because with human history, there is no dead end. Time always moves along and new births are always happening.

We are coming to the moment of mystery, a great mystery far beyond the ability of man to even imagine.

In the face of this mystery, man will be totally helpless. All the powers that he has taken into his hands will avail nothing. All his human wisdom will be as foolishness. In this moment of mystery, man will be confronted with supernatural powers.

How difficult to describe these supernatural powers to a world that is still stable and operating in its own power. All I can say is that one event will follow another. Gradually, mankind will see that its powers are of no avail. Some will despair. However, those with faith and all who want to receive my help (I will multiply their numbers) will call upon me, and I will more and more manifest my power as the Woman Clothed with the Sun.

Comment
Begin now. Do not wait. Give Mary power over your daily life.
Say the rosary. That is the chain that bonds you to her.

41

March 31, 2014
11. The Faith That Leads to Greatness

Revealing God's Plan

Mary

When the dust settles and the new realignment of Europe is completed, those countries associated with the West will have shrunk. New dangers will arise because the borders of Putin's powers will directly touch more of the West. It will be a new reality, totally unforeseen by the West, which was unprepared for these moves.

All of this will add much more quickly to the economic pressures, which already plague the European nations. One problem is added to another, all done very cleverly by a Satanic intellect that far outstrips human plans. I have explained the forces that have quickly risen to the surface. Many more are ready to come forth in other places and in other areas of human life.

When will these events drive man to his knees and to a return to the Catholic faith that so many have abandoned? Faith formed the West. Faith led to the greatness of the West. Faith sent forth missionaries and found new lands. The source of the West's greatness is the only source of the West's salvation. Return, O West, to your heavenly Mother. I await you. My arms are outstretched. You still hold a special place in my heart.

Comment
In spite of all these problems, Mary always ends on a note of hope.

The Importance of the Locutions

April 1, 2014
1. The Locution's First Word – The Family

The Importance of the Locutions

Mary

The world must struggle with so many problems. It has overreached and stretched itself too thin, believing that it can accomplish far more than its resources will permit. Its plans have gone beyond its true powers. I will now speak about these issues and what has happened.

From the beginning, God wanted the family as the central foundation of the nation. The child was to be born from the mutual love of a man and a woman, totally committed to their marital union, and willing to accept this responsibility for a new life. From the parents, the child would learn its language, its name and its place in the wider community. This was God's plan and the community was to foster this and keep the family as its primary goal, realizing that its strength and vitality came from family life.

The family is in shreds. Outside forces have destroyed it, placing pressures that so few can withstand. What can be done? The problem began with over-reaching and wanting too much. The families must scale back, placing their focus on intimacy and relationships, rather than on things and income. I will help every family who calls on me. The rosary is the means to accomplish this goal.

Comment

Even the strongest of families is pulled in so many directions
by the pressures of modern life.

April 2, 2014

2. The Locutions Speak about Human History

The Importance of the Locutions

Mary

Mankind always stumbles and falls, never reaching the heights to which God calls it. Human history is filled with frustrations. Goals are gained for a moment and then lost. Eras of greatness are soon followed by decline. The highest altruism gives way, in time, to selfishness and venality. Some make great sacrifices to gain peace, followed by others who squander the victory.

I do not speak of just one moment of human history, or of just one era. In all of history, growth turns into decline. What was built soon falls apart. Such is the human condition.

However, what is happening today flows not just from the selfishness of mankind but from the intelligence and hatred of hell itself. The very linchpins of civilizations are loosened. The structures themselves will collapse. What is happening is not just a cycle of human history which will correct itself, but a complete collapse from which there will be no return.

I must awaken the whole world. I must enlighten every intellect and stir every heart. Only the gifts placed in my Immaculate Heart can prevent and save. O reader, do not wait for others. Come and bring others to me. The rosary is the door of entrance.

April 3, 2014
3. The Locutions Speak of Satan's Plan

The Importance of the Locutions

Mary

In the great light given to me by the heavenly Father, I see all of reality. I see the causes of illness, of strife and of war. I also see all that sin destroys. I want to speak of these realities (which mankind takes for granted) and how they change the original plan of the Father.

All of human history is not what God intended. From the very beginning, human life was stolen from the Father's hands, pulled away from the orbit of his love and set upon this path which mankind calls inevitable, namely, the rise and fall of nations, the collapse of family life, the constant wars, and violence. These are inevitable only because mankind, from the beginning, walked away from heaven's blessings. From the beginning, the Father also promised a Woman whose Son would offer mankind a new moment of life, a way of reversing that original moment of sin, and a chance to be freed from what seems to be the inevitable cycles that plague human life.

However, this has happened only infrequently, when in eras of great faith, a new civilization was born, with ideals born from His words and His Spirit. The world has put away this gift and, instead, has plunged ahead into unimaginable darkness.

The world has not just come into a destructive moment in the cycle of history. Mankind comes to a moment of unbelievable destruction, carefully plotted out by the Evil One. He wants to tilt the whole world in his favor, so that all of mankind slides to him and only the few are able to gain God's life.

He sees this moment on the horizon. He is not interested in just a particular nation. He wants the whole world. He wants to complete the result of that original sin. He wants to destroy those helps which God promised immediately to Adam and Eve, specifically the promise of the Woman and her Son.

We are in a war, and sides must be chosen.

April 4, 2014
4. God Must Intervene

The Importance of the Locutions

Mary

The human person and human history are blessed when God comes first. This is the order of creation. When God is not given his rightful place, human life unravels and mankind falls into many unforeseen dangers. God himself is the very core of human life. When he is rejected, nothing fits together. All is subjected to destructive forces that inevitably bring about confusion and decay. At each of these moments, God must intervene to correct human life and restore balance.

This is what I have been describing so clearly. Because God no longer comes first, destructive forces have torn apart human life, which is constantly more vulnerable to even greater evils. Evil upon evil. Destruction and violence. Do you not see this every day?

However, I do not come to emphasize what you know, but to speak of what is hidden. As always, God wishes to intervene, to gather mankind, and to bring order out of chaos. Was this not his original intention in creation? When his creation was ruined by sin, did he not promise a Woman whom he would use to intervene? The Woman is ready. When she is invoked and when Russia is consecrated to her heart, order will begin to return to creation.

Comment
Without God, creation inevitably returns to chaos.

April 5, 2014
5. The Locutions – Mary's Stream of Light

The Importance of the Locutions

Mary

When man does not know or believe in God, the lights go out. Although walking in darkness, man believes that he sees. With great love, the heavenly Father pierced these clouds of darkness and sent his only Son, Jesus, who offers light to the world. However, time and again, mankind rejects this light and casts itself back into the darkness.

At this moment, fateful and irreversible choices are being made. Human history is different. The stakes are higher and the consequences are stark. So, the Father has sent me, the Woman Clothed with the Sun, to release a great light, never before given to the human race. At a moment when all could become total darkness, man will be able to choose the light.

I say this again and again. The hour of Jesus' death was a moment of darkness. This present era is a similar moment of darkness, and only heaven's light can save the world. Do not be surprised that I speak every day. The darkness will be so complete that the whole world will depend on these locutions. They will be my stream of light.

Comment
These locutions are extraordinary but they are helps needed
to understand what is happening.

April 6, 2014
6. Speaking Every Day

The Importance of the Locutions

Mary

"No one knows the day and the hour. Stay awake." So many sleep! They are taken up with the daily cares and engrossed in their own pursuits. "The heavenly Father knows all that you need. Seek first the kingdom of God, and all these things will be given you besides." This was Jesus' teaching.

I must speak every day because modern man hears so many voices. These voices penetrate his heart and bombard him. He cannot escape their constant knocking. They always vie for his attention.

I speak a different word, which contradicts the world's daily message. My word is about a kingdom that is coming in great power. God will come to save man in the day and hour unknown to everyone. Stay awake! Do not let your spirits be bloated. My word is daily calling you every day. Whoever stays awake will see. Whoever is asleep will miss out.

Comment
Mary wants a daily life of prayer. This is the only way to watch.

April 7, 2014
7. Roar like a Lion

The Importance of the Locutions

Mary

The days grow fewer. The time runs out when other solutions would have been possible. Soon, the only option that will exist is war, the final battle between heaven and hell, which will take place on earth and within human history.

Yet, the world goes along as if all is well. The battle cry that issues from my heart is heard only by a few. I have raised up many voices, but these are quieted and put in their place. "This is only private revelation," says the Church. "It can be accepted or rejected. It does not belong to the Deposit of Revelation." Such is the reply that I so often hear. Why do I speak, if people are not to listen? What good is a warning, if no one heeds my words?

This is my promise. I will raise up my special son and no one will quiet him. He will roar like a lion even though his heart is like a tender lamb. He will speak my words to the nations and all will hear. No one shall "put him in his place" because, suddenly and without consulting anyone, I will put him in my place and all will know that he speaks in my name. Such is the gift that still remains hidden in my Immaculate Heart.

Comment

When Mary speaks, especially when the Church has approved her word,
she expects people to act.

April 8, 2014

8. Locutions That Save

The Importance of the Locutions

Mary

Mankind is like a child lost in a forest, who long ago left the road to chase after the butterflies of momentary pleasures. Although the child realizes that he is lost, he knows nothing else but to continue seeking the passing delights. As the pleasures increase and as the way of satisfying his cravings grow, then the sense of loss is assuaged. He begins to enjoy the forest and forgets that he is lost.

However, a moment comes when truth forces itself upon him. Who will be there for him in that moment of his despair? Who will say, "All is not lost. A path exists to bring you back to the road of your childhood faith. Then, you can take up your journey to God as you did before."

I am that voice and these locutions are my words. They resound right now in your heart. O child of God, you are lost. You have set aside the goals of your faith. You have abandoned your religious pursuits for passing delights. But I have a new life for you. Do not believe that your past wanderings condemn you to remain forever in the forest of sin. Come, take my hand. I will lead you back.

47

Comment
Mary describes so many Catholics who have left their practices of faith.
These locutions are her motherly actions to recall her children.

April 9, 2014
9. The Surprising Light of the Locutions

The Importance of the Locutions

Mary

So soon! The events will happen soon. Many will be unprepared. Therefore, I must speak and speak and speak until the Church understands that this voice must be listened to, and even exalted, so that more can listen.

These locutions began as a tiny voice, heard only in the heart of the one I chose. "How long will they continue? What topics will they explain?" These were the early questions. It is clear that I will speak each day and I will speak on every topic that is important to the trials that face mankind today.

These locutions are a surprising light, which Satan never planned for. They are sent forth under obedience and made available immediately to the whole world. The locutions go step by step. They are bold, but not reckless. They speak of terrible events, but always with hope. They are my means of speaking quickly and accurately to the whole world.

These locutions are signs of my care and concern. They will continually pour forth and, in the moments of great darkness, their light will grow stronger. No one will put out this light because no one can stop me from speaking to the one whom I love and have chosen.

Satan will attempt to destroy this website, but those whom I have chosen will constantly find ways to communicate the messages.

Comment
Mary described her own work during these three years in speaking to the world.

The Modern Events

April 10, 2014
1. Putin – Satan's Perfect Instrument

The Modern Events

Mary

There is so much to explain. I will not stop. Because the world and the Church are entering into darkness, I will continually speak. Already, the events unfold which will only be understood later.

The evil in Russia, planted in its soil by the slain bodies of millions, has refashioned itself. It has survived the *perestroika* (restructuring) of Gorbachev and has been modernized by Putin. Putin is the important figure, fashioned by Satan as his perfect instrument.

He has surprisingly risen to the top. First, there was his training. When he was ready, door after door opened to him. He was planted early in Satan's heart and now comes forth, ready to release Russia's evils on the whole world.

He has absolute power and has surrounded himself with those who are faithful to him alone. He knows that he has built both the country and his political machine well, having removed whomever he could not trust. His years of conquest lie ahead. He has no restraints.

Satan feeds him his ideas and stokes his ambitions. Nothing will stop him. The West is in disarray and has no plan except to react in the moments of crisis. I was not mistaken in asking that Russia be consecrated to my Immaculate Heart. I am the only one who can stop Putin. No one else is his match.

Comment
Putin is Satan's instrument and he stands at the center of events.

April 10, 2014
2. Middle East Events (Special Locution)

The Modern Events

Jesus

When the withdrawal of troops is completed, the very bowels of Afghanistan will be rent asunder, spilling out everywhere in the Middle East. Iraq will continue to sink into its civil wars. The fires in Syria will burn and burn. Neither side will withdraw from the conflict. Pakistan is a nuclear powder keg that waits to be lit after the

49

government topples. Iran constantly rises, assuring its place in the Middle East by destabilizing its neighbors and fomenting unrest.

Iran is now surrounded by protecting treaties that have been negotiated in complete foolishness. These guarantees only embolden its plans. As Iran continues to satisfy the West (and it will make sure to do that), it is free to engage in all its undercover activities.

Putin is actively setting the agenda. He knows the path he has set for the Middle East. He stands in great contrast to the West, which stumbles along with no understanding of these events. These events are not just shaping the world. They are preparing the world for even greater, unimaginable events. I speak so clearly because time is running out and no one is listening.

Comment
Unless everyone responds, these events will happen.

April 11, 2014
3. The Supernatural Forces

The Modern Events

Mary

Because so many forces are at work, no one can see the many events that will happen. People are unaware of these forces because they reject the supernatural world of heaven and hell.

Heaven loves earth. The heavenly Father has already intervened in Jesus who sent his Holy Spirit upon the disciples. The Spirit is constantly intervening in every heart that allows him to work.

These locutions reveal another, very special intervention of the Father. This is the new age of my Immaculate Heart and my coming forth upon the world stage as the Woman Clothed with the Sun.

Hell also intervenes. (Is this not evident to everyone?) People give themselves to darkness. They are rewarded with earthly titles and earthly powers. Through these people, the darkness grows. I have pointed this out quite specifically many times. Even these people of darkness are kept in the dark, having no idea of how Satan is using them (and will soon discard them as he fashions greater instruments of his darkness).

All of this is frightening. Therefore, I must use these locutions to form the minds and hearts of those whom I will use in the great battle. For now, just remain close to me and keep your hearts away from every darkness.

Comment
By these locutions, Mary allows us to see the forces shaping world events.

April 11, 2014
4. The Wars of Heaven and Hell (Special Locution)

The Modern Events

Jesus

There will seemingly be no end to these events. One will follow another, like waves of the ocean, which have an inexhaustible source. Do not fear. Hell is limited. Heaven is not.

If my people call upon me, I will unleash the waves of heaven, blessings after blessings, which no one can imagine. I will raise up those of good heart, empowering them and sending them forth. I will place faith in some people's hearts, which will move mountains, and words on the lips of others that will turn many back to me. It will be a time of signs and wonders.

This war between the two forces, heaven and hell, will break out into open warfare with great tides of evil and destruction. At the same time, the greatest powers that heaven has ever unleashed upon the world will come forth.

Man cannot save himself. He will either turn to heaven and be rescued, or be carried away by the waves of hell. I speak because that time is near at hand.

Comment
The only good result of the events is that people
will grasp how much they need God.

April 11, 2014
5. Sending Forth the Locutions (Special Locution)

The Modern Events

Jesus

The locutions are a small but tested stream, given now for three years. They speak of political events and worldwide events but they do so only within this little stream of faithful readers.

It is time to take new action. The seeds of these locutions must be planted in the great field of the world itself. Many will be surprised as the prophetic words are verified by world events. People will understand that heaven is giving forth its light.

I want to march against the darkness that surrounds the world and dispel it. Let everyone who reads these locutions become messengers of the locutions. Take them everywhere – to the television stations, to the radio stations, to the newspapers and magazines. These locutions must be known everywhere.

I want these locutions to go forth first of all to the world, not to the Church. The Church has many streams of private revelations, and these locutions seem to be just one of many. However, if the locutions go forth to the world and the world shows great interest, then the Church itself will begin to investigate and see that these locutions are not just one among many.

As these locutions go to the world, I will increase their power and clarity so the world is convinced that heaven is speaking. I will begin with Russia and the Ukraine.

Russia will surround the Ukraine with its darkness and its fire. The pressure will be intense. As the time goes on, cracks will appear in the Ukraine and divisions will take place. The Ukraine has various cultures, with ethnic groups and sub-divisions, almost too numerous to describe (due to the centuries of its history).

Russia will apply its darkness by surrounding the Ukraine and keeping out the West. It will also apply its fire by the internal pressures that cause divisions. Very soon, many parts will appear and separate, all in different ways and in different degrees. Political unity will be shattered and its restoration will be impossible. New forms of political life will emerge. All will evolve into something new and all will be to Putin's gain. How much he will gain, no one can foresee now, but he does not need a crystal ball. He needs only to apply the Russian darkness and the Russian fire.

The Ukraine will self-divide because its political ties are already weak. Some regions will divide quickly and move politically out from under Kiev. Others will form a different relationship with Kiev. These first steps will not be the final steps.

Larger sections of the Ukraine will move more slowly but their movement will shake the Ukraine even more. The final stage of the Ukraine will be hard to recognize, far removed from the political arrangement that formerly existed.

April 12, 2014
6. Our Lady's Strategy

The Modern Events

Mary

So many sorrows, always mounting higher! When will it end? Satan's desires are never quenched. Suffering only feeds his hunger. Suffering, suffering, suffering. His kingdom knows only suffering. Victories for him must be filled to the top with suffering. Look out over the world. Sufferings are everywhere, a sure sign that the world is falling quickly into his hands.

I stand atop another mountain from which flows only light and consolations. Satan has covered over this mountain. He has turned people's eyes away from me. When I speak, he whispers, "This is only private revelation."

By these locutions, I descend from this mountain and adopt a new, surprising strategy. I knock on every door. I plead with every heart. People even ask, "Would Mary speak this way? Would she speak about world events? Would her words be so down to earth? She speaks so clearly, so easily, in teachings that all can understand."

Yes, I have left my mountaintop of light and have entered the valley of darkness only so I might lead the whole world back to my mountain. Only then will they overcome the mounting sufferings which Satan has planned.

Comment
The locutions knock at your heart's door. Open quickly.

April 13, 2014
7. Messengers of the Locutions

The Modern Events

Mary

I cannot wait any longer. The gifts in my Immaculate Heart must go forth. I will no longer use the established ways. I will go into the marketplace. I will cry out in the city square. I will walk the streets. My voice will be everywhere. I will use the messengers of the locutions. Armed with my words, fervent in their zeal, and using every means possible, they must take these locutions everywhere. The whole world must know about these locutions.

For years now, I have spoken and have gathered a large and faithful audience. They cherish my words and often discuss "the locutions." These faithful bearers of the word must now multiply their power and their presence. They must send these locutions everywhere. Let the media, the television stations, the radio stations, the newspapers and magazines know about these locutions.

I speak often about political realities and politicians. Let the mass media be aware. I want the whole world to listen. I will begin a new stage of the locutions. Names and places and events will be put into the open. All will be revealed. I can wait no longer. As these locutions go to the world, I will increase their power and clarity so the world is convinced that heaven is speaking.

Comment
For three years, Our Lady has spoken in this quiet way.
Now, she wants her voice to go public.

April 14, 2014
8. The Flood Waters of Immorality

The Modern Events

Mary

The events flow on but they are not like waves hitting upon rocks that easily turn them back and surrender nothing. These events are like floods that come and stay, ruining all that was so carefully built.

Mankind has welcomed these new moral evils that did not happen in earlier societies. After the original waves, came the deluge, the effects that man could not foresee. His city crumbles before his very eyes. The beauty is marred and human life descends to a lower level.

I speak now of all the moral ills to which society has opened its doors. These visitors will not leave. They have captured the day and are ingrained into society. There are always new visitors, and others that are soon to come. These enemies are not at the door. They are inside, like the floodwaters, and they will not leave. Society welcomes them, even votes to accept them.

Laws are ineffective and politicians are no match for their power. I must offer society a powerful light so that it sees what it has done. Only when there is a divine enlightenment will society turn back and begin to clean out these floodwaters.

Comment
These floods are mankind's own fault.

April 14, 2014
9. (Special Locution)

The Modern Events

Jesus

Pope Francis wants only blessings for the Church, and desires to make the Church a place where everyone is welcome. He wants to study the needs of the Church and has begun this process by calling a Synod, which will face the issues of family life.

There will be three stages. First, the time leading up to the Synod. Second, the Synod itself; and third, the Church after the Synod. The Synod will be a watershed. The desire to accommodate and to be open will come at a high price. People will speak up. Some guided by heaven and others guided by hell.

Before the Synod, survey results will be revealed by those who want to influence the outcome. At the Synod itself, some bishops will say things that will break with traditional morality. Others will make suggestions that cannot be followed. All of that will lead to the time after the Synod.

Some, to the far right, will have difficulty in accepting the tone of the Synod. The vast majority of Catholics will wonder what took place and just what was determined. There is a third group, which has advocated serious changes in the Church's teachings concerning family life issues. They will see the Synod as the vindication, at long last, of their positions (even though this was not explicitly said).

After the Synod, the Church will be known as the Church of Pope Francis. More than anything else, the Synod will put its stamp on this pontificate, just as Vatican II did for Pope John XXIII.

The Church, however, will not be ready for the fierce battles that lie ahead. It will not be a Church formed by the Woman Clothed with the Sun, nor will it be able to confront the great forces that are shaping the world. The Church of Pope Francis will not be ready. It will be a popular, accepting and open Church, but will not be ready for the future events.

Comment
The Synod will deal with Church issues,
but will not prepare the Church for the future events.

April 15, 2014
10. A New Role

The Modern Events

Mary

I must force the world (and the Church) to face certain realities. Even though these realities lie in the future, their time is at hand. They are not far away. The first waves have already lashed at the shore and more will inevitably come.

The world is in darkness and the Church is silent. So, I must take the initiative. My voice will ring out. My words will be heard by all. I will become the prophet of this age. Has this ever happened before? Has the virgin mother of God ever assumed such a role? No. Never. Previously, I have spoken in remote places and allowed my words to be carried by messengers. I have tried this, but the faithful messengers were not heeded. I can no longer use a messenger who is set aside.

I must come into the heart of the world and of the Church. I will come to both at once. My words will not be placed in the hearts of my messengers. They will be placed before the whole world. No one will keep my messages hidden. They will be given to the whole world in a minute, in the twinkling of an eye. There will be no cover-ups. No one can change or interpret my words away. All the world will know my exact words from the beginning.

Comment

Time grows much shorter. Our Lady's messages are kept hidden. That will end. Our Lady will speak directly to the world and the Church.

April 15, 2014

11. Putin and Western Europe (Special Locution)

The Modern Events

Jesus

Destruction is everywhere in the Ukraine. The very ground of stability is being pulled away, not just from the Ukraine, but from all of Western Europe. No natural wall exists that will protect it.

Western Europe is not dealing with an old Russia, based upon a corrupt Communist Party and a closed economy. Putin's Russia is different. It has infiltrated Western economies and welcomed Western businesses. Putin has removed anyone who was against him and has changed the political system. He has complete command.

In the Ukraine, he feels completely confident. Russia is geographically close and the Ukrainian economy compares poorly with Russia's. Many people are of Russian descent and seek to be reunited with Russia. The Kiev government is both new and weak. Putin knows that the Ukraine is his, and he has various ways of gaining it.

More important, these same factors hold true in other, nearby nations. Already, some peoples, who sought independence a few decades ago, are unhappy with the results, and believe that they would do better to return. Putin's formula has appeal in many places. All of this will shake Europe, and even America. All will be shifted. Putin is Satan's perfect instrument.

There is also the Muslim world of Iran, Syria, and others whom he has befriended. All share a hatred for the West and a desire for world domination. They will see themselves as more and more united in this hatred, especially as the West appears so defenseless and an easy prey. I have spoken before of international groupings that pay no attention to national boundaries.

Even the West will no longer have a stability. All will be destabilized. There will be many events, one greater than another.

Comment

No one can see how Putin's action will affect Western Europe and America.

April 16, 2014
12. Putin - The Hammer of Satan

The Modern Events

Mary

The story unfolds in a surprising way. What was thought to be stable and decided, namely, the allegiance of the nations after the collapse of Communism, is suddenly making a different choice. The tide is being reversed. Voices that clamored for independence now want to be united again with Russia.

Where does this force come from? What has turned the people around so quickly? Have they forgotten so soon what their former life was like? Do they know what awaits them?

What is taking place rests totally and completely in the soul of one man – Vladimir Putin. For years, Satan guided and protected him, keeping him out of the limelight and always fostering his career. At the right moment, he lifted him up. No one expected him to last long, but he moved quickly to grab, to consolidate, and then to cling to his power.

Putin sits in the very center of Satan's plans. He has kept alive the dictator in Syria and has provided scientists to Iran. He has fostered relationships with all who hate the West and has clearly made them dependent upon himself. He grabs wealth that is not his and fashions everything according to Satan's plans. The Western leaders are not his equal, even though their resources are much greater.

Putin will be the hammer which Satan uses again and again to weaken the West and cause unforeseen troubles. His stealing the Ukraine rips a massive hole in the protection surrounding Europe. At this point, nothing in Europe is safe. The European leaders thought they had built a strong city. Now, they do not even have a wall protecting their interests.

Comment
The events in the Ukraine threaten all of Europe much more than anyone suspects.

Safeguarding Human Freedoms

April 17, 2014
1. Against the One World Order

Safeguarding Human Freedoms

Mary

When did this begin, the moment when the course of world events no longer lies in the hands of mankind? Man has never been able to decide his own history. Unforeseen events have always happened, but these did not affect what man could decide. Parts of the world remained in his control and the human race would reestablish a center of order and culture.

Before this century, there never existed a truly worldwide power. Various empires rose up that conquered parts of the world, but much of human life was beyond their control. How the heavenly Father loves the diversity of nations and peoples! These guarantee the future of the human race. He wanted man to spread out over the entire globe, so no one person or one power could ever gain complete control. He guaranteed this at the tower of Babel with the multiplicity of languages.

Now, a one world order is emerging. Nations give up their uniqueness to enjoy a greater share in the world's goods. The growing crisis will only hasten this process which Satan is ready to use. As the one world order begins, the heavenly Father's plan for the diversity of the nations will be reversed. All will come together, but not to celebrate the banquet of the Lamb. The world will become like an army, trapped with nowhere to go, an easy prey for its enemies.

These are powerful forces that already are causing profound changes. Satan's crises will be used as proof and excuses that mankind must hurry along this path of one world order, one government, one currency. "Nations can no longer survive on their own," they will say. "National currencies and national interests must be sacrificed."

I say all of this so the Church understands that these worldwide forces will sweep the Church itself into its stream. When will the Church understand? Only the Woman Clothed with the Sun can stop the creation of a one world order and bring about God's original plan of diversity. Nations will flourish in their diversity as they truly help one another and allow each nation to retain its sovereignty.

God's plan and the world's plan are totally at odds. The world's plan is Satan's ploy. He wants a total, worldwide destruction, which he can accomplish in one swoop if only he destroys God's diversity. Only the Woman can thwart his plans.

Comment

This locution gives a powerful overview of Satan's plan and reveals where he is leading the world through his individual, destructive events.

April 18, 2014

2. Satan's Leaders

Safeguarding Human Freedoms

Mary

A tunnel of darkness lies ahead which mankind must not enter. Oh, how Satan wants the world to enter his tunnel. It will seem like the perfect solution to all the crises and events. The tunnel will be a leader whom Satan will raise up. I will explain his methods, which he is now using in the Ukraine and elsewhere.

First, Satan destabilizes a region. He causes unrest and protests. He causes sufferings and shortage so people grow dissatisfied. When he brings a nation to this point, he leads onto the scene a leader whom he has prepared. Even though people have many reservations, they willingly accept this leader, believing that he will end their hardships. Satan used this formula in Russia to raise up Putin, and Putin uses this to gain the Ukraine.

Right now, the West does not experience hardships like the Ukraine. Satan's powerful destabilizing action has not yet been fully released. However, events will begin, one after another, that will shake the West. Be assured that Satan already has his leaders prepared to come forth. They are hidden now but, at the right moment, they will begin to proclaim themselves as the saviors. Each one in a different place in a different situation.

People will surrender their freedoms and will accept a leadership that they would easily have rejected in more stable moments. This was the path taken by Hitler. People forfeited their independence and their human rights to gain stability. Instead, they entered Satan's tunnel and could not turn back. Only in the future will Satan's greatest leader arise. He will not be national or regional. He will be international and worldwide. It will always be the same formula. Worldwide unrest, and a leader who promises to be the solution when, in reality, he is Satan's tunnel.

I want to avoid all of this. I spell this out so the whole world is enlightened. Do not give up your God-given rights. Do not be drawn into false alliances. Foster diversity. Stand alone. Refuse to accept unworthy leaders, no matter what they promise or no matter how desperate is the situation.

People rightly ask, "How can we resist? How can we not go along?" You need the Woman Clothed with the Sun to help you. I can change world events and I will do so for those who call on my name. It is easy to surrender and difficult to resist. However, a moment of victory will come sooner than you think.

Comment

A powerful locution revealing Satan's strategy, which unfolds before our eyes.

April 19, 2014
3. Against Satan's Sufferings

Safeguarding Human Freedoms

Mary

Suffering causes man to set aside important values, even much of what he treasured and believed. Satan's plans always include much suffering so he can shake a person away from their beliefs.

In the twentieth century, he used the two great wars to tear Europe away from the church. The foundations of the people's faith were shaken because the established order was overturned. Instead of heaven, they saw hell on earth. Satan's plans for the future will be the same. He will fill the world with suffering. He will shake the established order so he can steal faith in God from people's hearts.

I hate Satan's suffering and I will raise up people who will protect the human race. Through them, I will cast my mantle over the whole world. I want the whole world to know that I am the Woman and my great interventions will come through people whom I place in high positions.

All must begin now in the West because until Russia is consecrated to my Immaculate Heart, my powers over that country are limited. She will continue to pour out Satan's sufferings.

Comment

Sufferings are always a mystery. Faith can grow amid suffering, but faith can also be endangered by widespread sufferings. This is one of Satan's tactics.

April 20, 2014
4. Staying Free

Safeguarding Human Freedoms

Mary

The time is coming when people will be willing to trade their freedoms for security. Then, the great doors of danger open, and changes can be introduced that no one ever conceived. The human race becomes like cattle, all herded into a common field. Diversity is stripped away. All are branded as if owned by others. How I want to avoid those moments and destroy the forces that bring them about.

Each person is unique, made in God's image. All creation exists so the human person can come to a fullness of God's image in a complete and individual way. Only the religious spirit resists the state. Only the religious spirit clings to God's plan. Those who want a one world order know what they must do. They must first kill the religious spirit of God in man.

I have come to awaken that spirit and to stir the hearts of all. If you want your freedoms, then worship God. Keep holy his day. Without God, no one is free, no matter how much they might claim their selfish freedoms.

Comment
The battle for freedom is no longer just in the
individual heart, but in all of society.

April 21, 2014
5. Opposing a One World Government

Safeguarding Human Freedoms

Mary

I must begin again, always raising my voice to protest what is happening and to direct my children before it is too late. In some parts of the world, human freedoms do not exist. They have already been stolen. In the West, these freedoms are supposedly guarded by constitutions and laws. However, all of these are endangered by the crises that have happened and, especially, those that will happen.

There is an inevitable march to a one-world order, in a future that is not too distant. I must speak clearly because God formed nations, giving each a particular culture and a distinct geography. Each nation is meant to prosper, and all are meant to help one another. Each people must be allowed to grow according to its own unique life. All governments must respect this individuality of each nation, fostering it and helping it to prosper.

Instead, people want to destroy these rights of nations and have them sacrificed for the sake of a new world order. This only plays into Satan's hands, gathering all the nations into a false unity and directly opposing God's plan. Why did God split the continents? Why did God create mountains? Why did he bring about various diverse languages? Because he wanted nations to evolve. The safety of the human race lies in its diversity.

When Jesus returns, he will gather the nations. Until then, any attempt to gather the nations into a one world order comes from Satan. It is a false gathering of the nations, a counterfeit, and must be totally opposed.

Comment
Mary outlines God's plan so clearly that we can see
the One World Order as a Satanic counterfeit.

April 22, 2014
6. A Song of Hope

Safeguarding Human Freedoms

Mary

I will place everything before your eyes so the world will see. Mankind marches to Satan's tune. He plays his sweet music and attracts the hearts of many, like a pied piper. Mankind only hears the music and pays no attention to his path.

So, I put forth these locutions. They have their own attraction. They resonate deeply in the heart. People say, "These words are true. I must listen more and more." The more I speak, the greater are the numbers who listen. They find in my words new lyrics and truths that give peace.

Come, my children, just listen and I will sing you a song of hope. My songs are of a new life that comes only by faith in Jesus. I will be the new pied piper and soon the world will hear two songs, Satan's song of death and my song of hope.

You will dance to my music and your hearts will be light. You will say, "Yes, it can be done. Mankind can turn away from selfish pursuits. He can live in harmony. Individual freedoms can flourish and goals be accomplished without surrendering our freedoms." The secret lies in the music. I am a different drummer, playing a new song. Listen for my music in your heart. It is already playing, the band has begun.

Comment
Very few understand the great joy of those who learn Mary's secrets.
She now reveals them to the world.

April 23, 2014
7. Preserving Human Freedom

Safeguarding Human Freedoms

Mary

Before all else, the heavenly Father desires the good of human persons. He created the whole universe for the human person and brought human persons forth as his final accomplishment. When sin had so destroyed his plan, he sent his only Son, Jesus, to restore the human person to freedom and dignity.

The human person does not exist for the government. The state must serve the good of the person, the full good of his body and soul. However, all of creation has been twisted and distorted, and the Father's plan set aside. Now mankind has enormous powers to form society against the human person and to take away his freedoms.

No one has the power to resist these forces or to turn them aside. All leads to centralization, to gathering of information and, ultimately, to total control by those who avidly seek this worldwide power. The human person is caught up in a powerful force that removes any choices.

Does not a mother love each of her children according to their individual personalities? Does she not delight in their differences? She does not force them all to be the same. As the Woman Clothed with the Sun, I want to prevent the forming of a one world order and to establish the uniqueness of nations, allowing each to flourish to their own genius. I must come quickly onto the world scene and pour out a new flame. It is late. It is so late. Only the gifts placed by God in my Immaculate Heart can save the world.

Comment
Our Lady continues the theme of the importance
of the human person's freedom in God's plan.

April 23, 2014
8. Special Locution

Safeguarding Human Freedoms

Jesus

Kiev is like a raw nerve. The main question in the Ukraine is how close will the fighting come to Kiev? What will happen as it approaches? The West has never declared its intentions concerning the Ukraine.

The Kiev government is new and weak. Many people still feel a loyalty to the ousted president and are now questioning that decision which Putin used as his excuse to seize the Crimea.

The new government and the West are totally unprepared for these surprising events. Who will broker any truce when Putin claims that this is a civil uprising due to discontent with the new government?

My message is this. Kiev is a great flash point that could easily burst open. Putin works with a demonic intelligence which mocks the West and grabs all that is left unprotected.

Comment

The Ukrainian situation is very dangerous, much more so than the West understands.
Just like Syria.

April 24, 2014
9. Closing Words

Safeguarding Human Freedoms

Mary

Events do not just unfold. Forces behind the events bring them about. I reveal these forces and their goals so that they do not unfold. Once a road is taken and once changes are introduced, they obtain a force that is difficult to dislodge.

Rich and powerful people want a one world order. They seek to control the world so that even sovereign nations are subjected to them (even though these nations still exist and seemingly are autonomous). When a one world order is established, all nations must feed into a higher, supra-national order and follow its dictates. Very little room is left for natural sovereignty.

Crises will be used to foster this one world government. There will be pleas that humanity will be better served if nations submit their particular goals to the greater one world goal and to these superstructures.

I have spoken clearly enough. Leaders must be elected who cling strongly to national sovereignty and foster close ties among nations that respect individual nationalities and refuse to erase the boundaries created by God's plan. Any other path is a road to Satan's goals of a counterfeit gathering of the nations.

Comment

Mary could not be more clear. Elect leaders who will resist the giving over
of a nation's power to supra-national structures.

A Grassroots Movement

April 25, 2014
1. Begin from the Grassroots

A Grassroots Movement

Mary

I will describe the future events clearly and the forces that will shape them. I will pull back all the veils so that the whole world knows how deeply I love the human race and all that I want to do for mankind. I must reveal the very depths of my Immaculate Heart so that everyone says, "Why should we not go there? What is holding us back from such treasures?"

In this way, many will see my love because they know my secrets. They will join with others in this search, like companions on a journey. In this way, they will not lose their way nor grow discouraged. Also, they will discover so much more. What one finds, all will possess, and their joys will multiply.

I will begin from the grassroots and, with the new means of social media, this can spread like wildfire. Come, I invite all of you. Listen to my song. Read my locutions. Let them claim your heart. I will speak every day to the whole world. Share these locutions with others. They will join your hearts. As your hearts are joined in my words, I will inspire you as to what steps you must take to increase this treasure. The beginnings will seem small but, after a few months, you will realize the great gifts contained in your small steps of faith.

Comment
Our Lady never delays. She acts now.

April 25, 2014
2. President Obama's Ideology

A Grassroots Movement

Jesus

All of these destructive events should not be happening this quickly. The timetable has been moved up because America has withdrawn from the world scene. All of this is due to the ideology placed deeply in the heart of President Obama. He rejects my plan for America. I blessed America so it would be strong and dominant and be a light to the nations and assume the role of a watchman.

He rejects my plans because of an ideology placed in his heart as a youth. For him, American dominance is the problem. For him, America has to be lowered in stature and become just an equal among other nations. This totally contradicts my plans for world peace. His actions show that American withdrawal allows the seeds of violence to grow unchecked.

America has elected a president whose heart is totally against all that I raised up America to be. So, I will not protect him, I will not support him. Except when America's good is at stake, I will allow him to walk his own path. He will not have my blessings or my protections. He is on more dangerous ground than he can ever imagine.

April 26, 2014
3. Tell the Whole World

A Grassroots Movement

Mary

There will be a great sweep to my actions. I will not limit myself to small-scale warfare. I will take on the enemy in the vast expanses of the mass media. That is why these locutions must go forth. They have been sown now in the hearts of many for three years. All are recorded. All can be read. They are like seeds that must bring forth a vast harvest.

My messengers ask, "What am I to say? What should be my message?" Just read all the locutions. See which ones I plant in your heart. That is the message that you are to take forth. Each will carry a different part of these locutions. I already have thousands of people who read these locutions and have studied them for years. Yes, there are many thousands. You are one of them and I commission you. I give you authority as Jesus gave his apostles authority to preach to the whole world. "All that I have commanded you," Jesus said.

Is this not exactly the same? Are you not with me on my mountaintop? I give you the same command. "Tell the whole world all that I have told you in these locutions." How great is this task. Accept it as your personal and sacred mission. Just as Jesus said to his disciples, so I say to you, my disciples, "I will be with you until the end of the world." All the gifts stored by the heavenly Father in my Immaculate Heart will flow out upon all who hear your words. Thank you.

Comment
The locutions must go forth everywhere by every means.

April 27, 2014
4. Fires at the Door

A Grassroots Movement

Mary

The fires burn everywhere, always more brightly and with greater destruction. What was considered safe, becomes endangered. O West, you think you are far from the fires. You think that they can be contained in the Middle East or in the Ukraine. Really, they are ready to consume your houses also. First, they will surround you on every side. As they continue to burn (because you have forsaken the only means to extinguish them), they will weaken your foundations, cut you off and isolate you. Your resources will grow smaller and you will even begin to say, "Let us begin to cooperate with this fire of Russia." This will be the fatal mistake, when you lose all your courage to expel the fire and you invite it to enter. At first, it will enter with its ingratiating smile, but then, the hatred and danger will appear. Your house is divided and a divided house soon topples.

As the Woman Clothed with the Sun I, alone, offer the waters needed to repel and, if totally obeyed, to extinguish the fires and restore world peace. Who even speaks of world peace these days? That is my promise, my total and complete promise. I will give to the world a time of peace. Who believes me? Who listens? Who acts? That is why I am raising up messengers of these locutions. The fires are at the door and the West has forsaken the only means which can extinguish them.

Comment
Our Lady's predictions are dire and her promises are clear.

April 28, 2014
5. The Fires of Darkness

A Grassroots Movement

Mary

Everything will happen so quickly. There are not just fires burning in so many places but winds that will spread Satan's fires. Walls of protection will prove to be useless. The fires will leap over these walls. There will be fires in front and fires to the back. With so many fires in so many places, how will they be extinguished?

I am not describing what is far distant. Look around. All can see the fires everywhere. (Even in Latin America which I love so dearly.) What is not consumed? There are some places where I am venerated in a special way. They will be a sign to you. I protected Portugal in World War II and Medjugorje in the Bosnian War. Let them be clear signs to you.

Only the Woman Clothed with the Sun can protect the world from the fires that will spread so quickly. Seemingly, they will be out of control. Really, they will be very controlled by Satan and by those whose intellects he darkens with his evil. The fires of darkness. These are the future forces being released. Can no one see or grasp? Human responses are like foolishness, child's play. The human race needs the Woman and I am ready to help all who invoke me.

Comment

This is a general warning. As the locutions proceed,
Our Lady will probably speak more concretely.

April 28, 2014

6. Putin's Method (Special Locution)

A Grassroots Movement

Jesus

Putin is rejoicing because he is inflicting suffering upon the Ukraine. Suffering is the key which he uses to steal what is not his. He inflicts more and more suffering until those in possession of the land and of the goods are willing to let go, so that the suffering stops.

Who is ready to stop him in his tracks? No one. The West, too, applies sufferings but compared to Putin's sufferings and the great gains that he is acquiring, they are as no suffering at all. So, he is rejoicing and he will continue to use this method. He will cause sufferings everywhere and will increase them until he gains what is not his.

April 28, 2014

7. An Appeal to the Polish People (Special Locution)

A Grassroots Movement

Mary

I give these locutions because I love the Ukrainian people and they love me. How they suffered under Stalin and Communism, more than any other group. Yet, their love for me did not waver. I hold them in a special place in my heart and I use these locutions to tell them, "I love you and I have not forgotten you."

The problem is that the West sees the Ukraine from a political point of view and that of the mass media. For the people of the Ukraine, this is not a mass media event. This is an event of blood, blood on their streets, blood in their towns and cities. This is about the sufferings of their young people and the total uprooting of their country. For the West, it is a matter of policy issues. For the people it is a matter of life and death, of darkness, of untold sufferings and of total despair.

The West will not help. The sanctions are not the answer. I must look around. To whom will I appeal? Poland loves me. They know that I have miraculously saved this nation on many occasions (as at the Vistula). To you, O people of Poland, I appeal. You know the true stories. You see the blood. Many of you have relatives. Do all you can. Reach out to the Ukrainian people. You are not powerless. Your hearts are strong and wide open. Reach out to the Ukraine. I will be with you and you will be surprisingly successful.

Comment

Sometimes grassroot actions are more effective than government initiatives.

April 29, 2014

8. A Totalitarian Russia

A Grassroots Movement

Mary

There is no time to waste. The supposed walls of protection around the West are like paper in the presence of fire. The destruction in the Ukraine will move much more quickly and decisively than anyone can imagine. What has been set in place (supposedly dedicated to Western-style democracy) will crash and a totalitarian regime will be quickly established.

Right before the eyes of the West, Russia has suddenly become once again a totalitarian regime under the control of one person whom Satan has led to the top.

I have promised the conversion of Russia when that nation is consecrated to me. Let all the world, not just the Church, know of my promise and what is still lacking. If the Holy Father and all the bishops of the world in union with him would consecrate Russia to my Immaculate Heart, I have promised that Russia would be converted and a great period of peace would follow.

There has been no such consecration and no conversion of Russia. There has only been the removal of a wall and economic intertwining. Satan still holds the country in his grasp. He will continue to use Russia as his instrument, just as he did in the past century.

Comment

Russia will grow as an evil force in Satan's hands
until the Holy Father fulfills Our Lady's wishes.

69

April 30, 2014
Poland, Baltic Countries and European Union
(Special Locution)
Jesus

Poland

Poland is weak, no longer the militant, aggressive Poland that existed under Communism and under Pope John Paul II. It has traded its militancy for the goods of Western society, becoming soft, penetrable and ready to go along. It is no longer resistant and ready to destroy any foe that would compromise its principles. With the events in the Ukraine, Putin now turns his glance to Poland. He enjoys a new window of opportunity in Poland. He knows the former Poland (the staunch ally of the Pope) and he knows the present Poland, no longer rooted in an iron-willed determination.

He knows how to plan his attack, which will be a mixture of threats, policies and enticements. He wants to change Poland's current status. He cannot do in Poland what he is doing militarily in the Ukraine. However, he will develop other plans to draw Poland closer to Russia. This will affect all of Poland, as people realize that their status quo is being challenged by a force that NATO cannot fight because it is not primarily a military force. This force will be even more real, a relentless force that cannot be destroyed and which always has access to people's hearts. Putin always manipulates the events so they serve Russia's purpose. Putin will be seen as a new force within Poland itself, a pernicious force that will not withdraw, like a wolf always seeking its prey.

Baltic States

A similar, but greater influence will extend to the smaller nations along the Baltic. They are more vulnerable because their population and their resources are smaller. These nations will experience Putin's newly revealed aggressiveness even more than Poland.

Destabilizing the European Union

Putin has his eyes set on destabilizing the European Union. Cracks have appeared in this European house because it is not well-built, or founded upon rock. This Union has never been built upon the Catholic faith. European unity is based upon self-interest. For many, self-interest in the European Union is fading quickly.

Putin knows that the European Union is a house filled with many cracks. He will apply every sort of pressure. He has one goal, to exploit those cracks and to increase

70

their power so that the whole European Union faces serious threats to its future viability. This is almost within his reach. Putin has a wrecking ball and wants to use it to tear down the European house. He wants to fulfill the dreams of Stalin, the collapse of Western Europe and the emergence of Russia as the world power.

All of this is possible and its fulfillment can happen much more quickly than any European or American leader can conceive. The timetable is moved way ahead and Putin, as Satan's perfect instrument, will not hesitate one moment.

I am putting the European leaders on notice of what can happen. In their foolishness, they have abandoned the faith and have built their secular union. They have no defenses against Putin, Satan's instrument. America will be deeply shaken by this destabilizing of the European Union.

April 30, 2014
9. Choosing the Wrong Woman

A Grassroots Movement

<u>Mary</u>

Before moving on, I must explain what has brought the human race to this point so that everyone understands my teachings.

Centuries ago, beginning with the French revolution, people walked away from the great faith that formed Europe. This revolution lifted up the false goddess of reason. The effects of this choice were like a knife in my Immaculate Heart. People would seek from the goddess of reason what she could never give. They would come away thirsty. Even worse, they would drink of her poisoned waters. Such has been the fruits of these 200 years in which man has chosen the wrong woman.

I quickly began to regain my place in men's hearts. The great age of the apparitions began, leading up to the phenomena of Fatima (1917). At Fatima, the heavenly Father himself, by the great miracle, proclaimed me as the Woman Clothed with the Sun.

Since Fatima, the West has continued to exalt the goddess of reason and to walk away from faith. What has happened? Look around. Untold destruction. Millions of people dead by violence. Now, the present situation. The West must understand the decisions made in the past. It has forsaken the Woman Clothed with the Sun for the false goddess of reason. Such is the foolishness of a child who has already destroyed so much.

You have chosen the wrong Woman, but it is not too late. I await your decision. These locutions will prepare many hearts, and when I begin to reveal myself more fully, all will understand that I am the Woman Clothed with the Sun who is coming to save everyone.

Historical Note

The French Revolution lasted from 1789 to 1799. In November, 1793 in Our Lady's Cathedral (Notre Dame) in Paris, the feast of the "Goddess of Reason" was celebrated. Later, the revolutionaries celebrated this feast of the Goddess of Reason in several other provincial cathedrals. After this, churches were used for meetings or for stores and not for Catholic worship.

May 1, 2014

10. Russia's River of Acid

A Grassroots Movement

Mary

Putin's Russia is like an enormous river of acid that can flow in many directions and change course at a moment's notice. This river has no fixed agenda, only the goal of Russian supremacy brought about by a great intermingling of nations that share its darkness. This flexibility presents the greatest hazards for the Western strategies.

The river of acid can flow anywhere, choosing its most susceptible targets. Once its corrupting power has sufficiently drawn them into the Russian mold, the river can flow out into other, less accessible places. This acid is filled with power and refuses to be diluted. It is corrosive and destroying, leaving death, destruction and evil of every kind in its wake. This acid has been flowing for almost a century and has taken many forms, sometimes assuming a militaristic confrontation and, at other times, a face that welcomes all visitors (as if it had changed).

A hundred years ago, I warned the Church about this destructive power of Russia and nothing was done. So, I now speak to the world. The source of your problems is not some unknown secret. Nor is the solution hidden from your eyes. These locutions will reveal everything.

Let everyone listen. This river does not yet have access to the very center of human history. However, if and when it does, then there will be an annihilation of nations. Only the Woman Clothed with the Sun can prevent this moment from happening.

Comment
Our Lady's plea is urgent.

May 2, 2014

11. When the Events Conclude

A Grassroots Movement

<u>Mary</u>

When this series of events concludes, a rearrangement of Europe will have taken place. The European Union will be diminished in power and size and the new reality will dawn upon everyone. Russia will once again emerge as an evil force, set upon its own path. How naïve was the West. It saw in Russia what it wanted to see and never made the effort to grasp reality.

It will not be a renewed Cold War because Putin has other means to gain his goals. The world is quite different than decades ago. The Muslim world, with its great hatred against the West, has come forth. Putin has friends in the Middle East whom he has cleverly gathered. He has multiple spheres in which to increase Russia's influence.

Such will be the state of the world when these events in the Ukraine and in Western Europe come to a cooling point, when what is gained or lost is finally settled. For now, all is still to be decided. Much depends on the determination of the West, which is so compromised and vulnerable.

In this current battle, I still sit on the sidelines. My only hope is to send these locutions far and wide. "O Church, you must awaken. Only you hold within your grasp the ability to have the Woman Clothed with the Sun come powerfully upon the world stage and call everyone to repentance and conversion."

Comment

Our Lady gives a picture of Europe after these events.

Our Lady's Plan for Saving the World

May 3, 2014
1. Rebuilding the World

Our Lady's Plan for Saving the World

Mary

I want to rebuild the whole world, but I cannot do it upon sinful structures. Nor can I use those whose hearts are taken up in darkness. Darkness and confusion permeate the West and the Church. Even believers cannot understand.

I begin with these locutions to cut away that darkness. Those who resist my words, claiming that my sword is too sharp, have no idea of the precariousness of the Western civilization. They do not realize the tremendous darkness which the West has embraced. I will use the sword of my words to cut away. I will cut deeply and surely. Those who accept my words, I will use to rebuild the whole world. Do not be surprised. All great movements begin with just a few hearts completely dedicated to a seemingly impossible goal.

My first concern is the unborn. Complete legal protection must be restored to them. No compromises. No clever political arrangements will do. They are persons and have their right to life, just as everyone else. Let us stop this flow of death that has poisoned the waters of life for everyone.

Comment
In America alone, 1.3 million babies are killed every year.

May 4, 2014
2. Wake Up to Fatima

Our Lady's Plan for Saving the World

Mary

At Fatima, I gave my important messages. All the apparitions of the nineteenth century led up to the Fatima revelations and all of my appearances since then have only extended the Fatima message concerning the great mysteries contained in my Immaculate Heart.

Now, all the events that I spoke about at Fatima are unfolding before your very eyes. People can hardly believe what is happening. They speak as if all of these events are new, unknown and little understood. They see the destabilizing of the world brought about by Russia.

I spoke about Russia nearly 100 years ago. Russia's destructive power and its central role in all the problems that have afflicted the world are no surprise to those who know the Fatima messages.

Wake up, O world. I have revealed much. Read the story of Fatima. Wake up, O Church, obey my Fatima commands. The secrets, the messages, my saving word are available to the whole world. Why act as if the Woman Clothed with the Sun had never spoken?

Comment
Those who understand Fatima clearly understand
what has happened and is happening.

May 4, 2014
3. Who Can Halt the Events? (Special Locution)
Our Lady's Plan for Saving the World

Jesus

Pope Francis opens the Church to study the issues and many rejoice that what formerly could not be discussed is now on the table. But, they do not see. The important question is all of the world events that are taking place. The events that have begun will lead to the annihilation of nations. The Egyptian revolution, the war on Syria, and now the turmoil in the Ukraine are not just isolated events. They are the beginning of a long series of events that will culminate in the annihilation of nations.

The important questions do not regard self-study of the Church, but who will stop these events? Who has the power to bring these events to a halt before the nations are annihilated? Only the Woman Clothed with the Sun can do this and only the Church can bring my mother onto the center of the world stage. No one seems interested in doing this. So, the timetable of destructive events moves along at a furious pace. She has already promised world peace if Russia is consecrated to her Immaculate Heart.

Comment
God has placed tremendous power in the Catholic Church
to bring forth the gift of peace.

May 5, 2014
4. Dropping the Atomic Bomb
Our Lady's Plan for Saving the World

Mary

How can I get the world to face all that is happening? The mountain of sins grows higher each day – personal sins, sins against the unborn, and sins against humanity itself. Widespread starvation is caused by the constant state of war on so many continents. There are untold human sufferings in an age that could wipe these sufferings off the face of the earth.

What is going wrong? The whole earth is off balance. All is shifted. Mankind falls into this darkness because he does not realize the past decisions that have put him on this path. He does not realize the forces that have been released.

When mankind used the atomic bomb to kill thousands of innocent people a shift took place that has never been addressed. There was no need for that action. The war was already winding down. The surrender of Japan was imminent. Satan saw, at the very moment when peace was to be restored to the world, that he had an opportunity to open an even greater door to violence. He lost his world war and peace was restored. However, he rejoiced that he had opened human history to nuclear arms and to the untold evils of the nuclear arms race.

Ever since that moment, the world has lived in the atomic era, filled with so many evils. Now it remains on the verge of atomic proliferation and evils that no one can imagine.

Comment
When one evil (World War II) ended, a greater evil began.

May 8, 2014
6. The History of Atomic Weapons
Our Lady's Plan for Saving the World

Mary

What began when that atomic mushroom cloud rose over Japan? Man had unleashed the ultimate weapons of war, the power to destroy earth and all of its inhabitants. After mankind had spread to every part of the globe, no power could destroy the human race.

Yes, the heavenly Father led the human race to constantly explore, to go forth to new regions and to populate every continent. In this way, mankind was safe. Even if wars or calamities claimed many lives in one part of the globe, the human race would survive in another.

With the atomic bomb, man now held in his hands the power to reverse God's plan, to destroy all the continents and all peoples, and to wipe mankind off the face of the earth.

For decades, man has had this ultimate weapon but has not used it. Only the

Woman Clothed with the Sun has held this back. Now, these weapons have fallen into hands that are more ready to use them. These weapons will be available to more and more. Can no one see the great precipice that mankind teeters upon?

I needed a strong and vigilant America. Instead, Russia stole the secrets and quickly joined the club. Other nations wanted to share these powers. Soon, there was a group of nuclear nations – the haves and the have nots.

Did they not think that others would want to join the club?

Now, many nations cling to their nuclear weapons, as if they could guarantee safety. Others look forward to the day when they, too, will have these powers. Is not this picture true? Look what has happened since August, 1945. Do you not need the Woman Clothed with the Sun?

Comment
Only because of Our Lady's protection, have we so far avoided nuclear war.

May 8, 2014
7. The Two Streams
Our Lady's Plan for Saving the World

Mary

Events flow like a continual stream, but where do they flow? History is not determined by the heavenly Father. From the very beginning, he has placed human history in the hands of mankind and has allowed him to write the story.

Oh, what a story he wrote – a story of wars and selfishness. Then, the Father, because he so loved the world, took pity on mankind and sent Jesus, his only Son, into the world. Now, there could be a different history, and a stream that flowed back to its heavenly source.

Again, mankind made its free choice and today, two streams exist, flowing side by side. The one stream brings hell and the other stream brings heaven.

In these locutions, I try to widen the stream of heaven and bring it close to every person. These locutions have no limits. They are not just heard in the churches, but flow out to all the world.

Comment
Our only hope lies in the power of heaven's stream.

May 9, 2014
8. A Child with a Loaded Gun
Our Lady's Plan for Saving the World

Mary

The world moves more and more into a darkness which it does not understand, unleashing forces that it cannot control. It is a world filled with unbelief, not realizing that heaven would gladly change its course. But the world is unaware of its need for my intervention.

Without faith, mankind can only look to its own powers and to its own leaders. O mankind, you do not have within yourselves the ability needed to change this fateful course of world events. You hurtle down this road, unable to stop what you see as the ultimate culmination of all the evils that currently afflict you. You are helpless, and you hold in your hands the ultimate weapons that can destroy you.

I take pity on your plight. You are like a child holding a loaded gun in your hands, not knowing that what seems like a toy, can totally destroy you. Yes, mankind, this is the true state of the world. You have discovered the ultimate weapons and these now proliferate, falling into the hands of those who would delight in destroying the earth.

"To whom can we turn? Who is able to help us? Who will save us from these cosmic events?" All is not hopeless. The heavenly Father has foreseen this moment of history. He does not want his creation to go up in flames. He has prepared my Immaculate Heart. He has clothed me with cosmic symbols, the sun, the moon and the stars (Rev. 12:1). These are signs of the role that he has given (assigned) to me. Take hope. Call upon me. "O Woman Clothed with the Sun."

Comment
At Medjugorje Our Lady has often spoken of the importance of Revelation, Chapter 12, to understand modern events.

May 10, 2014
9. Avoiding the Destructive Harvest
Our Lady's Plan for Saving the World

Mary

Will there ever be a springtime, when the darkness of this winter is over, when the road ahead is filled with light instead of the growing darkness?

Evil is buried deeply into the present age, and what you see are just the first evil fruits of what has been planted. This age is a time of a destructive harvest. The question remains. Will these seeds, sown for so many centuries, come to their full fruition of a devastating harvest, or will heaven intervene so that only a small portion of the evil comes forth?

Mankind faces this choice, either to reap what it has sown, or to be delivered from its past and present decisions by a merciful act of the heavenly Father. This is my constant message. The path to peace, the gift of avoiding what inevitably lies ahead, has been placed in my Immaculate Heart. The heavenly Father has prepared for this moment. He has no desire to see mankind destroyed. I have revealed his loving plan and await only to be invoked by all the Church and by all mankind as the Woman Clothed with the Sun. This will happen, but it will be late. Meanwhile, the destructive harvest grows each day.

Comment
Our Lady correctly calls the world events of wars, starvation and terrorism
a destructive harvest rising from past sinful decisions.

All Is New

May 11, 2014
1. Your Sufferings

All Is New

Can a tired, weary world, beset with every evil, become once more vibrant and living, filled with every faith and abounding in hope? Can I not speak a word to the weary? Yes, that is what I will begin to do. I will point out the plan of heaven, the helps that the heavenly Father will provide, and the steps that each and every person can take.

Turn your eyes away, for these moments, from all of the world events that you cannot control. Look to the Woman who would be your heavenly Mother. Realize that I have a plan for you, to save you and to bring you to a moment of great faith. Let us begin with all your sufferings.

Fill your mind with the memories of all that you have suffered. Are these memories not also in my heart? I remember every moment when you were disappointed, treated unjustly, and set aside. I remember every moment when you failed in your endeavors and you painfully saw all your limitations. I saw the relationships that did not last and those who even today take advantage. All of these are collected in my heart. I see you as wounded, frail, hurt, set aside, misunderstood. I see the pain in your heart and the failure of your hopes. All of this calls forth my greatest tenderness. That is where we must begin on this Mother's day.

Comment

Before beginning, Our Lady binds up our wounds.

May 12, 2014

2. Surprising Satan

All Is New

Mary

God is love, an infinite love that always pours forth blessings, like the sun that gives only light. If there is darkness, no one blames the sun. So, if there is evil, no one should blame God.

Somehow, his love has been blocked, kept out, and unable to enter.

In his secret plan, the heavenly Father has placed this love in my Immaculate Heart. He has told me, "Mary, go to the world. You will be more than just my messenger. Your heart will carry my love. I have so united your heart with Jesus' heart, that the two hearts are as one. You are so united that it would be more difficult to separate your hearts than to separate the sun from its rays."

So, I go everywhere with this great secret of my Immaculate Heart, a mystery kept hidden for centuries, but now revealed to a world that is plunging into darkness.

O mankind, the heavenly Father has united my heart with Jesus' heart. He has surprised Satan, who had no idea that he would be conquered by a Woman. Against my Immaculate Heart, he has no defenses.

He has not been able to plan for this surprise. He wants my words to be hidden, but by these locutions, I speak openly to the whole world. All is new!

Comment

In all of her apparitions, Mary reveals the secrets about her Immaculate Heart.

May 15, 2014

3. The New Lights

All Is New

Mary

My heart will sing of this heavenly glory which can restore man to the lofty existence which he once had. No tongue can describe what the Father will do right now within your heart. However, he will give me a few words that will give light.

When mankind sinned, he lost so much. The great lights fell from his heart because he had chosen the darkness. Now, at the very moment when darkness begins to cover the whole world (that is what is happening in these world events), the Father wants to place the lights that were given to our first parents into everyone's heart.

Do not be surprised by this because the Father already accomplished this great miracle in my heart and I share my light with you. All is new. I must constantly repeat those words. All is new. What did not exist before, exists now, a door into my Immaculate Heart and a total sharing in my light. Satan will hurl his darkness over the whole world but I will cast my light into hearts. The victory will be ours only because all is new. What a moment you live in. The Woman Clothed with the Sun is ready to place her greatest rays within you. Read on. My words will flow constantly, always telling of these new mysteries of God's love for man.

Comment
Those who study spirituality realize that God often gives new gifts.

May 16, 2014
4. Using More Than Words

All Is New

Mary

When the infinite God poured his blessings into my heart, I watched in astonishment, seeing so many gifts of the greatest variety. This abundance never ceased but has continued to this day and I must distribute these blessings to the whole world. How I weep when these blessings are unknown and rejected, and false blessings fill the human heart.

Words, can I only use words? What frail instruments to describe these blessings. I must use other means, which penetrate the human heart more deeply. I am not limited to words. I can touch the human mind directly. I can even capture the human heart so that all its desires center on these blessings. I can even speak within, in ways unknown to human teachers. This is what I must do because it is the time of blessings never before seen upon the earth.

O mankind, you have chosen the darkness and walk a path of your own choosing, but I will meet you there. When you think you are hopelessly lost, I will come and find you.

Comment
Our Lady teaches us now, so when she comes, we know what is happening.

May 17, 2014
5. An Emergency Light

All Is New

Mary

I will be pouring out these blessings until the end of time. Each year the blessings will get greater. Never has mankind experienced such an outpouring.

This began with the moment when I conceived Jesus, true God and true man. All can understand the blessing that his coming to earth has been. However, the continued blessings that the Father places in my heart are unknown.

During the months that he dwelt within me, Jesus left these blessings. They are Jesus' gifts. They belong to me only because I am called to distribute them. These are the mysteries that I am revealing.

Satan was surprised by the Resurrection of Jesus. He suffered his greatest defeat. He has regrouped his forces. He cannot remove the Resurrection, so he has decided to cover over its light, just as the clouds cover the sun, or better, how the night comes.

In this special time, when Satanic darkness begins to cover the earth, the heavenly Father suddenly brings onto the world stage a new light, all of the gifts which Jesus left in my heart, like an emergency light when the usual lights fail. I repeat. I am the Woman Clothed with the Sun and this is my moment in world history to become known to all. As this happens, I will bring forth a surprising light and all the world will know and rejoice.

Comment
These locutions awaken us to God's new and surprising light.

May 18, 2014
6. The Two Suns

All Is New

Mary

So many streams of new blessings flow down from heaven! I must awaken even those who believe. They must know what the heavenly Father has provided in these years of Satanic darkness.

I am the new Dawn. I do not arise in the East (where Satan has his forces of darkness ready to cover over the light). I arise in the West, for I am a reflection of Jesus' light, a shining mirror which perfectly reflects his rays. Satan is confused because he sees two suns, East and West. He will become a divided house that cannot stand.

Do not limit your heart to one Sun. Choose both the Son and the Mother, the true light and the faithful mirror. Let there be two suns, a fullness of light, both East and West. In these two suns, you will conquer and overcome.

I am the Woman Clothed with the Sun. Jesus rises in the East and I am placed in the West. There is no room for night, even here on earth. A new reality comes forth. This is the great mystery. Words cannot describe. Only images can.

Comment
The Age of Mary is just dawning.

May 18, 2014
7. A Shaky Economic Foundation (Special Locution)

Special Locution

Jesus

I must raise up this little voice of locutions to explain what is happening and to warn America. Otherwise, the events will take place and no one will see how they should respond. Even with this warning, many will pay no attention to this voice until after the events. Then, they will see the clarity of these words and take them to heart.

In America, there were always pockets of immorality. However, the nation held itself to a high level of goodness. My law was respected and life was ordered. One by one, these moral ties were loosened, slowly at first and, then, more quickly. At this point, there is no moral restraint. All the laws have been set aside. Immorality reigns supreme. Every kind of life style is praised. All has been torn asunder.

So, I must bring America to its knees. I must use the economy, because America only hears one tune, the song of money. I will stop the music.

America's economy is not strong. There are many weaknesses resulting from the 2008 collapse. In many ways, America does not hold its economy's future in its own hands. It is interdependent and is not ready for the next jolt. America, when your next economic collapse comes, will you finally listen to this little voice? Your economy will be in shreds because your morality is in shreds. You rebuilt your walls but you forgot about your foundations, as if you could have a strong economy and no moral base. O foolish children, you reject the wisdom of your eternal Father and have built a sand castle.

Comment
The 2008 economic collapse brought no repentance. The next collapse will be greater.

May 19, 2014
8. Heaven's Answer

All Is New

Mary

Who can tell the secrets of the King of Kings? Who knows what lies in the Sacred Heart of Jesus? For nine months, that heart, already filled with the divine nature and already possessing the Infinite love poured out by his Father, beat within my womb. This is the mystery I am portraying. Jesus left behind in my Immaculate Heart, the infinite love of the Father and the Holy Spirit's greatest gifts.

He knew that Satan would again lead the world into its darkest moments, when seemingly even heaven had no answer. Then, when Satan's darkness would cover over the Sun that rose from the East, suddenly another sun would arise in the West. All the gifts hidden for centuries in my Immaculate Heart, placed there by the yet unborn Jesus, could shine forth. The whole world will see that heaven had not abandoned mankind and that heaven had its answer ready when the new man-made darknesses were unleashed.

When will the Church exalt my Immaculate Heart? When will the faithful be taught that I am the Woman Clothed with the Sun? I speak in these little locutions, but these words must be magnified. Messengers of the locutions, take my teachings everywhere and darkness will not have the field to itself.

Comment

God has surprising gifts to overcome new evils.

Understanding History

March 29, 2014
11. The Two Greatest Historical Forces

Understanding History

Mary

No part of history is ever totally wiped away. People think of past eras, as if they are gone and forgotten. However, there is no such thing as a past era. Whatever happens in history leaves its effects. All of the past is stored up, the good and the bad.

To reject history, to forget about it or to set it aside, leads to blindness and an inability to understand the present forces or to foresee the future events. History is a stream and every event leaves its trace. This stream is carried both in the hearts of people and in the structures of a society.

I would point to two events, the fall of Adam and the death and rising of Jesus. These are the two most powerful moments of human history. These are the two polar events. The event of Adam affects the inner life of every person born into the world. The grace of Jesus is more powerful and is offered to every person, but it is frequently rejected or never understood.

This is an era of culmination. Will the powerful sin of Adam, planted in every human heart and constantly bringing forth evil, plunge the world into an unchangeable state? Or, will the grace of Jesus' Kingdom rescue mankind? These are the stakes. They are very high. They play out every day. All the world news reflects the clash of these two moments in history. I dare anyone to challenge my analysis of history. The Adam moment is relived and multiplied every day. The grace of Jesus is offered at every moment. Human history is a war, but the forces are often hidden and not understood.

Comment
Our Lady helps us to understand the two forces that battle for our souls.

May 20, 2014
1. Seeds Planted in the Field of History

Understanding History

Mary

All the events are bursting forth, but these are only the earliest beginning events. More and more events will follow.

The heavenly Father planted all the seeds for man's happiness deeply in the field of human history. These are the greatest glories which no one can imagine. At night, and in secret, Satan entered this field and planted the weeds. Since that moment, all history has seen both a good and evil harvest. Mankind has come to expect this.

As mankind gained greater control over creation, euphoria grew, as if mankind could build a perfect world and banish all evil. The euphoria has quickly evaporated because mankind has no power over the evil seeds. The world's field is now filled with the greatest weeds of war, suffering, terrorism and global insecurity.

This is my message. You have only seen the beginning weeds. Still hidden, in the bowels of the field, are seeds of destruction never before witnessed by man. These seeds, planted in the beginning, are making their way to the surface and are about to come forth. Some beginning seeds of destruction have already come to the surface. Many more will follow.

Oh, how the earth needs the great seeds of God's powers. These are also planted in the field of history. When will they come forth? I will use these locutions to speak of these seeds, waiting to burst forth. In this way, the greatest mysteries will be understood.

Comment
*Mary is applying Jesus' parable of the wheat and
the weeds to explain modern events.*

May 21, 2014
2. The Bountiful Harvest of Evil

Understanding History

Mary

The buried seeds do not all come forth. Many seeds of God's blessings bring forth no harvest. They are not accepted. Instead, they are rejected and ridiculed. This is the world's wisdom, which spurns God's true blessings.

In contrast, the seeds of evil find many hearts ready to accept their weeds. They appeal to all that is selfish and self-centered. They promise great delights and power. They entice and constantly force themselves upon mankind. They bring forth great harvests and a history filled with wars.

Children are born into this evil. People live and die in the darkness of poverty and squalor. Money flows to the rich. Power is concentrated in the hands of a few. Weapons are stockpiled.

Mankind has cooperated with these seeds of evil. You were totally unaware of these evil seeds, O world. Because you set aside the revealed word of God, I must use these locutions to educate you. I cannot ask you to change until I can get you to understand.

Comment
Our Lady begins a teaching to explain the revealed truth of original sin.

May 22, 2014
3. A Church Which Is Not Ready

Understanding History

86

Mary

I do not want to allow this evil harvest to continue. However, the Church is not ready for the good seeds to come forth. It would be like an early Spring, when the harvest comes forth too early, only to die and bear no fruit.

This is my message. Buried deeply in the field are the greatest seeds. Before I allow them to bud forth, I must send other graces upon the Church.

First, there is my special son, whom I keep hidden and closest to my heart, always preparing him. He will awaken the Church, releasing an expectancy so the blessings will be received.

Second, I must stir up movements, new and old. Some have served the Church well. These I will refresh and invigorate. New movements must also come forth, filled with greater gifts.

Third, I must lift up the whole Church. I will use these locutions to call every Catholic to return to the springs of living water. Years have been wasted, but it is not too late.

Although these gifts are buried like powerful seeds, ready to change the face of the earth and to turn human history away from the great darkness, the Church is not ready for the great gifts. Will they come forth? Will they bloom and flourish? All depends on the Church being made ready.

Comment
Our Lady spells out the Church's task.

May 23, 2014
4. The Winds of History

Understanding History

Mary

How quickly the winds of change blow. Suddenly, history moves in a different direction. Who is wise enough or clever enough to understand the wind? Who can chart its course or predict its path? Only the heavenly Father, who so much wants to protect his children. This is why I speak now. I will describe the winds that have blown mankind off course, and what is needed to regain the true path.

The first wind is the new technology and man's total absorption into that false world. How dangerous this is. It has already sparked upheavals and removed much of man's free will. This is a powerful new wind and mankind is herded like cattle that have no choice.

The second wind is the destruction of faith, the only power that frees man and allows him to stand firm while the mighty winds blow against him.

The final, and greatest wind, is the Satanic intelligence that cleverly has led mankind to this moment, where vast numbers of evil groups, equipped with devastating weapons, plot the overthrow of governments and the destruction of nations.

These are winds that blow so fiercely. Who can stand against them? Does mankind even see, or understand? You are children whose only hope is your heavenly Mother. I will never abandon you. In my Immaculate Heart are other winds, surprising and more powerful, ready to be released at a moment's notice. In the twinkling of an eye, I can change the entire course of human history. However, the Church must prepare. It is not ready for these new winds. It is a boat that does not have its sails in place. These sails of faith have been replaced by reason. Even in the Church, reason has replaced faith. O Church, regain your faith in your heavenly Mother and you will experience fresh winds.

Comment
Our Lady has much more to give us, if only we will believe

.

May 25, 2014
5. Events Leading to Other Events

Understanding History

Mary

Nothing in human history stands alone and isolated. All events converge. One event leads to another, setting the stage for a new good or new evil. All the events of these centuries have led up to the present age, in which a culmination will take place. These years are an extremely important moment in human history.

The events which you see – the revolutions in Libya and Egypt, the continuous civil war in Syria, the breakup of the Ukraine, and soon, the emergence of a more aggressive China, are the beginning. They are not just historical events. They are the door to unthinkable events, culminating moments. At least, that is Satan's plan. There will be an ever-more aggressive Russia and a Putin who enjoys the world's spotlight. There will be the hidden works of Iran, which has every reason to continue its nuclear program.

These forces now control the world scene. America is nowhere in sight. Europe is fearful and unsure. No human force exists to change this course of events.

My children understand this history. They see the events in their true perspective. They are not fooled. They will not compromise. They will not turn away. Their faces are turned totally to me and their hearts are completely mine. These will be my instruments. I must move quickly. I must raise them up and put them in high positions. I cannot wait any longer. I must have Church leaders who understand that I am the Woman Clothed with the Sun.

I will multiply the power of these locutions. I will use them to cry out in the loudest possible voice. Mankind is headed into indescribable darkness unless the Woman Clothed with the Sun is given her place chosen by the heavenly Father.

Comment
Our Lady will not be silent. The heavenly Father has chosen her
as his instrument to destroy Satan's plans.

May 26, 2014
7. Centers of Evil

Understanding History

Mary

Events twist and turn, as if no one is in control. They often involve many people, at times even thousands and millions. Yet, there is always a center to each event, good or evil. This is my theme.

An event whose center is evil will bring about evil. How great that the evil is will be determined by its own inner resources and by all the subsequent events that follow. Look at the so-called Arab Spring. Are the people better off? Has there not been constant turmoil? Did not the Egyptian army have to reject this Spring and take control, so as to limit the evil?

The inner resources of evil are still powerful in Syria, where the death and destruction continue, bringing great social evils to neighboring countries like Lebanon and Jordan. In the Ukraine, the evil center will continue its work. In spite of the presidential election, peace will not return.

This is my message. In the years ahead, greater centers of evil will arise, especially China, which will come more and more onto the world scene. As Russia sees China as a willing partner, these two centers of evil will cooperate and pool their inner resources to protect their interests and to insure that outside forces cannot turn them away from their goals. The constant rising of new centers of evil and, especially, their joining together, will cause the events that will shape the world's future.

Comment
Our Lady gives an easy-to-understand description
of the causes of the world's problems.

May 26, 2014

8. After the Ukrainian Elections (Special Locution)

Understanding History

Jesus

Even after the presidential election, the Ukraine will not enjoy peace. As the dust settles, Putin will see the true state of the Ukraine. He sees those parts which are firmly his, those parts which want to belong to Russia, and those parts that lean toward Russia. He also sees the weaknesses and divisions in those parts that choose the Ukraine.

His method will be constant disturbances. A government and its president must provide security or else they are seen as weak. By continuing to cause problems, Putin will constantly weaken these already shaky foundations. The Ukrainian government does not have great resources and would have difficulties even in times of peace.

Putin's method will be to constantly cause turmoil. He needs only to continue to disrupt in order to claim more and more of the Ukraine.

The election will not end these disturbances, nor bring peace. The election is on the surface while the divisions are deeply engrained into the Ukrainian culture.

Comment

The problems in the Ukraine will not end quickly.

May 27, 2014

9. The Shooting of the Pope

Understanding History

Mary

I can place my hands upon these evil centers; even though they might bring forth the event, the effects are limited. Look at the shooting of Pope John Paul II. This was an evil of the greatest magnitude. All the good that he was to accomplish in his pontificate would have been wiped away in one minute.

The event took place because I respected the free will of Ali Agca. However, I placed my hand on the event. Two things happened. The pope suddenly bent over to greet a little girl and the first two bullets missed his head. Then, I actually moved Ali Agca off course, so the other shots were not fatal. The evil took place, but the full effects were limited and repairable.

This was an act of the Woman Clothed with the Sun, the Woman of Fatima. Let this be a sign to all the world that I will protect all my children even in the face of the greatest threats.

It is my prerogative to limit the effects, even when the evil event takes place. I reveal this so all know to constantly invoke my help.

Comment
Centers of evil cause evil effects, but we do not have to experience or suffer
all the effects of these events. The shooting happened on May 13, 1981,
the feast of Our Lady of Fatima.

May 28, 2014
10. The Unseen Forces

Understanding History

Mary

The forces that bring about these historical events are not irrational. However, they are hidden and easily escape the light of man's understanding. Often, people are surprised and wonder how an event happened, but the seeds of good or evil were planted, sometimes years or even centuries before. I want to enlighten everyone.

God's kingdom of light offers man every possible help. Satan's kingdom of darkness wants only man's destruction. The two kingdoms battle over every single person. Some persons are more important, meant to play a greater role in history.

However, every person is a battlefield. Every person makes a decision for light or for darkness. According to this decision, they enlist in God's army or in Satan's, able to be used to bring about God's plan or Satan's destruction.

Each person is aligned with other persons, sometimes at the highest levels. Forces are released in history, like waves upon the shore. Each force leaves its mark. Human life is changed, for good or evil. More important, history is tilted one way or another, to good or to evil.

It is quite easy to see the present tide of history. Whole nations fall into chaos. Wars, revolutions and uprisings happen in so many places. Countries that were strong and in the light grow weak, and move into darkness.

Remember, one event leads to another. An evil event prepares for another, sometimes for far greater evil. History is never quiet and still. These forces, good and evil, never rest. The battle is always raging. Human history is a constant battlefield.

Mankind considers itself the author of its own history, but the clarity of my vision reveals the helplessness of man. Left alone, he cannot survive.

Comment
Our Lady pulls back the veil and reveals the forces
that truly form human history.

May 30, 2014
12. Wake Up!

Understanding History

Mary

I have given you a sweep, a quick overview of history. Do not forget or put aside what I have said. As you realize the forces that form human history, you will not remain passive.

I want to wake you up. While you sleep, the forces of evil claim more and more. Only as you awaken and take action does the power of Jesus turn mankind away from darkness.

Just listen carefully to my words. You need light because you do not even know the way. You need others, because alone and unaided, you cannot persevere. You need the Church with all of its sacraments. You need my words in these locutions. Most of all you need me as your Mother. Come to me and I will provide all the rest.

I speak so clearly because the time is short and when the events begin, no one can prepare. Remember the ten virgins. Only half were ready to meet the bridegroom. Did Noah build his ark when the rain started to fall? Not at all.

Begin now, at whatever stage you are. Return to Mass. Pick up your rosary beads. Wear my scapular. Especially, find others who also realize the need to prepare. I will be there as you gather. I will bless even your smallest efforts. Every step is a victory. Not to prepare is to accept defeat as inevitable. The enemy is at the gate, but I am at your side.

Comment
Our Lady ends this series with words of direction and hope.

May 31, 2014
13. The Woman in World History

Understanding History

Mary

Before the world began, the heavenly Father thought of me. He dreamed of the moment when he would create me, and bring me forth from the hiddenness of his own heart. How many centuries he waited and waited!

He had promised my coming from the beginning. I was the Woman who would conquer the Evil One by bringing forth Jesus (Gen. 3:15). The centuries passed. The sins of the world increased. The powers of Satan spread. Finally the moment had come – the moment of my Immaculate Conception. At last, he had created the Woman. Still, all was hidden. Even while Jesus lived on earth, I was still hidden, present but always in the background.

So, it has been for the centuries of the Church. Now, all is changing. How the Father has looked forward to this moment in history, the moment of the Woman, the moment of the battle, and, yes, the moment of the victory of the Woman. There will be my victory. The heavenly Father has ordered this and will bring it about. When? When? When? That is the question and why I speak in these locutions. I speak to hasten the victory, to prepare the way, to awaken the Church and to prepare for the moment when I will bring my priest son onto the scene. He will know exactly what to do.

Comment
The Church has always venerated Our Lady.
In this century, God's full plan for Mary will unfold.

The History of the Woman

June 1, 2014

1. Preparing for Pentecost

The History of the Woman

Mary

I was with God from the beginning of his ways, always in his thoughts as the Mother of his divine Son. After the Evil One claimed his victory over Adam, God thought of me: "I will put an enmity between you and the Woman, between your offspring and hers" (Gen.3:15).

This plan was hidden in the Trinity, known to them alone. Yet, human history proceeded along its way. The great moments of evil were erased in the Flood, and then God gave the covenant to Noah and later to Abraham.

This covenant was just a shadow of the reality that would come forth in the fullness of time and the new covenant, the permanent relationship of God with man.

From the very beginning, the Father said to me, "Protect this new covenant for I have placed it in the hands of men tainted by original sin." So, I was with the apostles in the

93

Upper Room preparing them for Pentecost. Even then, I was the Mother of the Church and they were my children. I knew the Holy Spirit. He was already my spouse and I told them all they could understand about his secrets. I prepared them for Pentecost.

Comment
Our Lady prepares us for her self-revelation.

June 2, 2014
2. The Purification of the World

The History of the Woman

Mary

All over the world, the battle takes place, sometimes hidden within the person's heart and, at other times, seen by the whole world. Who understands this turmoil or the forces that bring it about? I will explain.

As the evil stirring takes possession of the human heart, the person accepts this force as if it were their own will. Really, it is not from them. They have become an instrument, many times unable to free themselves. They rejoice in this evil and in its fruits. Soon, however, they are trapped, unable to be set free.

After that, they continue on this course, often destroying themselves and others as well. These forces are not seen, nor are they understood. Only when the evil fruits come forth, can all realize what seeds have been planted.

O mankind, you are helpless. These seeds have been planted for centuries. They have brought forth evil fruits, and these fruits have spread their own seeds. The whole world is now a field, ready for the harvest. However, the harvest will be of destruction, of death, and of a world completely changed. The seeds have been planted and planted and planted. They are everywhere, in the hearts of the people, in the structures of society, and in all the weapons now sold and distributed.

No human force can possibly remove these seeds and these fruits of evil. God alone can purify the world, and this purification must happen. It cannot be canceled. How will it happen? If I am invited by the Church and the world to come upon the scene, then the purification will be complete and done quickly.

If I am still set aside, the purification will be prolonged and filled with darkness. Whole nations will come before the heavenly Father to be judged. I speak out now, asking the Holy Father to consecrate Russia so this type of purification is set aside.

Comment
The purification is needed and inevitable.
Our Lady enjoys the prerogatives of softening it.

June 2, 2014
3. Our Lady's Three Sorrows (Special Locution)

The History of the Woman

Mary

I have three sorrows. The first is President Obama. It is not that he has turned away from me because he has never really known me or claimed to be my son. He is my sorrow because he has such great power and controls so many people by evil. They rejoice in their evil and he protects the evil for them. He is their great advocate and they see him as safeguarding their evil. Because he controls so many, he is my great sorrow.

His hands clutch many things, but I will beat upon his hands and loosen his grasp. He will not possess great power. I will do this through the scandals. There will be more and greater scandals. In trying to extricate himself, he will only get more entangled.

My second sorrow is the growth of terrorism. In this release of five prisoners, the terrorists see a victory. Terrorism grows because America has withdrawn from the fight. To fight terrorism comes with a high price, but there will be a higher price to pay if its advance is not stopped. Now, no real fight is being waged. The terrorists have free access and no fear of America.

My third sorrow is the Church and my enemies within the Church who constantly refuse to accept me as the Woman Clothed with the Sun. They deny me my rightful place, even though they profess to be my sons. They are depriving my Church of the full light and causing it to operate in semi-darkness.

Comment
Our Lady has spoken often of these sorrows. Now, she explains them clearly.

June 2, 2014
4. Putin's Ascendency (Special Locution)

The History of the Woman

Jesus

Putin is in the ascendency. No need for Satan to find someone else. Pieces of the world will be broken off. These will be on the borders, on the frontiers. Like a person devouring a loaf of bread, he will first break off the parts that are easily in his grasp. This has already begun in the Ukraine. However, the Ukraine is not enough to satisfy his hunger. He eyes the Baltic states, especially Estonia and Latvia. Even with their ties to NATO, they are endangered. Putin will see how big a bite he can take. He will test the resolve of the European powers and will be surprised by their feeble reaction. Europe does not want to risk a war. Yet, the risk will be greater, if Europe is not strong.

Comment
Russia and Putin are the main problems to world peace.

June 3, 2014
5. The Inner Voice of the Woman

The History of the Woman

Mary

Before all the upheavals occur, I must give my children the words of life. These words will live within them. They will be the voice of the Woman. Blessed will they be if, before the upheavals, they have already learned to listen to me. In this way, my voice will multiply, be stronger and clearer.

They must not listen to the voices of fear, or to the voices of selfishness. In all of the upheavals, large and small, I will always speak as the Woman. In these special trials there will be special words. Let me begin now, for the time is short.

From now on, you must prepare every day, just as Noah built his ark every day. Only in this way, will you be ready. To prepare, you must be still and quiet and seek my word. You must learn how close I am to you, and gain great faith that I am the Woman Clothed with the Sun. All my other gifts will flow freely from this faith.

Do not look for me in the sky. Later, will come the signs and wonders. Right now, the great gifts are flowing from my heart to your heart, and you can receive them by believing my words.

Comment
Our Lady is already speaking to you. Learn to listen.

June 4, 2014
6. The Two Fires

The History of the Woman

Mary

Which fires will light up the skies, the fires of the earth or the fires of heaven? This is the question which mankind will face in the next few years. Yes, I must say the next few years because this question will be answered soon.

Out of love, the heavenly Father has constantly postponed the purification of the world, always hoping and hoping that the Church would choose me as the Woman

Clothed with the Sun, and that the world would also embrace this truth. Now, these many years have passed by and the Church has still not responded to my command. So, the destructive fires of earth light up the skies. They burn brightly and their darkness covers more and more of the earth's surface.

If I am lifted up and acknowledged as the Woman, I will release heavenly fires from my Immaculate Heart. People will see. They will be enlightened. They will repent. They will change their ways. They will bring about deep and lasting social changes. There will be great movements of the Holy Spirit.

The soul of man is capable of great deeds, heroic deeds. Touched by the heavenly fires, mankind can bring about a new era. This will be my gentle purification. Without the heavenly fires, mankind can only bring about the great destructive fires which will envelop whole nations. This will be a different, more painful and more destructive purification. Which fires will light up the skies – the fires of heaven or the fires of earth?

Comment
What a promise – heavenly fires that change the world
by touching each person's heart.

June 5, 2014
7. Waiting and Waiting

The History of the Woman

Mary

The world is filled with confusion. No one can understand the events. All, however, realize that this is not a time of peace, nor does anyone even know a road to peace. When I speak about future events, I cannot speak of victories. I can only speak of defeats. Do you think I want to speak only about the new darkness or the new destruction? Do you think I want to speak only about the spread of terrorism, the problems in the Ukraine, and the growing strength of Putin?

This is not the news that I want to bring to the world, but I must honestly speak of what lies ahead. I must truthfully describe the road that mankind has chosen.

So, I must say again that there is no force present in today's world that can stop the spread of terrorism and destruction. I wait on the sidelines, my Immaculate Heart filled with every power of the heavenly Father. (This is the mystery I am constantly revealing), ready to blind Satan and to rout his armies, ready to free mankind and to usher in an era of unprecedented peace.

I wait and wait. Someday I will be invited, but the constant delays have been costly. Much has already been lost. I invite people to cooperate and they consider something else more important. Soon, I will just have to act unilaterally, sweeping aside those who do not understand and giving authority to the one whom I have prepared.

Comment

Until Russia is consecrated, Our Lady sits on the sidelines.

The Catholic Church in World History

June 6, 2014
1. The Catholic Church and Terrorism
The Catholic Church in World History

Mary

In these locutions I have poured out my heart as the Woman Clothed with the Sun. I have tried to explain all that is happening, why the reign of terror constantly expands, and why those who should be standing firm are retreating.

I have tried to show the ever-growing power of these forces of evil. Formerly, they were isolated fires, but in recent years they have joined together, entwined in their evil relationships. They have multiplied by their new unity. They see the weakness of the West and they understand that opportunities which they never conceived before are within their grasp.

They have found a friend in Putin, who has launched his own surprising offensives that have distracted the West. They recruit very easily because the young see them as the future victors. They terrorize and kill those who oppose them. Any means that gains their goals is legitimate for them. They are like the scourge of Babylon which destroyed Jerusalem, the boiling caldron ready to overflow.

Can I speak any more clearly? I have placed these truths squarely before everyone. Nothing is safe from their evil. Nothing will satisfy them except the complete domination of the world. Their tactics are well known. First, they terrorize (using just a few people). Then they assault, sending in those who can do constant damage. They plant their friends among unsuspecting peoples. At a given moment, these friends rise up and the whole society is shaken from without and within. What was stable is destabilized. Unrest grows. Governments are powerless. All of this has happened before your very eyes, time and again.

What is my plan? I must remove the current leadership of America and raise up those whose hearts belong to me. Only the Catholic faith saved Europe and only the Catholic faith will save America and the world.

Comment
Catholics must understand the great gift contained in their Church and in their faith. The world desperately needs Catholicism.

June 7, 2014
3. The Blood of Martyrs
The Catholic Church in World History

Mary

For 2000 years, the Catholic Church has preached the gospel to all creatures. Today, this Church extends throughout the world, with a hierarchical communion of the Pope with his bishops, with their pastors and their people. This worldwide organization has been built upon the sacrifices of so many who, over these 20 centuries, have left their native lands to preach the gospel in the far corners of the world. Many who believed their word, have shed their blood for their faith. Today, this shedding of blood takes place more than ever, especially in Muslim countries that kill in the name of their Allah.

You, who have killed and continue to kill my children, the martyrs' blood is on your hands, but it is a saving blood. I remember every single drop and hold each drop as holy. They are with me now and, in the spirit of Jesus, they plead for your salvation. Their blood has divine power and cannot be washed away with water. This blood is buried in your streets and in your cities. It cries out to me, not to condemn you, but that I should come to you so that Jesus is also in your hearts and on your lips. That day will come sooner than you think.

Comment
Our Lady will reveal the great power present in the worldwide Catholic Church.

June 8, 2014
4. The Church and History
The Catholic Church in World History

Mary

What began in Jerusalem 2000 years ago, with a small group of Jesus' disciples,

99

anointed with the Holy Spirit, has now become an enormous Church, with members everywhere. How this Church has suffered! First it was cut in two (1054 Orthodox division). Then many parts were broken off (1517 with Luther). Now these little parts continually split into many Churches.

The Church has also sustained internal sufferings, the betrayal of its own members, and the sins even of its popes. Still, the Catholic Church remains the true bride of Jesus, beloved in his eyes and special in my heart. We direct our gaze of love toward her and place our hope in her mission.

She is the Church of history, going back to the apostolic times. She also carries the sins of her history, the massive burdens that other Christian Churches have thrown off. I have a special gift awaiting her. She will be freed of her past sins. While retaining all of her historical blessings, she will suddenly leave behind the sins of her past. She will be old in her wisdom and young in her freedom. Only the Father can bring this about.

Comment
History is both the Catholic Church's claim and its burden.

June 11, 2014
5. The Church's Greatest Moment
The Catholic Church in World History

Mary

In the early, dark hours of the morning, the sun is making its way bringing the light of a new day. Such is my action within the Catholic Church. Deep within the Church lies the great Sun of Justice, a gift not shared by the other churches. Right now, this special light is preparing the Church for its greatest moment in history.

As the present darkness makes its way to midnight, the light of the Church will be seen as the only hope. The greatest moment in the Church's history will come as the world plunges into darkness and actually comes closer and closer to the full darkness of midnight. Then, the great lights which I am preparing in the heart of the Catholic Church will shine for all the world.

This preparation is two-fold. Some already know and are preparing to be my great instruments of worldwide light. Also, every Catholic must know that their Church has been assigned this great task and they will be part of this light for the world. Oh, Catholics, begin to prepare. Live as children of the light and a moment will come when you will share in the Church's greatest moment.

Right now, as the world moves into darkness,
Our Lady calls all Catholics to live in her light.

Special Locutions on Iraq

June 11, 2014
1. The Shockwaves of Iraq

Special Locutions on Iraq

Jesus

I told you that the timetable for the spread of terrorism would move ahead quickly with the American withdrawal. The terrorists would be international and not limited by national boundaries. They would join forces and no longer be isolated. They would see victories in their grasp that they thought would be years away.

The events in Iraq will send shockwaves. Other governments will realize how helpless they are. As the terrorists claim great victories, they will recruit many more.

Europe thinks that it is far away, but the collapse of Iraq will be such a blow that even Europe will tremble. All is ablaze, but far sooner than anyone imagined. The timetable is moved up. No one will grasp the depth, the magnitude, and the results of this collapse in Iraq.

Comment
Our Lord has often said in these locutions that the American withdrawal has moved the timetable of terrorists ahead. The collapse of Iraq will spread their power.

June 12, 2014
2. The Papacy's Greatest Moment

Special Locutions on Iraq

Mary

I want to speak of the pope's role in world events and his relationship to world leaders. The papal office is worldwide. The pope travels and is welcomed everywhere. He is, truly, the only universal figure on earth.

I want to speak of three phases of the papacy. Centuries ago, the pope was a central figure in the formation of Europe. As Europe sent forth its explorers and its missionaries, the role of the pope was also extended.

All of this gave rise to the modern papacy in which the pope, by his travels and the means of communications, is seen and heard all over the world. In spite of this high profile and worldwide recognition, he is not seen as integral to world events. This role is given to political leaders who make the daily decisions which determine war or peace, prosperity or poverty.

I speak now of a third moment, a future moment close at hand, when political leaders will be completely helpless in the face of the events. In this moment of great darkness, every political leader will be powerless.

At that moment, I will raise the papacy to its greatest height. When mankind asks, "To whom shall we turn?" suddenly the great light of the papacy will shine out upon the world and all will realize, once again, the great gift of the Catholic Church.

Comment
The modern papacy is held in high esteem but while the world believes that it has light, God's full gift is not yet revealed.

June 13, 2014
3. Satan's Enticements

Special Locutions on Iraq

Mary

The Catholic Church has existed for centuries and will continue to exist until the end of time. This is Jesus' promise, "I am with you always, until the end of the age" (Mt. 28:20). But it is about the next few years that I must speak. In these years, Satan will attack the Church as never before. She is the last and final bulwark that prevents his worldwide domination. If he destroys her, he would have no adversary that is his equal.

He will entice the Church with the false goals of popularity, acceptance by the world, and acclaim by world leaders. The world will welcome the Church with open arms. Currently, the world criticizes the Church for its moral teachings. The world says the Church is bigoted and out of touch. The world wants the Church to compromise, to adapt, to change, just as so many other Christian Churches have done.

The Catholic Church loves all mankind. It is universal and reaches out to everyone. However, how can the Church save a drowning world? Must it join the world in the water? Should it not stay on firm ground to throw the world a lifeline? The enticement is to adapt, to jump in and to be more immersed.

Comment

The world appreciates the Catholic Church's many works of education and charity, but does not like many of its moral teachings. In the near future, the Church will have to make important decisions, as at a crossroads.

June 13, 2014
4. Events in Iraq (Special Locution)

Special Locutions on Iraq

Jesus

The events in Iraq are not just moving up the timetable. They are a breakthrough of such magnitude that no world leader can foresee the consequences. This is the breakthrough which gives new life and new existence to terrorism. Now, they will take over a whole country with all its resources. They will establish Sharia Law and claim a victory of great magnitude. Other governments will fear and world markets will be affected. The magnitude of the breakdown taking place in Iraq is difficult to describe.

Mary

I can only use the word "magnitude" because the terrorists will bring about the collapse of an existing government. World leaders do not grasp the hearts of the people who have been told so many things which they no longer believe.

For them, reality lies with those who are waving their weapons. The terrorists are experts at causing fears. Even though their numbers are small, they can overwhelm many who fear and no longer believe the promises of their government.

Comment

Both Jesus and Mary use the word "magnitude" to describe the events in Iraq.

June 15, 2014
6. A New Role for the Pope

Special Locutions on Iraq

Mary

After Pentecost, as the apostles set out, I went with them. This was a gift given to me by the Holy Spirit. For all these centuries, I have been the Mother of the Church. Nothing has happened in the Church, the great moments and the sinful moments, that have not been recorded in my Immaculate Heart.

Right now, I want to reveal the Church's present situation, the dangers that surround it, and the events that are coming. I want every Catholic to know this revelation. It is not to be secret and sealed for years, only to be revealed later. This time is short and the whole Church must have this revelation. The more Catholics who see and understand, the safer will be the Church and the world.

The Holy Father heads the Church but the papacy should not just be a teaching office. These events have a role to play in world history. This role has been removed from the papacy over the recent centuries. However, the events have already begun which will throw the world into the greatest confusion. These events will have a secondary result of making the papacy grow more and more important. This will be a surprising shift. Only as events bring the world to its knees, will the world look again to the papacy and the Catholic Church as the one source of light out of the darkness.

Comment
The pope is certainly a world figure, but world leaders
jealously guard their power to control world events.

June 15, 2014
7. Satan's Worldwide Plan

Special Locutions on Iraq

Jesus

I must speak out. I can no longer hold the words in, because the world and its leaders do not understand all the events that are taking place in Iraq and Syria. These events are just flashpoints. Satan has his pot of evil boiling over, first in one place and then in another.

Right now, Satan foresees the possibility of setting the whole world ablaze. He does not yet possess all that he needs but, for the first time, the possibility of pouring out his flames upon the whole world is becoming possible.

To explain, I must speak about World War II. That, too, was Satan's pot of evil boiling over. However, at that time, Hitler and Mussolini did not contain the amount of evil that is now present. Also, there was a faithful and firm America that was a wall against that fire. Satan, however, did win a great victory when the atomic bomb was discovered. As the door of one evil closed, a greater door opened.

Satan sees two things. First, he sees the extent of his evil powers. He sees all the people whom he holds and all of the weapons which they possess. In assessing his own strength, he knows he does not yet have enough evil to cover the world.

Second, he sees President Obama, who singlehandedly has neutralized America which now sits on the sidelines and merely follows the events. As Satan sees these two realities, he knows what he must do to seize this opportunity to bring about the moment when he can set the world ablaze. When that moment arrives, he will act immediately.

I must also speak clearly about the Church, which has so failed the gift of Fatima. Sister Lucy was a faithful messenger. As World War II began, she alone knew why. My mother had told her that this war would break out during the reign of Pope Pius XI if the Church did not listen and heed her messages.

The work of Fatima and the task of Sister Lucy were meant to be fulfilled during her lifetime, but the Church did not listen to her. She was a religious, who lived a hidden convent life. She could only send messages. When these were rejected, she just sent more messages.

I will no longer send messages to the popes. They have never listened and they still do not listen. Instead, I will send a pope who himself is the messenger. He will need to deliver the message to no one. He knows what he must do.

I say all of this because no one sees the magnitude of what is happening in the Middle East, nor how close Satan is to gaining the power to turn the whole world into his hell.

Comment
The world knows that the events in Iraq are serious
but they do not see them in light of Satan's worldwide plan.

June 16, 2014
8. Oil on the Lampstand

Special Locutions on Iraq

Mary

The future of the Church will not be an easy path. First, the Church has suffered from so many sides. Its critics rejoice because their voices are so strident and their words are so well received. Second, the Church has inner enemies who are hidden and do their work without being seen. They want to strip the Church of her supernatural elements so she can appear a fully modern institution. Yet, of these I do not speak.

The Church will share in events which will shake the world. Not only nations but the Church, also, will be shaken. The structures, the finances, the very work itself will be endangered by these events.

However, the Church will have the strength of faith not shared by the nations. This is why I must speak now. When the events begin, fears and even panic can enter into the Church. However, a moment will come when a great light of faith takes hold. The Church will say, "It is for this very moment that we exist. In the darkness, we will be the light to the nations." There will be a fresh resolve. The events that should destroy the Church will be used to lift her up and place her light on the lampstand. At last! At last!

June 17, 2014

9. Prevailing over Hell

Special Locutions on Iraq

Mary

All see the Church's organizations and its institutions. However, what really is the Catholic Church? Why is it so important at this moment? We must go back to Jesus' promise, "You are Peter and upon this rock I will build my Church and the gates of hell shall not prevail against it" (Mt.16:18).

Does any other institution have that promise? Has it been given to any nation or union of nations? Only the Church has the promise, "Hell shall not prevail against you."

As hell pours out its fire, and as Satan seeks the total destruction of the world, he knows that only the Catholic Church has Jesus' promise. "Prevail" does not just meant "to survive," it means to overcome, to conquer, and to gain the victory.

If the world were just a group of nations, even strong nations united perfectly, Satan could still win the victory. However, the Church exists. It is in the world (as Jesus said). It lives in history, just as the nations do. It suffers. It bleeds. It sorrows. It lives and it prays. That is the Catholic Church. Someday, in the very midst of the great battle that lies ahead, when Satan attempts to reduce the world to ashes, the Church will also prevail. The Catholic Church is the only hope for mankind and Satan knows Jesus' promise.

Comment
Our Lady has tried to reveal the great and hidden mysteries
placed by Jesus in the Catholic Church.

June 18, 2014

10. Leading to the Ultimate Fire (Special Locution)

Special Locutions on Iraq

Jesus

Keep your eyes focused on the Middle East. I told you a long time ago that the war in Syria would not end quickly and, because it would continue, that many structures would be destroyed. This ripping apart of stability would open the door. Syria was always the fuse even though the explosions would take place elsewhere.

This violence is rooted in two things, the centuries of memories and religious beliefs. This Middle East fire is so deep, so strong, and involves so many people that no human power on the face of this earth can put it out.

What happens when fires cannot be put out? They continue. They grow. Moments of greater and greater destruction take place.

From now on, there will be no peace. These fires will never be put out. They will lead to greater fires and ultimately, to the great fire. All of this is true unless heaven begins to act.

Comment
At this point, the fires in Syria, Iraq and throughout the Middle East
have passed the point of being controlled by any human force.

June 20, 2014
11. The Voice of Light

Special Locutions on Iraq

Jesus

In the middle of this darkness are many voices of light, but so many of these voices are tiny. They are voices of lay people, of children, even of religious women who are given words from heaven. These are important voices, little rays of light, but they are ignored by many. Your locutions are a big voice because of [your spiritual director] and the stature that I have given to him. Early in his priesthood, I sent him a little girl with heavenly messages.

Then I led him to Padre Pio and later, to Mother Theresa. He has held worldwide positions and is known everywhere. People cannot ignore the light that has his name attached.

When the terrorists raise their flag over all that they will control in Iraq, a new level of terrorism will begin. They will have their own land and their own resources. This is new. They will not just be a government that allows terrorists. They will be a government of terrorists. They will not govern in order to bless their people. They will govern to destroy the world. No one can imagine the new level of this threat.

Comment
As the situation grows more dangerous,
heaven's voice must become stronger.

June 21, 2014
12. Mankind Is over the Brink

Special Locutions on Iraq

Jesus

Formerly, mankind was on the brink. Now it has gone over the brink. The previous century was filled with many evils and mankind was advancing into the darkness. Although these evils did not lead mankind over the brink, the constant delays in seeking heaven's help caused that moment to come even closer.

However, even with all that had happened, the evil was still contained and could be avoided. Now, the evil is no longer contained. It has spilled out of its container and is everywhere. When did this happen? Only recently, as the Syrian revolution destabilized the whole region and allowed the terrorist groups to emerge, knowing that they would meet no American resistance.

It is too late for earthly solutions. Only heaven's light and heaven's power can save the world. For this reason, I have raised up these little locutions. No one else sees what has happened nor understands what is taking place. Mankind is no longer on the brink. It has gone off the brink. The evil is no longer contained. It has broken out of its container. Earthly light is no longer enough. Mankind must begin to follow heaven's light.

This darkness will continue and mankind will go deeper and deeper into the darkness. At some point the world and the Church will remember my words that only heaven can save mankind.

Comment
Often we think that the evil events are just a long line in a series.
We do not understand that recent events were a turning point.

The Human Person

June 18, 2014
1. Call from God

The Human Person

Mary
Every human person has a call from God, a word placed in the deepest part of their

person. God places this call at the moment of their conception, when he directly creates the human person. For so many, this call is a seed that never opens and the person's talents are spent on other goals. Even with great worldly success, the person might never have fulfilled their divine call.

God's whole purpose in creating mankind was that each seed would come forth. This seed is the person's identity, who they are meant to be, what they should become, and the good they should accomplish.

When society is ordered and filled with faith, many understand and respond to their call. When society is confused, then the person finds this difficult. I am speaking now for two reasons. First, people must become aware of this divine power placed within them. Secondly, people need help to understand and to fulfill their call.

Come, this will be an exciting journey. We will travel to the very center of your personhood and discover who you are. You will set aside the false images that flood your mind and grasp what is true.

Comment
Even amid our confusing society, Our Lady can help
each person discover God's call planted within.

June 19, 2014
2. Deprived of Divine Light

The Human Person

Mary

I want to bring you into the deepest mystery. The human person has God's plan stamped forever on the soul. This is man's hidden identity, unique to each individual. Discovering and fulfilling this destiny was meant to be easy, like a journey on a road filled with light. Sin changed all that. The straight road became difficult, narrow, twisting, filled with obstacles and plunged into darkness.

Jesus came as the light of the world. Many walked in that new light and society was bathed in light. Cultures of light came about. Many began to know God's call and live it out.

Now, the darkness comes. The lights are extinguished, one by one. Yet, each person retains this force within themselves, this divine call. When darkness comes, people wait for the light to act. However, the divine call never waits. It persists. It cries out. It wants to shape every decision. This is the dilemma of modern man. He carries within himself a divine call but is deprived of the divine light. That is why I speak. My locutions will offer you, O reader, the light which your culture should have provided you. Listen carefully to all my words.

Comment
These extraordinary locutions are needed because the world has rejected God's light.

June 20, 2014
3. The Mystery of the Person

The Human Person

Mary

The human person is infinite, able to exist only by a unique act of God's will. The person is formed in the great mystery of the Trinity of persons, Father, Son and Holy Spirit and is called to a greatness, which is hidden in God's will but gladly revealed.

How does each person arrive at their own greatness? This is the mystery I will explain. Every person is born into a culture. If the culture is devout and filled with light, then the person can more easily find their way. God acts within them from the earliest years and the soul sets out in the greatest light. If, however, the person is born into a culture of darkness, they do not realize what God is doing within them. Their inner divine light is covered over and their choices are limited to earth.

This is the great struggle now taking place between the Woman and Satan. Millions of people live all their lives in darkness, their divine call is lost. As this darkness has spread, many have abandoned their faith and many more have never received it. So, I use these locutions to cast an inner light. They pierce the darkness and offer everyone an opportunity to discover God's call.

Comment
The human person is caught in the conflict between light and darkness.

June 21, 2014
4. Personal Light in a Darkened Culture

The Human Person

Mary

Before a person can discover their call, they must be awakened. What a special blessing that is, a moment when the veil is pulled back and the great door opens. This moment comes at different stages. Sometimes, the person is very young (even a child). For others the blessing comes in adolescence or young adulthood.

As the years slip away and the opportunities are no longer present, it is more difficult, but not impossible, for a person to be awakened and to realize, "This is my call. This is why I was created and to this I will give the remaining years of my life."

This awakening is God's gift. (What a special moment.) The moment is always prepared for. Those who receive the enlightenment as children usually have devout parents whom they obeyed. Those who receive this in adolescence or young adulthood have either been faithful for years or have had a conversion.

Right now, I speak to the whole world. My Immaculate Heart is pouring out extraordinary gifts of light. The growing darkness has covered over the usual ways of this awakening. I will circumvent the culture. I will conquer the darkness that surrounds you. I will come directly to your heart. Even though your culture offers you no door to God, you will know that I have given you a light. While darkness surrounds you, a new light will fill you. You will know this has happened, and by these locutions you will know what to do.

Comment
When the culture was filled with light, God worked easily
within each heart. Now, people need this extraordinary light
flowing from Our Lady's Immaculate Heart.

June 22, 2014
5. The Mystery of Human Existence

The Human Person

Mary

God does everything so that the human person discovers the mystery that God has placed in his heart. Unfortunately, each culture is filled with darkness and so many do not have the needed light to read what is within, to understand these inner mysteries. That is why I speak.

Within you, O reader, is an intellect which shares God's power to know. You also have a spiritual will, quite independent of your lower desires. Do not confuse the two because they war against each other. Inside you also is a power deliberately placed there by your Maker. He made you for himself. Deep inside that power is your call, who you are meant to be, whom you are to love, and to work with, and what you are to do to fulfill your call.

All of these are powerful forces within you that lead to your happiness. God calls you to the deepest joys, the greatest accomplishments and, finally, a place with Jesus forever.

You are not free to rip these mysteries out of your soul. You cannot say, "I will no longer be a human person." Even your death will not end your human existence. I come to you to help you. Together, we can discover the road to your happiness.

Comment

Man has no choice. He is created without any choice on his part.
Our Lady promises that she can bring each person to eternal happiness.

June 23, 2014

6. The Center of Material Creation

The Human Person

Mary

The mystery of the human person stands at the center of material creation. All was created for the human person who alone can thank God. Does the heavenly Father just like to paint beautiful skies or form planets? Is he like a child in a sandbox building castles? God is a person and has created the human person to know and love him. He wants the person to become like himself and to live forever.

Like Adam, who enjoyed paradise but felt lonely without human love, so the heavenly Father wants the human person to give him divine love. The greatness of the human person is his capacity to be divinized, to be made like God, and to love God as God loves himself. This call can only be fulfilled by the Holy Spirit of God poured out by Jesus.

Jesus stands at the center of all history, nailed to the cross from which he gave up his Spirit. The mystery of each human person is found only in Jesus' opened heart. Go there and you will find your name written. Stay there and you will discover who you are. Surrender to Jesus and you will fulfill your call.

Comment

Every person is a unique mystery and discovers
the answer to that mystery in Jesus Christ.

June 24, 2014

7. The Correct Surrender

The Human Person

Mary

I come to the heart of the problem, which is the heart of each person. The human person is like a fortress, with their will at the highest and most protected place, a free will that makes the final decision of what to surrender to.

It is faced with daily decisions and says "yes" or "no" a hundred times a day. From these decisions, comes success or failure.

112

O soul, you say "yes" to this and "no" to that, but I am knocking now at the door of your will. A heavenly visitor has come. I offer you a heavenly choice. I offer you a chance to surrender to what is above you. The heavenly Father wants to lift you up and rescue you from the frustration of human life. (This is his plan for the human person.)

Comment

Nothing on earth can satisfy the human person.
God made the heart for himself.

Lessons To Be Learned

June 25, 2014

1. The ISIS Terrorists

Lessons To Be Learned

Mary

Once more the destructive forces have broken forth in Iraq. This time the effects will not be reversed. The country will be divided. The goals of the terrorists will be gained and the terrible darkness of violence will now have its own territory.

So many are at fault. The blame lies squarely at their feet. They refused to act and to make Iraq secure. They set aside the warning signals and had no will to become engaged in the battle.

I will once more describe what is happening in these events:

1. This battle is between Satan and the Woman.

2. Satan's war against the Woman is inevitable. It is the only way to drain off his forces and enter an era of world peace.

3. The battle is worldwide.

4. Because mankind has walked away from God's law, it has come under the power of the Evil One.

5. These events, which are now getting the world's attention, are only the beginning stages of the birth pangs.

6. Only mankind turning back to the heavenly Father can mitigate these events.

Since mankind is not ready to do that, the events will continue. The destruction will spread and no human force is present to prevent this.

I will save all those who come to me.

Comment
Our Lady makes clear the truths that she has taught so often.

June 26, 2014
2. An Infection That Needs Cleansing

Lessons To Be Learned

Mary

Why are these events taking place? They are not the birth pangs of life with a normal sequence and purpose. The breasts do not get ready to feed a new child. Do not look for new life from these events.

These events have the same source as the two world wars which drove mankind off course. After World War I, the seeds for World War II were planted in the peace treaties. After World War II, the evil seeds were placed in the atomic bomb.

Each war opened out to a new and greater evil which has never been purged from the human system. These events are not birth pangs. They are a powerful infection that must come to the moment of crisis. That is where the events are going, to a moment of purging, to a cleansing that will inevitably take place. However, how will this happen? Who will be the doctor? Who understands the illness? Who knows the remedies?

O mankind, do not trust yourself to human leaders who are unskilled in the ways of heaven. I will be your doctor, if only you seek my services.

Comment
Only heaven understands what is going on
and how to eliminate the infection.

June 27, 2014
3. Satan's Intelligence and World Leaders' Ignorance

Special Locution

Mary

What is happening is totally beyond the power of human intellects to grasp. They see only the pieces, the fragments, the individual events of destruction. Even then, they see only what is most evident and on the surface.

The only ones who see are those involved in destroying the earth. They see because they are demonic, enlightened by the Evil One. He gladly reveals his strategy. He reveals the weakness of the defenses. He shows them safeguards that have been foolishly set aside. He shows them what is ripe for destruction and what must wait for a later moment. He shows them what weapons to use and what tactics to employ. He teaches them how to lie and deceive, and how to be protected by false treaties.

He clouds the minds of world leaders and compromises them by their sins. He always holds before their eyes the political consequences of any move they might choose. In this way, he paralyses them and forces them to hold back.

So effective has Satan been, that he can hardly believe that a world which had been so strong, has become weak and ready for a complete takeover. He owns the whole field. He has no enemies, especially no strong America, to oppose him. All of his strategies come together. What he has planned for centuries is coming to fruition, a harvest of disruption, distraction and untold suffering.

He has only one real enemy, the Woman, whom the heavenly Father announced from the beginning (Gen. 3:15). I have not delayed. I never delay. My work is hidden. I am raising up my army. Reader, I invite you and the whole world to enlist. When you see an opportunity to gather with others in my name accept it immediately.

Comment
Our Lady reveals what world leaders fail so miserably to see.
As she gathers her army, all must join.

June 28, 2014
4. The Cancer of ISIS

Lessons To Be Learned

Mary

No one sees. No one understands. A country is torn apart and divided. A group, whose heart is totally evil and dedicated to destruction, quickly rips apart Iraq and claims a part for its own. Now its evil heart takes on a full body. It has its own country with land and resources, a firm base for its operations.

This group is like a new cancer that has entered the human body. It is powerful, totally dedicated to evil, and now it has its own life. Can no one see the newness of this situation? A cancer is small compared to the whole body but it contains death within its cells, an evil quickly carried by the blood stream to other parts.

So it will be with ISIS. Do not think that they will just be content with Iraq. They see the whole body, the entire world, and they want to bring their cancer everywhere. I no longer say that it is late. I say that it is too late. The world leaders have failed miserably to contain the evil. Now it is out of its container. It has broken loose. Only heaven has the antidote. I speak now so that when all happens, the world has faith that heaven is more powerful than hell.

Comment
World leaders continue to do absolutely nothing.
Now it is too late for effective action.

June 29, 2014
5. The Two Paths

Lessons To Be Learned

Mary

Gaping holes open up. Defense strategies mean nothing. How can the whole world be defended? Is there a fence large enough to keep out the intruders? O mankind, your world has been invaded by the forces of hell. You yourself have opened the doors by throwing away the security that only religious faith can provide.

Now it is too late. Your defenses have been pierced and the evil pours into your system. I do not want to say these words but you have a demonic infection and your fever will go up and up. I can only point out to you what will happen in the future.

The Muslim terrorists see this as their hour, the moment they have awaited for centuries. They have been told many stories of the past and the dreams that have not been fulfilled. In their hearts, they see this dream of their forefathers coming into view. Their dream is of worldwide domination, when all the infidels have been conquered and Allah and his prophet, Mohammed, are raised on high. Realize that you are facing demonic power and intelligence united with hearts which carry centuries of memories. These forces carry the Muslim terrorists down a road of destruction and the whole world will be dragged down that same road.

I speak now, while it is still in its beginning stage, still limited to the Middle East chaos. I invite all to learn of my plans and to follow my path. There are only two paths. Whoever rejects mine, will be taken down the other.

Comment
Our Lady is now speaking more seriously than ever before.
Her messages always hold out hope, but each person and
the whole Church must do what she asks.

116

June 29, 2014
6. Tomorrow's Supreme Court Decision (Special Locution)

Lessons To Be Learned

Jesus

Tomorrow the Supreme Court will deal a great blow to the Obama Healthcare Act. The decision will contain some surprising thoughts. In this way, I will continue to destroy President Obama and all those who have cooperated with him. He will look and see that all are discouraged. He will act foolishly to regain his stronghold but this will be his fatal step. He will stay in office but will be stripped of all meaningful power.

Suddenly, I am giving America another chance. America will be free to use the polling places to choose different leaders. This is so important and it will happen quickly because I need America to be a force on the world scene. This must happen quickly.

Comment
The decision fits in with all the other events
that are stripping the President of power in his remaining years.

June 30, 2014
7. The Wounds in Iraq

Lessons To Be Learned

Mary

Other nations have been drawn into the conflict because the wounds in Iraq are so severe. The country is dismembered, and gaping holes appear. These nations are beginning to realize how this will affect them, even though they do not border Iraq.

The nations in the region are more deeply shaken. Lebanon and Jordan have already been destabilized. As the conflict continues, with no end in sight, these countries cannot foresee the final results.

This great evil is now whistling aloud. Countries, near and far, are hearing the sounds. They look at Iraq and see a country devoured by its enemies and abandoned by America. Will not the pattern continue in the Middle East? Previously, the hatred and the militancy determined relationships, but the governments remained stable.

All of that has changed, beginning with the Libyan and Egyptian revolutions. The Arab Spring was no Spring at all.

Comment
The Middle East events are different. There was always
hatred and violence, but governments remained stable.

June 30, 2014
7a. Implication of Supreme Court Decision (Special Locution)

Lessons To Be Learned

Jesus

The Supreme Court Decision does not seem to be earth-shattering. However, it is much more powerful than anyone can see for two reasons.

First, it is a continuation of events that are weakening the power of President Obama. He had hoped that a favorable decision would reverse the present tide. Instead, the tide against him grows stronger and he finds himself swimming against the current when previously everything flowed in his direction.

Much more important, no one can see the implication of the Supreme Court decision. How many others qualify for this exemption? How many others see the possibilities of new exemptions? This new decision has not yet been applied by the courts to other questions. To how many others will it bring freedom from the Healthcare law?

The fence has been cut open. What good is a fence when it has holes allowing people to climb through? There are many who are searching for this opportunity and many others who want to make the hole bigger. This decision is far greater than anyone realizes and far more important than meets the eye.

Comment
The decision is very important with many ramifications.

July 1, 2014
8. A New Day for America

Lessons To Be Learned

Mary

Many do not see it, but the first rays are appearing on the horizon. I am speaking of a new day for America, a surprising gift coming from my Immaculate Heart. This moment has already begun as I strip President Obama of his power and the darkness which he has cast over America. But there is much, much more.

As the hold of darkness is loosened, a new light will arise in America, a surprising return to its religious stream. Already the beginning waters have come and the beginning light has dawned. I speak so that the signs of this new day will be understood. People must know and respond. The churches must be ready. I will speak quickly to each group.

I want political leaders who totally protect the lives of the unborn. If this is not on your agenda, then I will not use you for the new light.

I want priests to pray with their people. Why are your churches closed all day? Should you not be there with your people, adoring the Blessed Sacrament?

I want people who respond to my initiatives. I am pushing back the darkness so you have a freedom but you must use this freedom to bring about a new day when the purified Church is again exalted in people's hearts. There is much more to say.

Comment
*This locution is a real surprise because these years have contained
so much darkness for America and the American Church.*

July 2, 2014
9. Baghdad – Caught in the Crossfires

Lessons To Be Learned

Mary

President Obama seeks a political solution to the problems besetting Baghdad. However, the President of Iraq will not go along and the two presidents are at odds. Meanwhile Iran, and even Russia, enter the scene while the invading armies try to strengthen their hold and decide upon their approach to Baghdad.

The people see these multiple forces, the invading armies, and the division among the political leaders. They find it impossible to decide whom they should trust. They only know that they are in the middle of forces which they cannot control.

Such is the continual state of Baghdad, a situation that cannot be resolved. Who can bring stability and peace when there is fighting even among the leaders?

Baghdad is caught in both military and political crossfire. It also sits as a great prize, easily able to be stolen because not controlled by any one group. Its fortunes will continue to sink and its power to defend itself will slowly dissolve. Its final fate will not be decided quickly.

Comment
Our Lady spells out the multiple problems and the uncertain future.

July 3, 2014
10. Finger in the Dike

Lessons To Be Learned

Mary

President Obama will send some troops, but this is like putting his finger in the dike, a woefully inadequate solution. His actions will have little effect on the final outcome.

The region itself will suffer from constant dismemberment. Powerful groups will carve out their own spheres of control. Nations will break up and a new map of the Middle East will be drawn. All of this will strengthen the terrorist groups, who will act like governing bodies over a definite geographical region. This will prepare for a new level of terrorism all around the world.

I have many purposes in speaking these words. All of this evil is satanic and the Evil One has these powers because the world has rejected my Son, Jesus. The tide will turn as the world returns to the heavenly Father. World leaders so seldom talk about God.

Comment
Our Lady summarizes the forces and shows the future dismemberment of nations.

July 4, 2014
11. Terrorism and Europe

Lessons To Be Learned

Mary

Where are the European leaders? I must speak to a Europe that has left its Father's house, abandoning faith and placing all its confidence in economic progress. I must say this with loud words.

You are in the direct line of fire, totally unprotected, a continent waiting to be destroyed and engulfed in the fires of terrorism.

When the terrorists settle into their new home in Iraq, after they have quelled any insurrection, after they have established themselves firmly, they will immediately cast their covetous eyes upon your riches, knowing that you will be an easy prey, ready for the plucking.

First, they will destabilize by violence and cast fear by their atrocities. The new birth pangs of death will grip your countries. Foolish children, why did you leave the heavenly Father's house? There is still time to return and enjoy a protection that will save you from the greatest sufferings.

Comment
Europe will be the next major target.

July 5, 2014
12. Satan's Perfect Storm

Lessons To Be Learned

Mary

Satan has created a perfect storm. He has moved the most powerful destructive forces into a perfect place and he has removed all those forces which in any way would mitigate the evil that will now begin to pour out.

The world has not as yet seen the explosion of terrorism in the Middle East. It is only witnessing the gathering of the fuel and the growing capacity to launch the fires everywhere in the world.

How clearly I have spoken in these locutions of those forces that are still hidden, but soon to be revealed. Therefore, my words must go forth to all the nations. People must understand quickly, even instantly, the hidden powers behind the events. This clear and worldwide knowledge will be the best antidote against the destructive fires that will soon be lit in every corner of the globe. Human intellects cannot cope with this perfect storm, which will happen in many situations.

Comment
As the destructive fires spread, so must these locutions.

Path to Peace

July 6, 2014
1. The Beginning Words

Path to Peace

Mary

Is there no path to peace? All the exits from war and terrorism seem to be blocked. No safe haven exists. All can be set ablaze. Some would say, "The heavenly Father would never allow this to happen," as if relief comes without any efforts or that the sins of mankind which have created this situation can be instantly removed.

Certainly, a path to peace exists and I will explain the steps which must be taken. However, I warn you that many will ignore my words (as if they are not from heaven). Others will not think they need my words (as if the world will just continue to be safe). Others will believe that mankind can find its own way to peace (as if mankind has no responsibility for what has happened). Others will hear my words and postpone taking these steps (as if the dangers are far away and will not happen in their lifetime).

Only some will rejoice, knowing that there is a path to peace and the beginning steps are within their reach. (Yes, I will reveal only the beginning steps.) I speak for the benefit of these good people whose hearts are already fixed upon me.

Comment
Having spoken so much of worldwide terrorism,
Our Lady launches us on her road of peace.

July 7, 2014
2. A Blocked Path to Peace

Path to Peace

Mary

The path to peace is hidden from your eyes and the words that I will speak will seem like foolishness to many. Even those who love me will not understand them fully. Yet, I must speak now so that the words are recorded. Later, as the events begin, people can return to these words as firm guidelines to peace.

The problems of gaining world peace are quite new and different because a new reality has emerged – worldwide terrorism. Formerly, the various groups could be brought together to resolve a conflict peacefully, in the interest of both sides. Terrorists have absolutely no interest in peace. Their very name reveals their goals – to spread terror. They exist for war and destruction. Therefore, the usual path to peace is blocked and, really, does not exist.

Formerly, an aggressor was met with force and, as the force increased, the aggressor could be led to the bargaining table. But this method is not effective with terrorists. They are not a nation with national interests. They have no citizens to feed, and no children to protect. Their eyes are always upon what they can destroy, not what they need to protect. These are the difficulties in finding a path to peace.

Comment
Our Lady begins by outlining the new and unique difficulties.

July 8, 2014
3. Understanding the Evil of Terrorism

Path to Peace

Mary

Regarding terrorism, world leaders are in great confusion about the path to peace. They do not understand the way the terrorists are joined together or the internal forces that suddenly explode into external acts.

Terrorism is like cancer. The number of cells is so few compared to the entire body, but the cells are so joined in their evil power that they can destroy the body.

Terrorists are not joined in seeking good for their members. They look outward at what exists and they plot to destroy. They are willing to postpone satisfaction and even, in some cases, to offer their own lives to destroy.

In these circumstances, the path to peace is not clear. I must outline the steps because they are not self-evident. My steps are different. They speak of a different world. They speak of faith, of God's help, and of a new charity. Many will say that these steps are ineffective, but remember that I am outlining only the beginning steps to peace, the foundations that need to be restored. Terrorism feeds upon sins, especially the sins of those who are fighting terrorism.

I ask the world leaders, "Are you ready to begin with your own sins?" If not, you cannot walk any path to peace.

Comment
Our Lady reveals what is different in the terrorist threat
and where the path to peace begins – by acknowledging our own sins.

July 9, 2014
4. The Few Who Control the World

Path to Peace

Mary

In seeking their own interests, people act immediately, but when thinking of others, action is postponed. Tomorrow seems acceptable. However, the time is short and the first step to peace is to pay attention to the great discrepancies between rich and poor.

I now cast my eyes to the greatest and to the most powerful evil in the world of economics. The entire world financial markets lie in the hands of a powerful few. For decades, they have tilted the world. Their money always increases because they control the rules and the regulations. Even elected leaders of great nations come under their control, unable to act without their consent.

From these few people come every kind of evil. They control world events for their own financial interests. They begin wars, destabilize legitimate governments, and fund countless hidden, covert operations. These few people who control the finances of the world are the main obstacle to world peace. They want to bring about a one world order where their power is supreme. However, their fortress is not impregnable. There is a path to removing them from power.

Comment

Control of the world's money lies in the hands of a small group
of unbelievably wealthy and powerful people.
They are the main obstacle to world peace.

July 10, 2014
5. The Terrorism of Abortion

Path to Peace

Mary

I take you quickly into the very center of the darkness which has come over America, the great darkness of abortion. O foolish America, you build walls against terrorism while your own terrorists kill the unborn.

A darkness has been forced upon America, a darkness accepted and even canonized by your Supreme Court. A darkness that says a mother can kill her unborn son or daughter. I will say this clearly, "As long as you do not protect the unborn from your own terrorism, I will not protect you." You have brought this evil upon yourself. You have opened the heart of America to the greatest darkness.

There is a path to peace but you have no desire to walk it. Even so, I will raise up a new stream of life. I want political leaders to protect all the unborn without any compromise (as if some unborn are less worthy of life than others). I make this truth so clear. Protect all of your unborn and I will protect you. Abandon the unborn and I will abandon you. Why should I protect you from terrorism when you allow terrorism to go unchecked in your abortion clinics? I outline the path to peace, but who wants to walk that path?

Comment

Almost no one sees the connection between abortion
and God taking away his protection over America.

July 11, 2014
6. The Personal Road to Peace

Path to Peace

Mary

The more the world tries to find the path to peace, the more confused it

124

becomes. Its efforts bring forth few results and the darkness grows even greater. The heavenly Father has decreed that the path to peace must pass through my Immaculate Heart. He wants to exalt my Immaculate Heart and he wants all the world to understand the prerogatives and powers which he has placed there.

Although the path to peace cannot be walked overnight, I must explain the beginning steps. First, the world must understand how helpless it is, that it cannot even find the path to peace, let alone walk that road. Second, it must believe that there is a path to peace and it can be found in my Immaculate Heart.

Peace begins with repentance. Each person must realize that they have caused division. Let each person examine their own conscience. Let them remove anger and dissension within their own heart. Let them always seek peace in their home and in their relationships. This seems such a small step, compared to the long road to world peace, but the person who chooses to walk this road of peace will be constantly lifted higher, be given greater power and authority, and will become a great instrument of peace to many. These are the beginning steps.

Comment
Do not wait. You begin to bring world peace
by deliberately walking your personal road of peace.

July 14, 2014
7. The Long Difficult Path to Peace

Path to Peace

Mary

Many set out on the path to peace but are quickly diverted by selfish interests. Seeing advantages that they can gain, they forget the goal. This only hinders peace. When one nation or group takes advantage over another, this becomes an issue, an obstacle to peace.

No, you cannot take your eyes away from the goal. You cannot allow short-term gains to divert you. You must sacrifice all that is selfish to bring others to the vision of peace. All selfish interests which jeopardize peace must be set aside.

You can see the road to peace is not of one day or of one year. It might not even be of one lifetime. It is a long and arduous road, walked only by those whose hearts are firmly set upon peace. This is a path of sacrifice, of thinking of others, and of seeking their good.

In this light, look at your weapons. This has been the false path to peace. Weapons, weapons, weapons. They are everywhere, even in the hands of children.

This is my promise. If even just a handful take up this road of peace, if they do not abandon it, if they truly try to bless others, if they seek no self-interest, I will bless their work. All will see the great results. Even if only a small portion of the world walks this path to peace, I will keep them safe.

Some might even lay down their lives for peace.

Comment

Our Lady speaks honestly that the path to peace is long and difficult.

July 15, 2014

8. American Arms Sales

Path to Peace

Mary

The diplomats get on planes. They travel here and they travel there. They talk and discuss. However, how many nations are ready to change their own hearts? To them, peace is like a chessboard.

Is world peace a series of moves and countermoves? This is called a manipulative peace, as if peace could be engineered or manufactured.

The path to peace is much deeper than diplomatic travels, because the causes of war lie in a nation's decisions. World peace cannot be pulled out of a hat like a magician's rabbit and it cannot be brokered by astute diplomacy and clever moves.

People have memories. The sins of the past remain alive, powerful and uncontrollable forces which constantly boil over.

The world is now faced with intelligent, powerful, coordinated and growing forces. Satan has placed these in the hearts of millions. The fires you have witnessed are as nothing compared with the fires that are still hidden, and these fires cannot be extinguished by flying diplomats. They are only fought by a complete turning back to my Son Jesus, the Prince of Peace. But nations do not want to hear these words. They do not want to hear about their own sins, their own fires and their own dishonesty.

Let me end with one single question. I ask everyone who reads these locutions to demand an answer. In the past 40 years, "How many billions of dollars has accrued to America by selling weapons to other nations?" Your greed, America, has fueled the fires and your weapons that are used everywhere. You sell weapons and then send your diplomats to play their chess games.

Comment

Every year, America leads the world in selling weapons abroad.
For decades, America has armed the whole world.

126

July 16, 2014
9. The Path to War

Path to Peace

Mary

It is too late when the fires of war break out. The task of peace is when there are no wars. This demands vigilant hearts, nations that are sensitive to justice, and leaders who are filled with charity.

If human life is always a clash of interests, a domination of rich over poor, and control by the powerful, then wars are inevitable. These wars destroy valuable resources. The victor claims what he wants. The vanquished are worse off and the seeds of future wars are sown deeper into people's memories. Such is the cycle of war.

When I propose a different path to peace, people and nations cry out "unrealistic." As they reject my path of peace, only the path to war remains. The world travels this path so quickly these days.

Comment
Our Lady's plan is not superficial.
It demands changed hearts and changed policies.

Treasures in Mary's Heart

July 17, 2014
1. Receive without Cost

Treasures in Mary's Heart

Mary

In my heart are many treasures and I invite the whole world to come, seek and find. Even if a person searches for their own selfish interest, this is not important. I will grant their requests and will use this gift to attract them to my more important treasures.

Some will come to my heart, receive their gift and walk away. Others will come and receive their blessing. However, they will notice that my heart contains many other gifts. They will stay in my heart and seek my deeper gifts. In this way, I will attract every heart.

There will be a third stage when my heart reveals its deepest gift, a sacrificing love that serves others. This love is the treasure placed in the field, the pearl of a great price (which no one can really pay for but was already purchased by Jesus' blood). What a gift, the ultimate and greatest gift, to love God with all one's heart.

I will begin to explain the gifts in my heart and invite the whole world to come and receive. Do not forget. Jesus has already paid for them by his death on the cross. As the prophet Isaiah wrote, "Come, without paying and without cost, drink wine and milk" (55:1).

Comment
All of God's treasures lie in Mary's heart and she will reveal them.

July 17, 2014
2. On Shooting Down the Plane (Special Locution)

Treasures in Mary's Heart

Jesus

You see Satan's evil, his plan always unfolding, always surprises, always much suffering, and always unforeseen ramifications. Some say that Putin has made a mistake, but Satan has not. All is according to Satan's plan.

Putin will withdraw more and more from the West. As this happens, he will become more dangerous. These events show that the time is short and the timetable has again been moved ahead.

Putin will rely more and more on the spirit of nationalism that is sweeping Russia. He must show results to his people because they suffer from the sanctions. He must enter new alliances. Because the West is closed, he will turn East to China.

The downing of the plane will radicalize the Ukrainian situation. He is forced back to the table because the pro-Russians will be attacked and he cannot let them be beaten. They are his constituency.

July 18, 2014
3. The Trinity's Gifts

Treasures in Mary's Heart

Mary

When you seek the treasures in my heart you will find gifts from the Father, the Son and the Holy Spirit. The Father, who created, has placed the fullness of life. This fullness was meant to be given to everyone by Adam, the first father of the human race, but he lost these treasures by sin. So, the heavenly Father has placed the fullness of life in the safety of my heart, knowing that I would never commit sin and lose this life.

The Son has placed all of his virtues in my heart. In these gifts, each person can live as Jesus did, in perfect union with the Father's commands.

Finally, the Holy Spirit has placed his gifts of fecundity. By his power I was able to conceive. By the Spirit, new blessings will burst forth in surprising ways.

For many people, the Three Divine Persons are a hidden mystery, but if they enter my heart and receive my gifts, I will share with them the greatest gift. They will come to know and experience the Father, Son and Holy Spirit.

Comment
The greatest of all gifts is a relationship
with the Father, Son and Spirit.

July 19, 2014
4. A "Yes" to God

Treasures in Mary's Heart

Mary

How do you get to my heart so you can discover my treasures? You are already there because I hold the whole world, and every human person, in my heart. I carry all your sins and failures. I carry all your hopes and desires. Most important, I carry God's will for you. When I said to the Angel Gabriel, "Let it be done according to your word," I said those words for you. I accepted fully God's will for myself and for the whole world.

When Eve, and her husband Adam, said "no" to God, human history became a vast and resounding "no." Then, the light of revelation began, a beginning "yes" in Noah and Abraham and the prophets. Divine revelation came to its greatest moment when Gabriel revealed that God would become a man and I was chosen to say "yes" for the whole human race.

At that moment, you were placed in my heart. More important, your "yes" to all that God wants for you was placed there. That is my gift for you today. Do you always want to say "yes" to God?

Here, take your gift. I place it right now in your heart. Quickly, you will experience its divine power. You will be attracted to the light. You will want to forsake the attractions of evil.

Just say "yes" to this new gift in your heart. That is what I did all my life – a constant stream of "yes."

129

*Your life is filled with decisions. May you always
say "yes" to God's will for you.*

July 20, 2014
5. Past and Future Secrets

Treasures in Mary's Heart

Mary

In my heart you will find all of God's secrets. The Father has placed your secrets in my heart and wants you to find them there. These secrets are his plan for your life.

These secrets are both past and future. Concerning the past, they will reveal to you why certain things have happened to you. Some were blessings from God. Others were the results of your own decisions, good and bad. You will see your life as God sees it. This is a moment of great light.

Once you have opened and received this gift, the secrets of your future are easy to discover. In this light, you can see the path to walk. You must accept this full light about your past and, in this light, choose the correct future path.

After this beginning gift, there will be many more secrets, all that God has planned for you. These cannot be revealed until the conversion light is received and accepted. When Jesus said to Peter, "Come, follow me," he was revealing a secret that was important for Peter. Only because Peter accepted that secret and followed Jesus, could he receive all the other secrets that were in Jesus' heart, that he was to be the rock on which Jesus would build his Church.

All that God intends you to be, all the many blessings for your whole life, are secrets hidden in my heart but so quickly revealed if you but search.

Comment
*For each person, Our Lady's heart holds unique secrets,
the mystery of each life and its purpose.*

July 21, 2014
6. Revealing God's Plan

Treasures in Mary's Heart

Mary

God's plan for your life is hidden in my heart, kept safe and waiting to be revealed. As you enter my heart, I will share with you my greatest gift, a deep desire to know and to do only God's will.

Before I reveal God's will, I must purify your heart of all your other desires, for if you cling to them you will not treasure God's plan. When you want only God's plan for your life, then I will reveal the first step.

You will see what you should have been doing all along. You will understand who should be in your life and who should not be with you. You will see the enormous amounts of time that you have wasted on useless pursuits. You will see the decisions you must take and those who can guide you.

As this light comes, you must act. Do not delay because I want to reveal the next steps in God's plans for you. As your mother, I do not want you to get lost on this road of life.

Comment
Our life is successful if we fulfill God's plan. Otherwise, we have wasted our years.
There is always, always time to find God's road.

July 22, 2014
7. Every Needed Gift

Treasures in Mary's Heart

Mary

My heart holds innumerable gifts for you. These are very personal gifts, designed by God himself to bring you to as full and complete happiness as is possible on this earth, and to eternal happiness in heaven.

You must search, not from time to time, but every day. Seeking your gifts in my heart must be your daily task. Why do I say this? All that you can become and all that you must accomplish on this earth is already contained (and paid for) in my heart.

Why purchase by fruitless labor what I provide as a gift? Why try to bring about in an imperfect way, what has already been perfectly fashioned for you and is waiting in my heart?

This is the mystery that I am revealing. People take charge of their own lives. They set their goals. They choose their paths. They give themselves totally. Then, they are disillusioned.

Years go by and they cannot understand why they feel so empty. They have constructed their own image of themselves while the true gift lay ready for them in my heart.

Seek everything in my heart. I will reveal to you what you should do, how to accomplish it, who will help you, and how you can avoid failures. Come, it is not too late. Before you make any decision or take any action, ask me and I will give you the gift for that moment.

131

St. Louis de Montfort teaches that when we learn the secret of Mary, we accomplish everything quite easily. Also, she makes our sufferings so much less.

July 22, 2014
Events in Iraq and Israel (Special Locution)

Treasures in Mary's Heart

Jesus

The path to peace will continue to narrow. Doors will close. Options will be taken off the table until mankind realizes that no path to peace exists. Even at that moment, I will not act. I will delay and delay until the whole world realizes that mankind is powerless and that no human force can restore peace. Then, and only then, will I act. All the world will know that peace came only from heaven.

The Iraq terrorists are cleansing the cities of all who do not hold their faith. They are gaining much ground. Even more important is what is happening in the hearts of the people who are not terrorists and have no sympathy for terrorism. They see the flow of the tide. They see what happens to those who do not agree with the terrorists. They see that America has withdrawn and will not come to anyone's aid, no matter how valiantly they resist.

An inevitability sets in. The people lose all hope and any will to resist. In this way, the terrorists gain far greater victories over the people's hearts.

Also, the impact of the temporary closing of Israel's airport cannot be overestimated. For the first time, the West has withdrawn. A message has gone forth and the Hamas have won a signal victory. They have accomplished by their offensive what had not been done before. People's eyes are open. Israel, with all its military might, cannot fully protect its citizens and its interests. The wound is not deep, but Hamas has drawn blood which all can see.

Israel is rightly upset by this decision of the West. Satan has cleverly used the shooting down of the plane over the Ukraine to get the West to close down air traffic to Israel.

Comment
All the Mideast events are interlocked in Satan's plan, which is now unfolding quickly.

July 23, 2014
8. An All-Encompassing Gift

Treasures in Mary's Heart

Mary

For every person in the world, I have a surprise gift, which is not revealed at first. This gift lies deep within my heart and is given only at the moment when the person is ready to receive. This gift is God's most important secret for each person, the whole reason why God created them. This gift encompasses everything and carries with it the greatest of blessings.

This gift is the person's divine call in which God can totally bless them and bless many others, even thousands.

Many people never receive this gift. They have not searched in my heart nor have they cooperated with the earlier gifts. A few discover the gift but, surprisingly, they reject it (like the rich young man who did not sell all his possessions).

Some embrace their gift totally. They aid many others. Even generation after generation are blessed. You can see how important is this gift. My promise is this. Such a gift exists for every person in the world. If you just seek the beginning gifts, accept them, and do what they require, I will lead you to this special gift that contains your identity, your fulfillment, your life's work and your eternal happiness. I want you to find it. I want you to accept it. I will then help you to bring the gift to fruition.

Comment

If you have never discovered the call of your life, or have never searched, or have rejected the gift, return to Mary's heart and seek God's gifts waiting there for you.

July 24, 2014

9. Treasures of the Kingdom

Treasures in Mary's Heart

Mary

I bring forth these gifts for everyone. All are included. My arms embrace the whole world and my heart has gifts for everyone, a secret that I am constantly revealing.

The heavenly Father created a world in which man had gifts that precluded suffering. Suffering was brought into the world by sin, which caused the first parents to lose God's grace and these special gifts. Thus began the sinful and suffering-filled stage of human history.

The heavenly Father held on to his dream of the original creation. Jesus spoke of the kingdom of heaven and proclaimed that the kingdom was at hand. This is the secret which I proclaim. God has placed all the gifts of the kingdom of heaven, all the gifts that Jesus brought to this earth, in my Immaculate Heart. These gifts will do everything. They will protect, guide, purge sin, and lift to greatness. All of God's treasures are present in the kingdom proclaimed by Jesus and all of these treasures are in my heart, waiting to be given away. Unfortunately, many of these gifts will not be claimed, even by those who love me.

Comment
Jesus spoke about "as it was in the beginning" when man's internal and external worlds were in order, due to special gifts. These gifts can still be found in Mary's heart.

July 25, 2014
The Fire Leaps to Europe (Special Locution)
Treasures in Mary's Heart

Jesus

The world is not yet in total darkness. However, it is on a road that leads away from the heavenly Father. Inevitably, the future holds more and more darkness. Many see the problems, but few see the road that lies ahead. In the Middle East there are many fires. These burn brightly but are still separate. Satan's goal is to have one, unified conflagration, even though the terrorists' groups are diverse. When there is one united fire, then the flames will jump to Europe.

The terrorists have their eyes upon Europe, especially those countries with a sizeable Muslim population. For centuries, Muslims have dreamed of controlling the European countries. Now, these populations see that the terrorists destabilize and bring about fear. This hastens the day when they will no longer be denied many rights. They dream of taking control of these countries. What happens within the heart of a person who sees their dream suddenly come much closer? They are ready to make any sacrifice.

Europe looks stable, but this is fiction. They cannot defend themselves like Israel.

Comment
Sooner than expected, the Middle East fires will leap over to Europe and find a Muslim population that will see a new opportunity.

Mary Speaks Her Mind

July 25, 2014
1. An Even Clearer Word

Mary Speaks Her Mind

Mary

Many who read these locutions are surprised that I would think about and express my thoughts on so many issues. Am I just a heavenly figure? Did I not live on earth? Did I not conceive and give birth? Did I not share in all the sufferings? I am a mother, who takes everything into her heart and brings forth a wisdom. That is what I am doing and people should not be surprised.

I know that so many delight in my words and anxiously await the daily locution. Those who read them all are formed by my thinking and I bless them.

Now, I will embark on an even clearer road. Up to now, I have revealed my heart. Now, I will speak my mind. No one will have to read between the lines or conjecture what I mean. The words will be both pointed and true. They will cut through the darkness and give light. They will chastise but always offer the grace of conversion. When I finish, no doubts will remain about where I stand and what I think. Let no one interpret away the clarity of my words.

I will speak to a Church which has failed me, to world leaders who have deceived their people, to the rich whose gold has made them an abomination, to the powerful who have manipulated the structures of power, to the average Catholic who has been swept along by the world, to the little ones who need my encouragement and to you, the reader, who are so anxious to find your way. To the whole world, I will speak my mind.

Comment
Mary's words have always been to the point.
Now, the words will become more pointed.

July 26, 2014
2. A Place with Mary in the Desert

Mary Speaks Her Mind

Mary

I speak first to my Church, born when the heart of Jesus was pierced by a sword and filled with the Spirit on the day of Pentecost. I was there at your beginnings and I will be present at the grand culmination when the angels gather all the elect.

What a history you have had, filled with sinners and saints, moments of divine greatness and moments of the most shameful behavior. Yet, you are mine, the child of my womb, and I will always clasp you to my breasts and give you life.

Now, I must speak my mind in words only a mother could say. "You must repent and turn back to reclaim your former glory, the glory of serving the world by being its light. Once you were small, persecuted, trodden underfoot by the power of the world, but I loved you for your fervor and your fidelity."

I say to you what Jesus said to the Church of Ephesus. "I hold this against you. You have lost the love that you had at first" (Rev. 2:4). That is where we must begin. Like Israel, I must lead you back into the desert where you can again recover your first love.

"What about my worldly power?" you ask. I say, "What good is your worldly power? Soon, you will see all the power of the world collapse. Will you be caught up in that destruction or will you have escaped with me into the desert of your first love?"

God prepared a place for me in the desert (Rev. 12:6). That is where I will take you. Do not delay in the city where you think you are so needed. If you come into the desert with me, I will prepare you. In the moment of the world's great darkness, you will be its light. This is my message of hope.

Comment
Where else could Our Lady begin? She calls us back to our first fervor.

July 27, 2014
3. Mother of the Church

Mary Speaks Her Mind

Mary

The Church must learn the wisdom of my heart. So often, the Church seeks wisdom from its learned men and women. It seeks wisdom from all the human sciences. It studies the wisdom that the world uses in its business enterprises. Why does the Church reject the wisdom of my heart? It chooses broken cisterns that cannot bring forth living water.

The Church has a great strength. It has openly proclaimed me as the Mother of the Church. Well, come back to your mother. The mother gathers the family and embraces all the children. The mother keeps the household together, always inviting her children to return.

Do not reject me. Do not set me aside. God's plan began with me (I was with him in the beginning of his days) and God's plan will end with me, the Woman Clothed with the Sun.

O Church, I will heal your divisions. I will bring back your children. I will purge you of your sins. I will make of you the new Jerusalem, the light on the mountain.

The heavenly Father has declared these times as the Age of Mary, but you have not yet understood or even believed the words of your own prophets and saints.

Comment
The Church certainly needs help and Our Lady
wants to be the Church's mother.

July 28, 2014
4. The Age of Mary

Mary Speaks Her Mind

Mary

Return to your first love. When you were a child and held no possessions, when you were small and had only your faith, when you were persecuted, and loved one another, I watched over you. I saw you spread to all the nations. I watched you cling to my Son and proclaim him even when this brought sufferings and death.

I saw your acts of charity. You were revered even among those who did not understand your beliefs. You were truly a light to the nations, waiting to be put upon the lampstand.

Now, I have put you on that lampstand. You are known throughout the world, the largest of all the churches, but your light has dimmed. It is now mixed with darkness. Many know you but they scorn you and reject you. Even your own sons and daughters, born into your bosom, walk away from you. You watch them leave with great sorrow. You are quite aware of your state. You know the reality, like a parent disappointed in the decisions of their children. I know your failures and how distraught you are.

I have a question for you. Are you ready? Are you willing to take my hand, to walk my road? Are you ready to trust your mother and to do what I tell you? Are you ready to inscribe me on your heart and to decide firmly, "I will walk the road of Mary"? I challenge you at this grave moment in human history, when the world will need the Church more than ever. Do you truly believe that this is the Age of Mary? If you do, I can make you the light of the nations. If not, your own resources will prove too little and too late.

Comment
The Age of Mary holds unbelievable gifts of the Father,
but the Church has never committed herself fully to that gift.

July 29, 2014
5. The New Flame

Mary Speaks Her Mind

Mary

I go now to the depth of my heart to find the most consoling words for my Church. Among your members, I find the little ones, those whose hearts are firmly set upon me. I find your missionaries who have left their native lands to preach the gospel in difficult circumstances. I find mothers and fathers who fulfill their sacred duties, and I find ministers of the word who live out their commitment. At every level and in every situation I find these people of good will.

This is my promise. I am ready to take all of them into the most sacred fire that burns in my Immaculate Heart. They will be the first ones to whom I reveal the gift. I am not asking them to do more. I am asking them to receive more, to take this new flame into their hearts. I know their hearts and if they take the new flame it will burn brightly. That is why I invite them first.

However, they must accept the invitation or they will be left behind, not ready for the difficulties that lie ahead.

Comment
Whatever we have received from God, we must be open to greater gifts,
this new flame in Mary's heart.

July 30, 2014
6. The Less-Traveled Road

Mary Speaks Her Mind

Mary

I will speak gently to world leaders, because if I fully exposed all of your sins, you would cover your ears and shut your eyes. Instead, I will speak about what you are able to do. All I ask is good will.

First, look at your heart. Why have you sought this high position? What led you to public office? Only you can examine your own heart and be honest. Expose your own selfishness, your own pride and ego. I am not asking you to step down. I am only asking you to change.

You have made many decisions in darkness which you would never want to come to the light of publicity. You have two lives – your public life and your private life. One for the people to see, and one which only you can see. Right now you are entangled. I do not say hopelessly entangled because I will help you.

I must ask you: "Are you willing to walk a different path, one that is less-traveled?" If so, I will do two favors for you. I will free you from your entanglements and I will lift you up to a much higher position. If not, I can only leave you mired in your world that will inevitably destroy you. Such is the nature of worldly power.

Comment

Power corrupts unless God continually purifies the world leader.

July 31, 2014

7. A New World Order

Mary Speaks Her Mind

Mary

To lead the world is a matter of the heart and you leaders of the world have hearts that are too small. So, I offer you the gift of my heart. I have a plan for every person. I know what they need so their life can fulfill all that God intends.

I dream of a new world order, where weapons are put aside, and where nations cooperate. I dream of a new economic system where all share in the goods of society.

I must raise up new world leaders whose hearts are quite different, leaders who dream of blessing others. I need a veritable army, fashioned in a different mold, claiming a different vision, and refusing to set aside their firm beliefs that every person in the world must have the necessities of life.

Where are these people? I will go and look for them. When I find those who are committed to my dream, I will open doors for them. They shall rise quickly in every field of human endeavor. Only those formed in my heart can truly bring about a new world order.

Comment

Changing the world results only from leaders
whose hearts are attuned to the heavenly Father.

August 1, 2014

8. Lazarus, the Beggar at Our Door

Mary Speaks Her Mind

Mary

Let us stop for a moment and remember that getting to heaven is the purpose of earth. At the moment of death, the human person leaves this temporary human existence and enters into an eternal state. Jesus never exalted earth or human life, but constantly reminded all that earthly life ends.

139

"What does it profit a man to gain the whole world and lose his soul?"

"If anyone should save his life in this world, he will lose it in the next."

"Thou, fool, what good is it to have stored up all these treasures, when tonight you will die?"

Yet, Jesus was sensitive to earthly needs. He fed the hungry and healed the sick. He promised that if a person seeks first the kingdom of God, the heavenly Father would care for the necessities.

Do you not see Satan's plan? He wants only sufferings so that people cannot find their way to heaven. Taken up in the trials of earth they lose faith in their heavenly home. So, I speak to every Catholic, to every believer, to every person of good will. You all have a Lazarus, a beggar, at your door, a needy person. Care for them and you will both arrive safely in heaven.

To the rich and the powerful, to those who control great amounts of earthly resources, I have placed all these in your hands so you can help many on their road to heaven.

Many voices of the poor cry out to me and I search for those who can answer their needs. I will come soon and ask for your help. Blessed are you if you hear my voice, open your heart, change your ways and give of yourself by helping the needy.

Comment
Man is made for heaven but his search takes place amid earthly needs.
Helping others is the surest road to eternal life.

August 2, 2014
9. Promising a New Light

Mary Speaks Her Mind

Mary

I will speak from my heart, bringing forth the deepest feelings. I weep abundantly. I see my children walk away from all that Jesus taught. I see them cast aside their baptismal gift and to think nothing of their loss of faith. I see them enter deeply into the immoral ways of modern culture and be swept up in its mighty current.

Those who have been called to a deep Catholic faith and to the highest of Catholic values are never even taught the basic truths. Their rich heritage has been stolen from them. They were never shown the path to goodness. The darkness of the culture has obscured everything.

I must provide another light because the lights of the powerful Catholic culture have become too weak to light the way, and the road has become far too dark.

This is my message. I will provide extra lights which you must freely choose. Seek these lights. Look for my new lights. Do not be content with your current light. Seek for yourselves and your children. Write this on your heart, "Mary has told me that I need more light. She has promised to provide this light. I must search for this new light, like the Wise Men searched for Jesus, the light of the world."

You will find. I promise that you will find the new light I have prepared for you.

Comment

Our Lady sorrows over the great darkness but promises to provide. We must search.

August 3, 2014
10. Rain Clouds of Hope

Mary Speaks Her Mind

Mary

I see the world in such anguish. Never before have I so desired to pour out my gifts. I must always repeat the message. The heavenly Father has placed all of his treasures for the world in my Immaculate Heart because he foresaw this moment in human history when the fires of hell would break forth from beneath the earth.

He placed them there because my heart is so easily broken open and his gifts can fall like raindrops upon the fires. When fires are burning out of control, are not rain clouds a joyous sight? Do they not hold out hope that soon the fires will be overcome?

The Church must see my heart in this way, filled with heavenly rain, waiting to quench these demonic forces that are evident everywhere and to everyone. Is there not a demonic source to all the wars, to all the diseases, to all the acts of terrorism, to all the hopelessness?

The Holy Father must consecrate Russia. The rain will fall there first. From Russia, peace will go out to the whole world.

Comment

For almost 100 years, Our Lady has said that for world peace Russia must be consecrated. Events are showing that Mary was right all along.

August 4, 2014
11. Special Surprising Lights

Mary Speaks Her Mind

Mary

Usually, I pour out my gifts in great order, the small ones first and later the greater ones. Now, however, a greater need exists to which I must respond. I must take people who are not fully prepared and give them gifts far greater than usual. Like children in an emergency, who are pressed into action and asked to do works usually reserved to adults.

What a special time this will be! Many will wonder. People of good will who have just begun to live devoutly will be given great powers, usually reserved for the perfect. Those who are spiritual children will lead many to great faith. Others, who have just begun themselves to love my Immaculate Heart, will be foundation stones of strong communities.

New movements, filled with the greatest lights will arise. Fresh spiritual leadership will emerge. These are the fruits of the new lights that will suddenly begin to push back the world's darkness. As always, these secrets lie in my Immaculate Heart.

Comment

In these days of extraordinary darkness, Our Lady must take surprising actions.

August 5, 2104

12. Being Set Aside by the Church

Mary Speaks Her Mind

<h1 align="center">Mary</h1>

Who can know the sorrows of my heart unless I speak openly and reveal what is hidden? I see the many difficulties of the Church. A Church that was strong and flourishing has now been set aside, and often is the object of ridicule. The young are no longer formed by its teachings and many of the older generation have abandoned its truths. The Church cries out in the marketplace but its voice is not heard. Its teachings have no impact upon the modern mind. How has all of this happened?

I must speak honestly. I have been set aside. The Church flourished when I was exalted. Many gave themselves to the priesthood and religious life when the Church rejoiced to be my child. Then, new waves of thought washed upon the shore. The new agenda erased the deeply ingrained devotions. My appearances, my visitations and my words no longer occupied the Catholic mind. How different would these decades have been if I had not been moved to the sidelines!

I must speak honestly. It is late. The weapons of war explode. Some roads of peace narrow and even end. The world's resources turn to destruction not to life. At this point, no one can perceive the power of the coming darkness, nor how close it is at hand.

I will try again. I will send out greater invitations. I will use more messengers, in even higher places. They must be faithful to the message, "There is only one path to peace, the road that leads into the center of my Immaculate Heart." There will be new

142

movements, new beginnings, new fires. I have not abandoned my Church and I refuse to sit on the sidelines while Satan claims his victories.

Those who heed me, I will use. Those who believe they have a better plan will waste their time.

Comment

This is a very strong locution that sums up Our Lady's feelings.

Casting Light upon Cultures of Darkness

August 6, 2014

1. Casting Light upon Cultures of Darkness

Casting Light upon Cultures of Darkness

Mary

Through these locutions I want the whole world to see the sufferings of my Immaculate Heart. These sufferings result from the complete failure of the world to gain the true goal of human existence, which is eternal life in heaven.

To see poor people without food, to see sick people without medicine, and to see lonely people without spouse or friends is a deep sorrow. But my greatest sorrow is to see an immortal soul be lost forever in the pains of hell. The atoning death of Jesus on the cross was of no avail. They spurned this gift. They chose the darkness. They gave their hearts to their own selfishness.

These are the decisions made every day in a world that rejects the path of faith. Because the darkness of the culture brings this about, I must cast new light. So, I begin anew. Read my words.

They will cast out this terrible darkness that has come upon the modern person, so given to only what reason can reveal. I will cast a great light of bold faith. Take my hand and we will walk. You will see as I see and believe as I believe. Then your hearts will easily choose the light.

Comment

Our Lady sees every soul after death. She sees where they will exist for all eternity.

The modern cultural darkness is the greatest cause of eternal damnation.

She will address that problem in this series of locutions.

143

August 7, 2014
2. The Good Samaritan

Casting Light upon Cultures of Darkness

Mary

I search for you, wounded soul, who are not yet dead, but bleeding profusely. If I do not find you soon, your enemies will claim you forever and I will have lost another child. Yes, yet another. This need not happen, but you must cry out and place my name on your lips, with words spoken from the heart. That will open the great door. Just a little opening is enough.

Such is my search. Where do I go? To the bars, to the houses of prostitution, to the places of greatest darkness, to homes torn asunder by evil. This is where I search. Do not say that I am far away. Do not think that you must find a church. I need hear only your cry for help. I will be your Good Samaritan bending over your bleeding soul, pouring out the medicine of grace.

Then I will take you to the Inn and place you with those who will care for you until you are spiritually strong.

Comment
Conversion might end up in church, but it seldom begins there.
Mary seeks her children everywhere.

August 7, 2014
3. Putin as Satan's Instrument (Special Locution)

Casting Light upon Cultures of Darkness

Mary

I must speak quickly and urgently so the world understands. Even more, my Church must understand because only the Church has the keys of the kingdom to release a flood of peace and to bathe the world in light.

I must speak of Putin who has placed himself on the world stage, using all of his resources to reposition Russia as a world power. The West does not understand his actions because reason does not guide him. Another force, a satanic power, possesses him, just as it possessed Hitler and Stalin.

Often he will make decisions that seem to harm his own people or work against his own interests. This does not matter to Satan, who ultimately desires that everyone be destroyed, including Putin. Satan has one goal and he will use many instruments. His goal is the annihilation of nations. See the world events as a road to this ultimate moment of annihilation. Then you will understand these events as steps along the road.

With all the wars taking place, Our Lady reveals their ultimate purpose.

August 8, 2014
4. Avoiding the Annihilation of the Nations
Casting Light upon Cultures of Darkness

Mary

I must take up the same theme, but this time I must speak to the Church, to the Holy Father, and to the bishops of the world.

I do not expect the world to discern the Evil One because the world has not been given that light, but I do expect the Church, the Holy Father, and the bishops, to see clearly the satanic powers which lay behind the terrible destruction taking place before your eyes.

I have a question for all of you who guide my Church. Did not Jesus establish his Church as the Rock that will prevail over the gates of hell? In these wars, is the Church to step aside, to stand on the sidelines, and to think that the world powers can establish peace? The Church has been formed for this moment. Only the Church can avoid the annihilation of the nations. Only the Church can release the fires of peace that are stored in my Immaculate Heart.

You know what to do, yet you refuse to take the steps. What will I do with you? Do I allow the nations to be annihilated? Why do you set aside the pleas I made at Fatima?

Comment
Our Lady at Fatima spoke clearly of the possible annihilation of the nations.

August 6, 2014
5. On the Brink (Special Locution)
Casting Light upon Cultures of Darkness

Jesus

In the coming months, Putin will push the world to the brink. Even Putin will be on the brink, in danger of collapsing. In these moments, the world will not know what is next. His purpose is to test the West. After these months of "going to the brink," there will be the next stage of Satan's timetable. These months are not the culmination, nor will there be a world war. The West seriously miscalculated Putin. All of this will show that Russia is the problem and, for now, Putin is Satan's instrument.

Comment
Many do not understand Putin's moves
because they do not come from human reasoning.

August 9, 2014
6. The Hypocrisy and Charade of America's Political Leadership

Casting Light upon Cultures of Darkness

Mary

How gaping are the wounds and how small are the consolations. Amid these events, who is able to have hope? Violence spreads everywhere. Multiple wars. Steps toward peace that are of no avail. I must speak to this problem.

Efforts toward peace will multiply. Meetings will be convened. Diplomats will make every effort. However, no one sees or grasps all that I have tried to explain. The forces of violence and destruction are a mighty river flowing from the inner circles of hell. Man's sins, especially the killing of the unborn, prepare the way. They open the door. They invite hell's powers to enter human history.

Look at the hypocrisy. America decries violence and speaks out against the killing of innocent civilians. Tell me, who is more innocent than an unborn child? Yet, America refuses to protect them. What a charade. To send your diplomats all over the world to protect the innocent, while at home you sacrifice thousands each day. America, I established you so you would receive the poor and helpless. Now you allow them to be killed.

My words are solemn, and as these events continue to sweep the whole world, I hope that they get an attentive ear, especially from political leadership. You must protect the life of every unborn American. The moment that you make that decision, the tide will turn.

Comment
Most people do not realize the history of the Civil War. Abraham Lincoln wanted only to save the Union. He had no interest in freeing the slaves. As the Union armies were constantly beaten, he saw the important spiritual battle and, in prayer, decided to issue the Emancipation Proclamation.
Then, the tide shifted and America was saved.

August 10, 2014
7. A Demonic West

Casting Light upon Cultures of Darkness

Mary

I see hearts that are shut tight and minds that refuse to give up their ideas. People will not change. Terrorists cling to their violence. The West clings to its lifestyles. There is no room for God and no willingness to submit the heart to the fullness of love that would lead in a different direction.

The West sees the violence of the terrorists, but does not see its own hardness of heart. Who is saying, "Let us repent of our sins"? Who calls out, "Let us turn back to the Lord. He will save us"?

I say this to the West. You have buildings with no foundations, and paths with no light. You have built your city without God's law. When you banished Jesus, you invited the demonic. Now the demon springs his traps. When he pours forth his violence, you have no light. You lack all understanding. I must come to rescue you with greater light and stronger fire. Yet, even with these signs, will you give up your ideas and open your hearts? The future will tell the story.

Comment
The news focuses on the terrorists.
Our Lady focuses on the West banishing Jesus.

August 11, 2014
8. Almost 100 Years Ago

Casting Light upon Cultures of Darkness

Mary

With the gaping wounds in my heart come individual sorrows. I see particular people whom I have called to high places in the Church, but they are ashamed of me and do not proclaim me to the world as they should. My greatest sorrow comes from those who do not believe my promises and do not understand the truth I am trying to proclaim. So, I will say it again.

From the very beginning, the heavenly Father foresaw a constant war between the Evil One and the Woman. He promised that the Woman would defeat the Evil One and crush his head. The heavenly Father foresaw this moment of human history and prepared a victory (even against these powerful forces) in my Immaculate Heart. As these events began nearly 100 years ago, I announced my victory, openly and publicly for all the Church to hear. My messages were increased and multiplied. The more they multiplied, the more they were set aside.

But I will not be set aside. The battle is far too serious and the victory is guaranteed if my Immaculate Heart is honored. So, I will begin to pull down those who do not believe. I will remove those who are obstacles to the consecration of Russia. What am I to do, allow the annihilation of the Nations?

Comment
The 19th century saw Marian apparitions at Rue de Bac, Lourdes, and many other places. They led up to the great apparitions of Fatima in 1917. This has been followed by Medjugorje and others. The message about the Immaculate Heart has been constant.

August 12, 2014
9. A New Joan of Arc

Casting Light upon Cultures of Darkness

Mary

I pour out my sorrows. I want all the world to understand. I see where each event leads. I see the path that Satan has chosen. I know his mind. I know his plans. I know those who help him. I watch as he cleverly moves each person, every step of the way.

I see the foolishness and the mistakes of those who seek peace. Only when they look back do they see the wrong decisions they have made, allowing the violence to spread.

Sadly, it will all continue, at an ever-increasing pace, one clever move after another by the terrorists, and one foolish move after another by those who are trying to resist. So many mistakes in the past and so many political decisions in the present!

Should I be like Joan of Arc, guiding your armies to victory? What kind of intervention is needed? I am ready to lead. Do not look to the heavens, but at your own hearts. Am I totally unprepared for this moment of crisis? Indeed, I am the only creature whom the heavenly Father has prepared. I am his plan of action.

I want my light to pour forth out of the Church and into the marketplace. I want all to know that the Catholic Church is the repository of God's special light at this moment of world crisis.

My greatest sorrow is that the Church herself does not understand the light that I want to pour forth. At this moment, the Church needs someone like Joan of Arc, led by a divine voice, to take the bold steps needed for the victory of peace.

Comment
St. Joan of Arc (1412-1431) began to experience visions at 13. These heavenly voices told her that she would save France from the English. She convinced everyone and was allowed to lead the French army in recapturing Orleans and Troyes (June 1429). In July, Charles accepted his role as King of France. She is called the Maid of Orleans and is the patron saint of France.

August 13, 2014
10. An Ocean To Put Out the Fire

Casting Light upon Cultures of Darkness

Mary

There are many paths, leading in different directions which mankind chooses. Often, he feels that he has chosen the best path, when really he has chosen his own destruction. Such is life upon earth, a veritable landmine of darkness, filled with false lights that attract powerfully and lead to the first steps that doom many.

Never before has this been so true. The world is filled with the greatest weapons, with powers never before available. The darkness settles and abides, one darkness leading to another.

Mankind is in an endless tunnel with no doors, caught and enmeshed in webs he himself has constructed, like a fisherman caught in his own net. Really, words cannot even describe the present state of the world.

In some places, life goes on as usual, seemingly immune to the darkness. Other places find themselves at the very center of the boiling pot. The world is like a house which is partially on fire. Does it give comfort that one part of the house is not yet ablaze? Or is the fire an alarm signal for all in the house?

My words are that signal, trying to awaken the whole world before the house burns down. "Awaken! I say to my Church. Awaken to me so you can pour out a fresh light upon this darkness. Awaken so the fires of hell can be extinguished before they consume more and more of human life."

In you, my Church, I have placed powers which reside deeply in your soul, a mighty ocean which alone can put out these fires. I have placed them nowhere else. They do not abide in any other church. They do not rest in any world organization or in the hands of any world leader.

I want to exalt my Church. At the moment of the greatest fires, I want these waters to be freely released, so the whole world can see the divine prerogative of the Catholic Church. I wait for you to act. Someday, that ocean will be released, but how much of the house will be burned down before it happens?

Comment
*Certainly, the world is a house on fire. All can see that. However, we need
Mary's words to know about her mighty ocean hidden in the Church.*

❖

When Russia Is Consecrated

August 14, 2014
1. When Russia Is Consecrated

When Russia Is Consecrated

Mary

When I speak, I want the whole world to hear my words. So, I must raise up a special son who hears my words and proclaims my words to all mankind. This will be a special time when my words pour out like a mighty ocean, flowing directly from my Immaculate Heart.

Only these words will save the world. They will cast out the darkness, point out the failures of those who lead the world, encourage the good in all their efforts and, most important, reveal the paths to peace.

What a time that will be! By then, the war between myself and Satan will have broken out for all to see. I will no longer be on the sidelines. He, in his daring, will set aside his disguises and allow himself to be seen by all (what foolish pride).

The great battle will be played out in the sight of all, but with this difference. My powers will no longer be restricted. Russia will have been consecrated to my Immaculate Heart, just in time for the victory that I have promised.

All my words and all my promises will become clear. All the gifts that I have promised will flow forth, able to be received if the person's heart so desires. Not all will take advantage of my gifts but every person will be able to receive. I will speak more about this consecration.

Comment
Our Lady has promised that Russia would be consecrated but that it would be late.

August 16, 2014
2. Waiting for the Consecration

When Russia Is Consecrated

Mary

Even though I speak as clearly as possible, it is only when all the events culminate, that the world will see what I have been trying to describe. Present in the world today is the great evil planted in the soul of Russia in 1917 with the Communist Revolution. This evil has gone out to the whole world, resulting in the horrible deaths of millions. That evil continues, in a new but unabated form. Russia fuels the revolutions and the unrests. It arms many of the terrorists and does everything possible to destabilize the world.

In October 1917, at the little cove in Fatima, I planted the great seed of peace which was to come forth as the antidote to the Russian poison. There was to be a great victory and an exultation of the Catholic Church which would provide such a great power. None of this has happened because my request for the Consecration of Russia has not been fulfilled.

Now, I must speak of the future. The Russian evil will continue to spread through all of its friends. As these events culminate, Catholics will see before their eyes what I have been describing. They will also remember that my words always carried a message of hope. There was always time, always a way, because of the mystery of my Immaculate Heart. So, the clamor will grow. Prayers for the Consecration will increase. More important, I will hear these cries. I will use the evil events themselves to open the door. Finally, the Consecration will take place according to my request.

In all things, a timetable exists. These are not fixed hours or days, but rather the goal that will be reached as the forces of good or evil are released. The timetable depends on the free will of every single person. When many hearts deeply desire and pray for the Consecration, the time of its fulfillment grows closer and comes sooner. To pray and sacrifice for that moment is everyone's task.

Comment
Both the great Fatima sign and the Russian revolution happened in 1917.
On July 13, 1917, Mary had revealed the need for the consecration of Russia, and
on June 13, 1929, Our Lord and Our Lady told Lucy that the time had come
for the Holy Father to fulfill her request. This has not happened. So, evil spreads.
Our Lady prophesied that the Consecration would take place, but that it would be late.
She has promised victory but needs our prayers and sacrifices.

August 17, 2014
3. A New Culture of Peace

When Russia Is Consecrated

Mary

After the Consecration of Russia, the beginning gift will be a conversion of hearts of those who control the nations. New ideas of peace initiatives will surface. World leaders will see that peace is in their self-interest. They should have seen this earlier but were blinded by Satan. Nations will move to true peace agreements, not the false pieces of paper they now call treaties.

The hearts of the people will move in the same directions. The hunger for war and the use of weapons to gain natural interests will be seen as outmoded ideas, the products of the past, foolish concepts that have no life in this new thinking.

The wisdom of true peace that was set aside in the selfish pursuits will regain its rightful place. Peace will be a constant, powerful light, set upon the lampstand. Even those whose hearts are not touched will be forced to walk on this new path by the power of the new culture of peace.

Comment

The world has a spirit of war and self-interest. The consecration of Russia will change individual hearts and create a new culture of peace.

August 17, 2014

4. The Stirring in Russian Hearts

When Russia Is Consecrated

Mary

When Russia is consecrated to my Immaculate Heart, there will be a stirring in the hearts of all, but especially in the souls of the Russian people. They will receive an inner light and will understand what forces of evil were planted in their nation by Satan's instruments.

As their hearts are stirred, more and more light will fill them. They will reject both what has been forced upon them and what, to some degree, they themselves have chosen. All of these evils have formed their nation and their leaders into instruments of darkness, death and destruction. In this new stirring, they will fully reject what they have become and what they had been forced to accept.

This stirring will grow greater as it manifests itself in outward demonstrations of a growing desire to return to its religious roots and, especially, to return to their devotion of my Immaculate Heart.

No one will be able to stop this movement, because their nation will have been specifically consecrated by the Holy Father and by all the Catholic bishops of the world. I have put my seal of promise upon this act of Consecration, and the graces flowing from it will not be turned back. Even though the most frightful opposition will arise, the stirring in the hearts of the Russian people for this new light will not be turned back.

Comment

Our Lady begins to sketch out the new Russia, formed by the special graces still hidden and locked in her Immaculate Heart.

152

August 18, 2014
5. The Overcoming of Separation

When Russia Is Consecrated

Mary

I will place such great gifts in the hearts of the Russian people that they will not be satisfied with superficial changes. Instead, they will wipe away the divisions of the centuries.

They will realize that I have released an ocean of graces which have changed their darkness into light. They will realize that they have been freed from the past century of diabolical control. They will also know that this great gift has come through the consecration of Russia made by the Holy Father in communion with all the bishops in the world.

They will begin to question why they are separated from the Holy Father. Would all of this darkness have fallen if there had been no division? They will cry out for unity with Rome. This ocean will be so deep and so powerful that it will sweep away all opposition. The Russian people will overturn the centuries of division that have been forced upon them.

That is why the Holy Father and all the bishops must make this Consecration in a public way and must specifically mention Russia. The Russian people must know the source of the gift. This is also why I wait and wait, even though the Holy Father delays. I must have the Holy Father act in the name of the Catholic Church so the Russian people know that the Catholic Church has released this gift. In this way, they will desire and bring about union with the Catholic Church.

I unfold these revelations so all the world, especially the Church, can see what I intend and why I ask what I do.

Comment

For the first 1000 years, there was only one, united Catholic Church.
In 1054, the Archbishop of Constantinople withdrew from this union with the pope.
Thus began the division into Roman Catholic and Orthodox Catholic Churches,
the great schism that lasts even today.

August 19, 2014
6. Better To Wait

When Russia Is Consecrated

Mary

Before the consecration of Russia takes place, many events will happen that will change the earth. Why do I wait? Why not act immediately? If these powers for the good of mankind lie in my heart, why not pour them forth now?

When seen from earth's perspective, the ways of heaven are often difficult to understand. Why did the human race lie in darkness for so many centuries before the Father sent his only begotten Son? Jesus came in "the fullness of time," the earliest moment that the human race could receive. Heaven waited because earth was unable to receive.

Before Jesus began his ministry, Israel needed John the Baptist to prepare the way. Otherwise, Israel would not have been ready for the gift of Jesus. Only heaven fully understands what must be done. Earth gains only glimpses of the full reality. By my words, I pull back this veil. Yet, even when I reveal heaven's secrets, who believes? Who accepts the messages? Who acts? Who responds?

I speak clearly. Heaven has a plan. That plan has been revealed. Promises have been made that will be fully kept once the conditions are fulfilled. Heaven does not change its plan just because earth does not accept it. Why do I wait? Certainly, it would be much better if the Consecration of Russia had already been made and the gift released. However, to release the gifts before the Holy Father and the bishops consecrate Russia would ruin the fruitfulness of the promises. It is better to wait.

Comment

Heaven wants to bless earth, but why pour out this water
if the Church and the world will not be ready to receive?

August 20, 2014
7. Our Lady's Hidden Actions

When Russia Is Consecrated

Mary

I speak, I act. I lead those who would do my will. I enter into every conversation. I touch every heart in the world. I act everywhere and every moment. Yet, man remains free and this freedom is greatly limited by the darkness of his own selfishness and of his culture.

Violent forces have now been released, flowing from one heart to another. Tremendous pressures exist. Man is free but he is not free. He is pulled and forced to go along. He is intimidated. He is not shown all of his options. He is hurried and harassed. Event follows event, cleverly leading him to countless decisions that allow no turning back.

I see a mankind subjected to powers that want his destruction, that cleverly force him to choose their path. If he hesitates at all, new pressures are brought upon him. I watch this happen in one place after another. I see this same pattern in every area of man's life. The stranglehold is pulled tighter and tighter.

It is no longer a matter of mankind needing to respond to God's grace because mankind has been robbed of his freedom. Can a family live at peace when war is all around them? Can a person walk in light when all is midnight? Mankind has passed the point of no return. Mankind cannot save itself. Too many evil forces have been released. They are now imbedded in human life. Some are seen. Others, especially the most powerful, are still hidden. They have not yet come on the scene. They lie in wait, looking for the appropriate moment. This moment is different from any other moment in human history, filled with unimaginable and uncontrollable evils.

I wait, yet I refuse to wait. Oh, I must wait until the Holy Father acts, but until then, I will act. First, I must breathe upon the whole Catholic Church (whose teachings exalt me) and call forth fresh devotions to my Immaculate Heart. I must stir the bishops. They have a role in the Consecration of Russia. They must raise their voices and speak out. Finally, I will continue to prepare those who will actually make the Consecration.

In the middle of all the evils, in the face of all the delays, no one should lose heart. I am actually bringing about what I have asked to be done.

Comment

This locution reveals the whole picture, a mankind plunging helplessly into darkness, the Consecration of Russia not yet made, but Our Lady, always filled with hope, promising that she is actively preparing for that day.

Understanding Human History

August 21, 2014

1. Man's Helplessness

Understanding Human History

Mary

Human history is a powerful stream which is difficult to understand, and even more difficult to control. Yet, some have risen up, hoping to control history and turn

155

the stream totally in their direction. In this they have failed, but they did leave their mark.

God wants human persons to help, to cooperate, and to participate in the shaping of human history. Even with this heavenly decision, it would be wrong to see history as the product of human labor. Other forces come into play which very much shape all human events. As the Church grasps this total picture, it will see its own role. As the world understands, it will not be entrapped by its foolish decisions.

So, let me try to explain the factors that make up human history and the forces which shape it, for good or evil. This enlightenment is absolutely needed so that the Church and the world can walk in light. Let us begin.

By himself, man cannot accomplish the good. He can do some good but, without God's help, that good will be corrupted, lose its power and even turn to evil. Such is the nature of the human heart and of human society. Man, without God, is helpless to bring about the purpose of human history.

Comment
Our Lady wants a large number of people to understand the need for God
in man's shaping of human history.

August 22, 2014
2. Who Shapes Human History?
Understanding Human History

Mary

At the opening of the story of mankind all was sinless. All was a "yes" to the decision of the heavenly Father to bring forth persons made in his image and likeness, a startling decision that flesh and blood would share in God's powers of knowing and willing. It was the grand experiment, and even the angels were amazed at this next step in God's unfolding plan.

They rejoiced to have man as their friend, knowing that man's destiny was to join them forever in heaven. The fallen angels did not see this creation of man in the same way. Their places were now vacant and God had chosen to fill these places with creatures much more lowly in stature than the mighty, but fallen, angels.

Thus, the contest began, a struggle that will continue to the end of time when, finally, Jesus will put all creation under his power and will wipe out death and sin forever. These are the shapers of human history. Although many shape the course of human history, man, of course, is at the center, the main actor, the one who ultimately must make the decision. However, these other forces are powerful. They, too, shape human history. I will unfold this story to enlighten all, because many are quite unaware of the powers they face every day and of the helps that the heavenly Father wants to provide.

Comment
Our Lady lays out the scene for her explanation of history.
This is very important for a mankind that has largely rejected these beliefs.

August 23, 2014
3. Reading Human History Correctly

Understanding Human History

Mary

I am speaking now of the course of human history, the path that it takes and the goals that it chooses to accomplish. This is the vision I want to implant in your hearts.

Many speak of human history as if they could judge its failures and its successes. That is not true. Human history has one Judge, Jesus Christ. He, alone, will draw all to a close, whenever He so chooses. It is only when Jesus Christ returns, when all gather before him, when all is revealed, when the human race is separated forever, some on his right and others on his left, with some entering into eternal glory and others trooping off to hell, that everyone, in that instant, will see the purpose of human history.

These are the mysteries I am trying to reveal now. I must do this through locutions because mankind has turned a deaf ear to the preaching of these mysteries.

These truths used to fill the culture. They were the very pillars upon which society built its daily life. Now these pillars are destroyed.

Comment
Mankind tries to judge history by human standards.
The only true Judge of what is happening is Jesus.

August 25, 2014
4. All Future Generations

Understanding Human History

Mary

Human history has many years to go. We are not at all near its end. However, the current generation will decide an important question. Will the future family of man be a tree filled with life or will it become a branch that lives in a withered form?

In human history, the future generation does not decide what it receives. The previous generations make those decisions and then they bequeath earth to others. What will be left? What will be handed on? These are the modern questions. What world will we leave to future generations?

The answers to these questions are not many years away. Earth will continue. Human life will continue. There are years and years to go before history ends. But answering the question of the future of the human race is not far away. I will say this with all of my strength, "The future generation, how mankind will exist for centuries to come, will be decided in this generation." That is how serious are the conflicts now arising in every part of the globe. The level of human life that is bequeathed for generations to come will be decided by this generation. Can I say it any more starkly?

This generation is the hinge upon which all future generations will swing – to life or to death, to light or to darkness.

Although all of these questions are far beyond the powers of mankind, mankind still believes in its own powers, trusts its own judgments and refuses to listen to heaven. That is why I speak and why these little locutions are of such grave importance.

Comment
This locution is startling but world events make it credible. This generation, the coming years (we do not know how many) will determine life on earth for all future generations.

August 26, 2014
5. Casting New Fire upon the Church

Understanding Human History

Mary

Human history continues on its path until some Movement arises, which points out a new direction. How many times such movements have saved the world and rescued human history before it succumbed to the evil of its own decisions. At the center of these movements were strong personalities surrounded by devout disciples.

They knew how to spread their ideas so that many others joined in their fervor. The greater their numbers and the greater their devotion to their cause, the more powerful would be their impact.

Such was the vision of Jesus, as he gathered his disciples and taught them how to gather others. Released into human history was the great movement called Christianity which turned the world away from destruction and formed a new way of thinking and acting.

What has happened to this Movement? It now embraces the whole world. Christians live everywhere in almost every culture. In some places and among some groups, the original fervor remains. However, in so many places and in the hearts of those who call themselves Christian, the fervor of Jesus has cooled down. Even the understanding of his goals have been lost. The Movement has been swallowed up. The light no longer goes forth. The fire has been extinguished. Many claim the name of Jesus but the throbbing power of his life does not flow in their hearts.

This is why I act. This is my goal. More than any other disciple, I received the divine fire. It never grew cold in my heart. It always blazed with its initial fervor. Now I want to pour out this fire upon the whole Church. I take for myself the words that Jesus used, "I have come to cast fire upon the earth." If I do not cast this fire of divine love, rousing all believers to a new life in Christ, the human race will be unable to turn aside from its rush into a fire that will destroy all.

Comment
Human history records many movements that changed its course.
Our Lady seeks the renewed fervor of the Movement begun by Jesus.

August 26, 2014
6. History's Final Scene

Understanding Human History

Mary

When human history ends, and all of mankind is gathered before my Son, Jesus, only then will the full revelation of the heavenly Father's plan be revealed.

At that moment, each person and each generation will see what they have done. All will see human history before their very eyes, like a movie in which they themselves are the actors, choosing to act according to the script of God or choosing to play a different role and become a discordant note.

Such will be that great moment. Every person will have played some part. Those who added to the story will be lifted up onto the heavenly stage. Those who rejected their God-given place will be left behind. They refused to be saved by the Lamb of God. Such is the final scene of human history.

Comment
When Jesus comes, we will all be there.
It is a command performance, the whole purpose of our human lives.

August 27, 2014
7. The True God of History

Understanding Human History

Mary

When all human history comes to a close in the presence of Jesus, every person will look into their own heart. They will find there all of their decisions, all the people who influenced them (for good or evil), and all the forces which shaped their lives. They will see themselves as they truly are, ready for heaven or worthy only of hell. What a frightful moment that is. The decisions, the choices, all have been made. The die is cast. What is can never be changed.

Contrast this final moment with human history, where decisions are made every day and nothing is final and all can be changed. That is my message to the world. While living in human history, you can change. On earth, none of your decisions are final until that final moment. No matter what darkness you have accepted, no matter what evil you have committed, nothing is final while you are still on earth. Human history exists so the human person might live forever. Such is the true goal. Seek this and you shall live.

Comment
Our Lady speaks because she wants you to live with her forever.

August 28, 2014
8. The Only Important Question

Understanding Human History

Mary

When all history ends with its final culmination, there is only one question: "O reader, will you be with me, forever?" Mankind thinks of the millions of people, but as a Mother, I think only of you. I want you to be with me forever. I want to share the joys of heaven with you. I want to be your mother and have you as my son or daughter.

You are mine. Yes, my child, I gave birth to you in the pain of the cross when I offered Jesus to the Father and accepted the beloved disciple. "Woman, behold your son," Jesus said. At that moment, I saw you and became your mother.

Nothing else is important. The joys and the sufferings of earth pass away. History culminates. Jesus returns. All gather. The Book of Life is opened. I have written your name in this book. I have written it in large and prominent letters. You are precious to me. I cherish you. I want to hold you forever and ever in my Immaculate Heart. I want

160

no one to steal you from me. That is why I speak each day. For you! Blessed is that person who cherishes my words.

Comment
*This series on human history ends exactly where all history culminates –
with the focus on the salvation of every human person.*

The Sweeping Modern Events

August 29, 2014
1. The Syrian Revolution
The Sweeping Modern Events

Mary

The world finds itself caught up in sweeping events that seemingly have no answer. Leaders are confused by the quick rise of ISIS and by Putin's activities in the Ukraine. Rockets have been flying into Israel and the destruction of Gaza has been brutal. China has begun to emerge as a nation on the move, emboldened and aggressive.

In the past, I have spoken about the timetable of events and how that timetable has been moved ahead because America has withdrawn. Now, the whole world can see the truth of my words. So, I will begin to speak again and to comment on all that is taking place. As the events continue, more and more will become students of my words which pour forth divine wisdom.

I will begin with Syria. I said clearly that the revolution in Syria was quite different from the revolutions in Egypt and Libya. Those revolutions burned themselves out quickly as the dictators were overturned. I prophesied that Syria would be different. That the dictator would not be quickly deposed, that the revolution would drag on and on, that the region would be destabilized and that larger terrorist groups, more unified, would emerge. All of this has now happened and the world is confronted with a totally new reality, a terrorist group that claims its own country, with all of its resources, a group that does not overturn governments but itself governs.

Listen carefully again to my words. I am the Woman Clothed with the Sun. Only my armies can overcome the Evil One. Where are my armies? I must gather them quickly. I must spread devotion to my Immaculate Heart throughout the whole world, in unprecedented ways. When you see these signs and events, know they are a call into my army.

Comment
Locutions speaking about Syria were given in 2012 on February 12,
and in 2013 on April 28, 29; May 5; August 23, 26; September 2, 4, 6 and 17.

August 30, 2014
2. The Mystery of Syrian Evil

The Sweeping Modern Events

Mary

Syria will continue to be the problem, the great mystery which continually sends forth evil. Syria is not just one evil, the evil of Assad. It has become a collection of evils. Because the revolution was not quickly ended by the overthrow of the regime, it became an attraction for evil. Various terrorists groups saw an opportunity to topple the regime and claim control of an entire country. It did not happen that way. Instead, the fires within Syria burned and eventually spread to other parts of the Middle East, just as I had said.

Now, Syria is a greater mystery. The West cannot figure out a strategy, how to use its weapons. This is the enigma that exists and the source is Russia, which saw Assad as an ally and continually strengthens his role, giving him the needed support to survive when so many predicted his quick downfall. Go back and read my locutions for I spoke of all these events in great detail even before they took place.

Comment
Our Lady was clear from the beginning that Syria would light the fuse,
although it will not be the place of the explosion.

August 30, 2014
3. Putin and the Ukraine

The Sweeping Modern Events

Mary

"Why wait," says Putin, "when all of the Ukraine waits for me to take what I can hold? I can redraw the map and gain what I have coveted for many years."

So, the Ukraine waits for the reaper who comes, not just to take its harvest, but also to claim its soil. Once these parts are swallowed up, they will not be returned in Putin's lifetime.

I have said before that he is Satan's perfect instrument. No need to look for another. No need to seek another source of evil. The evil flows from Russia, as it did throughout the twentieth century.

This is not a replay. Putin's Russia is quite different. He has many new alliances and has shaped a modern Russia that can withstand the obvious actions that the West will take. He has seen them all. Nothing surprises him. He has fashioned many other sources that can help him. He will remain on the scene, directing the evil wherever he sees weaknesses.

I have spoken of him before and my words were true. He is an adversary who will not go away. For years, he has plotted his course and has had no qualms about the means he needs to employ. The West has been deceived.

Comment

Our Lady has spoken often about Putin and the Ukraine.
Consult the following locutions: In 2012, October 5, 6 and 7;
in 2014, March 14, 24; April 10, 11, and 28; June 2.

September 1, 2014
4. Infection in the Blood Stream

The Sweeping Modern Events

Mary

Let the entire stream of events flow out so that all can see the evils contained in human history. They have been planted there for years by past decisions and wars. They have been fed by the fires of anger and injustice. They have grown, hidden from the eyes of all. Now, this stream begins to come to the surface, all that I have been speaking about. All see these events happening everywhere. The evil is not limited to one country or to one region. Evil is in the very blood stream of mankind, flowing to every part of the body, and growing more powerful.

The body is too weak, daily losing its battle to overcome the infection. Mankind tries to stir itself to battle. Leaders call for solutions. Yet, the evil grows and spreads. The body seems helpless. No aid in sight.

This is why I speak. You can see the truth of my words before your very eyes. Let my words be your comfort, and also your guide. Act upon my words. Look into your heart. You believe. You know that God exists. You have faith. Treasure that faith. Stir that faith into action. As all the events pour forth, you will wonder how you can be saved. Suddenly, your faith will take on a much greater value.

September 2, 2014

5. The Annihilation of the Nations

The Sweeping Modern Events

Mary

I must come to the deepest sorrow of my heart. Only reluctantly do I speak of the annihilation of the nations. This annihilation is not imminent. It will not happen tomorrow but it does loom on the horizon.

Right now, this annihilation cannot happen because the people who can bring it about are not yet in place and they do not yet have the weapons that are needed. However, everyone is quite aware of how situations can shift quickly. The pattern has now become familiar. What seems stable begins to shake. New factions arise. Leaders are toppled. Chaos and instability enter. A door opens for those who want to take advantage of the opportunity and they, who had no power, suddenly control a new portion of the world. This process, taking place everywhere, will open the world to a future moment when the annihilation of the nations becomes a distinct possibility.

My real sorrow in this annihilation is not just death, but the manner in which death takes place. Millions will lose their lives quickly. There is no time to repent, to prepare for death, no opportunity for God to use the time of sickness to pour out his graces of conversion or to help devout souls to better prepare for the moment of their divine judgment.

In the annihilation, all are caught short, both sinners and saints, both those with faith and those without. The divine mercy of God, which saves so many people as they gradually face the reality of their coming death, is robbed of this opportunity.

You can see my sorrow as I perceive the possible annihilation of the nations that looms on the horizon. I will not speak much about this now but I have to begin this revelation. Later, I will speak more fully.

Comment
A possible annihilation of the nations is seemingly part of the Fatima secret
that is still not revealed. If so, then it should be revealed.

164

6. The Woman and George Washington

The Sweeping Modern Events

Mary

I must begin to prepare, especially since all are seeing, for the first time, the extent of the evils and the possibilities for destruction that they hold. Many evils are still hidden, soon to appear, claiming even more of what seemed to be so stable. A hopelessness and an inevitability set in, as if the only choice is just to watch passively as this new force makes its conquests.

My message is quite different. "Prepare," I say. "Awaken to the powers that lie in your faith. Your faith alone can save you. This is my promise, 'Fill your churches and I will raise up leaders who will guide you in my ways. I will strengthen the hearts of the people and make firm their resolve. They will sweep away the years of debauchery. They will instill new ideals of morality. The hearts of the young will turn back to me (for they especially will see their future being taken away).'"

The Spirit of God must come upon America. The conversions must be true and deep. All of these evils would never have arisen if America had stayed true to the light. It is not too late but there must be no delay. An unprepared America will shatter into many pieces. An America prepared by an outpouring of the Spirit will respond. I prophesied these times to George Washington, the son of the Republic. Read my words. They will reveal a woman who has always cared for America and has promised her salvation.

Comment

One morning at Valley Forge, a woman appeared to George Washington and prophesied three events. First, he would win the Revolutionary War and bring about the union. Second, there would be a civil war but the woman would preserve the union. Both of these have happened. The third event concerns ten nations that come against the United States, which is saved only by the actions of the woman. This account was published in the Philadelphia Tribune and is available on the internet.

7. Mercy or Justice

The Sweeping Modern Events

Mary

Before continuing, I must reveal the secrets of my own heart. I saw creation as it came forth in all of its beauty from the Father's hand. I saw the power of the redeeming love of my Son pour out from his heart. I personally experienced the sanctifying fire of the Holy Spirit. I see all that God has done for the human race. I also see the pitiable state of mankind and, even worse, the future state, the path that he has taken because of Satan's deceptions.

I speak from this abundance of knowledge and I use these little locutions to share with all the world my own understanding. This is man's only saving light, to see the works of the Father, Son and Spirit, all that God will do, if only mankind turns, repents and seeks his intervention.

This is my message of hope. God will intervene. He is ready and waiting. He will not delay. He wants to find a mankind humbled and repentant so he can pour out his mercy. If not, when he intervenes, it will be his justice that pours out. This is why I speak.

Comment

Today's locution is a pause along the road to reflect with Our Lady.

September 5, 2014

8. A Day Claimed by Evil

The Sweeping Modern Events

Mary

You see events exploding in many different places. This is the way it will be because evil is spilling over wherever there are openings in the society. Evil resides in the heart of human history, placed there by men's countless sins. When this evil is not purged by repentance and God's forgiving power, it grows and boils over wherever the society is weak.

On September 11, 2001, this evil broke forth in an extraordinary way. America was damaged. The terrorist world rejoiced. Ever since that decisive moment, the terrorists have taken heart. They saw concrete evidence of their power. 9/11 has become their battle cry. They are emboldened and give the impression that the future belongs to them. The West is on the defensive. Even with its much greater resources, it has no battle cry. Such is the world without faith to unite hearts and to lead to victory.

However, the future is not determined. Man is free, and evil flows according to man's free decisions. If there is repentance and a turning to God, these events can be avoided. What voices are raised? These locutions are a tiny voice, but if their message is carried by others, then all the world can hear.

Comment

Each year on September 11, the West braces for new outbreaks.
Where will we be in 2015? We must act quickly to turn the world to repentance.

166

September 6, 2014
9. Help in the Trials

The Sweeping Modern Events

Mary

When all the events converge, the world will see Satan's plan emerging. Now, this plan is hidden. When it is revealed, the world will see its own mistakes, its poor choices and the helplessness of human wisdom. But a greater question exists: "Will there be any solution to the ever-increasing problems?" Efforts will be made. Mankind will continue to foolishly believe that it controls its own destiny. (That control has really not existed for a long time because these events go back almost 100 years.) All efforts will be futile. The powers and the intelligence behind the evil far surpass all human forces.

What will happen? I must speak clearly and loudly. My words seem small and reach only a limited group for now, but it is important that the words be recorded. Later, they will be flashed like headlines to the whole world.

I will never forsake mankind. I will always hold out my saving gifts. I will deliver all who call on my name, not from the evils that affect all, but from the despair that will accompany these evils.

The time is short. The preparations are already being made. Do not delay. Gather up your loved ones and say, "We must return to the Virgin Mary. She will sustain us in the trials." And I will.

Comment
Mary's messages always bring hope, but only if we respond.

Mary's Immaculate Heart

September 7, 2014
1. The History of the Light

Mary's Immaculate Heart

Mary

I know the plans which God has, his plans for peace and blessings. These plans should be easily fulfilled. However, when sin entered the world, the plans were torn to pieces. Only with great difficulty and with the help of God's revelation could man even glimpse these plans.

In the fullness of time, I brought forth God's Son. A new light entered the world. Man could see again his path to the Father. The Holy Spirit was sent and man was enlightened in a totally new way. Jesus' hope was to restore things as they were at the beginning.

Since those events, this light has had its own history. Sometimes accepted. Sometimes rejected. This is the mystery which I now reveal. The light of Christ is under attack. This has always been the case, as the centuries of martyrs prove. But now, the assault is from every side, the terror of the Muslims and the sins of the West. So the Father has placed this light in my Immaculate Heart for its safekeeping and for the light to shine brilliantly once again, as never before. Why seek this light elsewhere, when I tell you exactly where the Father has hidden it? Why not listen to my revelations? Then, all will find the light. The great mystery of this age is my Immaculate Heart, the depository of the light of Christ. I will speak more and more about this mystery.

Comment
In Mary's Immaculate Heart we can find the light of Christ more easily.

September 8, 2014
2. The False Economies

Mary's Immaculate Heart

Mary

I can no longer hold back the secrets that lie hidden in my Immaculate Heart. They must be revealed because the time is short. I will reveal places and events.

Much depends on the free will of man. Also, what God now decrees in his justice can be changed by his mercy. So much depends on how responsive man is to my pleadings. What is certain is that I must begin to reveal. To wait any longer would be foolhardy. The human race has long ago passed the point of no return. Certain events will definitely happen but much can be changed. Most important, the Church and all who believe can be spiritually prepared for these events.

All eyes look to the terrorists and to the Ukraine, but few now look to the economies of the world that are so shaky and ready to topple. No one tackles the difficult issues of restraining the false economic policies.

The foundation is eroded. The countries can no longer pay for their arms and their lifestyles. No one preaches restraint and the people have no desire to tighten their belts. In the time ahead, I will speak often, always more clearly, of the economic disturbances that will rock the markets. Do not judge by the boom. No solid foundation exists. All is debt driven.

Comment
Our Lady will point out the problems.

September 9, 2014
3. A Light from Mary's Heart

Mary's Immaculate Heart

Mary

When all the events begin, a light will shine forth from my Immaculate Heart. It will not be just a general or diffused light. This light will be clear and definite. The light will come from those whom I have long ago placed in my heart.

This light that will go forth will have a special power to attract. The light will be under obedience to the Church. No one will be led astray. The light will gather, console, offer warmth and peace. The light will strengthen in times of great weakness.

While all the world struggles, this light will grow stronger and stronger. People, and even nations, will walk in this surprising light, which continually flows out. The light will be a sign to all that I am the Woman Clothed with the Sun, able to overcome even the greatest victories of the Evil One.

Whatever darkness he pours out, I will give a greater light. Whatever area he touches, I will go there with my light. His darkness will be no match for my light.

There is only one condition. People must believe. They must accept the light into their hearts and walk by the light. If so, even in the darkest of moments, they will enjoy my light.

Comment
Words give light and direction. Mary promises
her light whenever the darkness comes.

September 10, 2014
4. Heart to Heart to Heart

Mary's Immaculate Heart

Mary

When my heart breaks open, every blessing will pour out. The world will see a new power, hidden until now in my Immaculate Heart. The world and even the Church have never seen these gifts even though, through my apparitions, small

169

manifestations have taken place. Only a few have tasted of this new wine. So much is still hidden that I must now speak quite openly.

Man's heart is good but entrapped, surrounded by so many evil choices and a powerful culture that pulls him away from God. The Church holds on valiantly, trying to preach the basic truths and to offer the powers of the sacraments. All can see that these are not enough. The hearts of many belong to the world not to my Church.

There is a need for a new stream which takes its place alongside the Church's teachings and its sacraments. This is the stream of devotion which captures the person's heart for Jesus. This is the mighty stream which I am beginning to pour forth from my Immaculate Heart, heart to heart to heart. From my heart to your heart that leads you to Jesus' heart. These powers will pour forth as my heart breaks open and the mighty stream comes forth.

Comment
All of our hearts can profit from this stream.

September 11, 2014
5. A Day of Infamy

Mary's Immaculate Heart

Mary

As I pour out my words all will know that they are gifts of my Immaculate Heart for they will be rich but simple, easy to remember, and always able to bring hope, even though they speak of dark events.

Let us walk into the future together. Through my words you can take my hand. My voice will always speak, and although darkness is all around, you will not be in darkness. A strange and powerful light will fill your heart and the evil will not touch you. From the light will come my voice which you will recognize. By my voice I will comfort you.

Today (September 11) is a day of infamy, of tragedy, and worst of all, a day that always inspires new and more violent acts of terrorism. Satan, who stirred up those who perpetrated the original acts, has laid claim to this day. Why? He is not the Lord. He has no right to a day. However, those who serve him have now claimed this day.

Can I not take this day back? Can I not reclaim this day for my Son? Next year is so important. Let my followers prepare and gather. Do not surrender this day to the Evil One, otherwise the terror will grow.

Comment
Our Lady wants us to prepare for September 11, 2015
and reclaim the day for Jesus Christ.

September 12, 2014
6. A Year from Now

Mary's Immaculate Heart

Mary

When the heart speaks, it holds nothing back, sometimes revealing what should be kept secret. Such is my heart, pouring out all my secrets.

By next September, much will have shifted. The terrorist groups will be stronger and better organized because the steps taken against them will not be sufficient or effective. The problems will not just come from terrorism. There will be sparks coming from new fires. These fires should have been put out but instead they have been put off, as if terrorism was the big problem. These fires are internal, especially the enormous debts and the economies with no foundations.

Time must not be lost. The Church must understand, through the prophetic gift, how to prepare its members and the world. This is a true gift of service which can alert without being sensational.

Too many merely watch and wonder what is going to happen. I am telling you what will happen. Before the events begin, the Church must call for prayer and fasting, for a renewal of fervor. People must flood the churches beginning now and not wait for these events. All must be ready and not caught unawares.

Comment

Our Lady speaks frequently of a series of events, in different aspects of human life, that will shift the world. She asks us to believe and, even now, to fill the churches.

September 13, 2014
7. The Fire of Mary's Suffering

Mary's Immaculate Heart

Mary

I wait and wait, unable to pour out all the gifts stored in my Immaculate Heart. How I suffer from these flames that long ago should have gone forth. They burn within me as unopened gifts. Instead, I see the other fires, the fires of destruction given free reign because my fire is bound and tied. When will my suffering end? When will the fires be allowed to go forth?

That is why I speak and why, O reader, I have led you to these little locutions that reveal so many secrets. These words have prepared your heart. You believe. You have faith and trust. You can receive my fires. Please take my fire. You will relieve my suffering.

171

"What can I do for you, O Virgin?" you ask. Just receive my fire. In me, these fires cause great suffering. In you, the fires will bring peace and zeal for Jesus' kingdom.

These fires do not belong in my heart. They belong in your heart. I am already full of grace. This is the mystery. The heavenly Father has placed all the fires meant for the whole human race in my Immaculate Heart. He wants me to distribute these fires so that Satan is humbled by being conquered by a woman. The greatest favor that you can do for me is to open your own heart and receive all the fires meant for you.

There is a second mystery. To those who are faithful, I will give fires meant for others, but rejected by them. These fires are tasks that must be done to save souls. Many reject their tasks but they must be accomplished. So, I look around for faithful souls and I give them tasks that should have been done by others.

You can see the many mysteries. As you learn the ways of my heart, you become my perfect instruments.

Comment

Today, Our Lady has revealed great mysteries in very simple words.

The Valley of Decision

September 14, 2014
1. Man's Free Will

The Valley of Decision

Mary

In these teachings, O reader, I want to take you into the depths of your own heart so you can understand the freedom of your will and how that freedom must be used. All freedom brings a responsibility to choose wisely, and the greatest freedom is to choose to live forever with God.

I call this the Valley of Decision. Valley implies mountains on every side, and this image brings home the importance of what takes place. A valley is central, the lowest, the deepest, and, at the same time, the most important.

Such is your will. It lies at the deepest point of the human person. It is central and the most important component of every human life. The will is the valley of decision, the unique power that man uses to decide for good or for evil.

I will shed great light upon this valley. I cannot decide for you. You alone must choose. But I can help you, flooding you with light and teaching you how to use your free will and gain heaven.

Comment
Our Lady has spoken so often about world events.
Now, she explores man's inner world.

September 15, 2014
2. The King and Queen of Material Creation

The Valley of Decision

Mary

I want to take you deeply into this great mystery: that God decided to create the human person, clothed in flesh, who had a will that could freely know, love and serve him. He so wanted man to say "yes" to him that he clothed these first two persons with special gifts. Their bodies enjoyed perfect and complete order and their souls enjoyed a unique intimacy with God.

In spite of these prerogatives, their wills remained free, free even from disordered passions and ambitions. They were the king and the queen of his earthly kingdom, meant to pass on their riches to all of their children.

It did not happen. They failed the test. The riches were lost and the inner order was shattered.

Such is the state of sinful humanity and the disordered history of mankind. O reader, you are plunged into this sin and disorder, through no fault of your own. How can you conquer? How can your free will, mired in sinful history, correctly choose your Maker? This is the mystery which I will unfold.

Comment
In explaining the will's freedom, Our Lady describes
the sinful state of humanity that hinders free will.

September 16, 2014
3. The Powerful Valley

The Valley of Decision

Mary

Too many wait and wait, allowing the forces of the culture to lead them. They are taken up with worldly ambitions and selfish desires. They never enter the valley of decision, the great valley where they encounter Jesus in the quiet of their heart. They never hear his voice nor experience his call. They never discover their destiny which can be revealed only by faith. This is why I speak to you, O reader, and by my words reveal to you this great valley.

All you must do is enter the valley where all else is left behind. The valley is holy and contains every gift. The valley will transform you, strip you of all darkness and clothe you with light. You will be free, and will discover all the helps offered to you— your guardian angel, the sacraments, and the word of God. I will be there in the valley, and all of my helps will flood your soul.

When you plunge into the world, you are alone, but when you walk into the valley you discover all the help that heaven offers you. This valley is in your own heart, the free will that resides in the center of your being. When you were baptized, the great valley of grace poured forth. That is the mystery I will explain.

Comment
O reader, you are not alone. God has formed this great valley
of his presence in your free will.

September 17, 2014
4. Living in Truth

The Valley of Decision

Mary

The way of integrity is the path of truth. Only truth sets the will free. Otherwise, it is bound by error and confusion, easily led astray and choosing false goods.

Truth is light but man loves the darkness which allows him to choose evil. I must make the truth attractive so you will always choose this light.

The first truth is that God gave you existence and that you owe everything to him. The second truth is that he sent Jesus, his only Son, to free you from sin and darkness. The third truth is that he sent the Holy Spirit into your heart to lift you into the kingdom.

This is your greatness, and when I speak of the beauty of the Valley of Decision, I am speaking about a free will immersed in God's Holy Spirit. This is your greatness. A Valley of Decision bereft of the Holy Spirit is a Valley of Darkness.

The first step of truth is to receive the Holy Spirit, the Spirit of Truth. The steps are easy. He comes by faith in Jesus and by holy Baptism. His presence is regained after sin by a good confession. His presence and power multiplies by constant Holy Communion, prayer, and a reading of Scripture. These are the certain and sure helps. Use them constantly and you will live in truth.

September 18, 2014
5. The Freedom in the Valley

The Valley of Decision

Mary

What a great gift when man enters the valley and understands his freedom in Jesus Christ. Man thirsts for freedom. He takes extraordinary efforts to be free. Alas, the freedom he seeks is often false, and he makes himself a slave.

Come, reader, I will lead you into the great freedom. You find this freedom only in the valley of your own heart when it is filled with God's grace and God's life.

The first freedom is to see how important you are to God. You are unique and precious to him. You must see all that God has done for you. He brought you into existence and sent Jesus to redeem you. He baptized you, and his Holy Spirit pours out his treasures. By entering this valley, you see yourself in God's ever-loving presence. Never can anyone degrade you because you are a child of the King.

You also see that your sins are forgiven in Jesus' precious blood. (Make sure you get to confession.) No one can accuse you. Finally, you are ready to live like God's child, offending no one, making reparation for whatever evil you have caused, and trying to help everyone along the way.

You are free. Just enter the Valley of Decision, which is your own heart, your free will by which you choose to be God's child.

Comment
Man's great longing for freedom is fulfilled only by Jesus Christ.

September 19, 2014
6. The Secret of the Saints

The Valley of Decision

Mary

In this Valley of Decision, the deepest part of the human heart, only one voice speaks, God alone. No one else has access. All other voices are silent. The incessant noise of the world cannot reach this valley. The soul is alone with its Creator.

The child is with its heavenly Father.

The person must visit this valley often, every single day. Otherwise, confusion reigns and the cacophony of many voices pull the person in different directions.

Let me explain this simple experience that is easily available. By grace, Jesus lives within you. He calls you into this center of your heart. He waits for you there at every moment of your day. It is a great secret to learn how to go in spirit and come into his presence, even for a few moments of what is solitude.

You are alone with Jesus, deliberately giving to him power over your free will. You are surrendering to him and seeking only his light. He refreshes you, assures you of his love and tells you to return often to this holy place where he dwells within you.

I have shared with you the secret of the saints in the most simple words. Hold these teachings in your heart.

Comment
Constantly being with Jesus in the depths of their own hearts
was the secret of every saint

Hell's Power over Earth

September 20, 2014
1. Going from Light to Darkness

Hell's Power over Earth

Mary

Come, I want to take you into the darkness of hell. Only then can you understand the events that are taking place and the hideousness of sin. There will be stages of this darkness and at the very end, we will come to the center, face to face with Satan and his legions.

The road from light into darkness begins slowly. It is like a twilight. The person still believes, still practices their faith, but in certain areas of life they begin to leave God's law behind. Attractions grow that were never tolerated before. Religious practices become secondary and routine. The flower is cut off from its deep roots of faith and no longer draws nourishment from the soil.

The person can no longer fight the culture and soon becomes one with it. The joys found in religious practices fade and the heart is consumed with worldly goals. The soul becomes powerless in the face of temptations and more and more succumbs to a lifestyle that it would previously have rejected.

The soul has not yet fallen into darkness but it skirts the edges, stumbles often, rises slowly and is greatly weakened while Satan waits for his moment, ready to claim a soul that had lived in the light.

Comment

O reader, if these words describe you, know that Our Lady loves you and is offering you the help you need to return quickly to the light.

September 21, 2014

2. Satan's Network

Hell's Power over Earth

Mary

Sometimes the earth trembles, the skies grow dark and the waves are in turmoil, as happens with hurricanes, earthquakes and tornados. All of these are symbols of the destructive powers of hell. A force is released which disturbs the existing order. Although some earthly manifestations have a satanic root, hell's greatest powers are shown in human events like anger, disputes, misunderstandings, breaking of promises, destruction of relationships, greed, scandals, sometimes a complete and sudden destruction of what seemed so stable.

These powers of hell do not break forth in natural disasters but within the human person. All are subject to these powers and many mistakenly believe that these are human misunderstandings or human errors. Really, hell is breaking loose and, if not overcome, the powers will keep spreading. Satan wants only to destroy, to tear down, and to ruin.

However, the powers of hell reach another level when they fasten upon hearts which are committed to evil, twisted hearts which have made evil decisions and deliberately chosen evil paths. Satan raises these people up, gives them places of authority, fills their pockets with money, lavishes upon them great political powers, protects them from their enemies, and keeps them in power until they no longer serve his purposes. These people are everywhere, in the world and in the Church, in business and in education, in politics and in science. Without knowing it, they form a network of evil that protects each other and fights for the same causes. They are intelligent, powerful, accepted by many, often well-groomed, highly educated and even charming.

They persuade others, lead causes, and are brilliant in speech. They have no love for the truth and see no evil in breaking God's law. All is expediency, whatever gains their distorted goals.

Society is on the brink because Satan owns so many thousands of people. Their passions are disordered and their egos dominate their thoughts. They are his vanguard, his instruments in leading the world over the brink, where it is now headed unless the powers in my Immaculate Heart are soon released.

No human mind can detect Satan's network and no human force can destroy it. Only the Woman Clothed with the Sun is his worthy adversary.

Comment
Our Lady gives a powerful description of what is happening
before our eyes but is really not seen.

September 22, 2014
3. Face to Face with Hell

Hell's Power over Earth

Mary

Before leading to the important conclusions, I must take you face to face with this kingdom of hell, for it is truly a kingdom, with a hierarchy and members, tightly knit and under the leadership of Satan, whose name as an angel was Lucifer, the bearer of light.

I must open your eyes and you must see. There can be no mistake, no claiming that the kingdom of hell is just a name for impersonal evils that inevitably happen in human events. No, the kingdom of hell is persons. Fallen angels are persons, with intellect and free will. They have used their free will to reject light and to choose darkness, to reject love and choose hatred, to reject service and choose pride. They are bound to each other by their "No" to Jesus Christ and to his kingdom of light. They contain every possible evil and seek only to pour it forth upon mankind of whom they are extremely jealous because human persons have a chance to replace them on their heavenly thrones.

This kingdom of total darkness and complete evil constantly breaks forth into human history, destroying the good and promoting destruction. This kingdom is intelligent and powerful, always keeping itself hidden unless it serves their purpose to be known and seen.

Unaware of this intelligent, powerful, evil, destructive, and well-organized kingdom, human beings cooperate with it, find some aspects attractive, dabble in its powers, and open their hearts to becoming a member.

All of this, I will explain further.

Comment
Our Lady tries to warn us of the enemy who wants to destroy us.

September 23, 2014
4. Turning the World into a Hell

Hell's Power over Earth

Mary

Let us pierce to the very heart of hell, which is the free will of all the angels who rejected the light. By their own choice, their wills are filled with an unquenchable fire. God made them angelic persons with the most piercing intellects and the firmest of wills, mighty angels in his image and likeness, far outstripping any human person. It is impossible to conceive the perfection of the angelic beings or the great powers which they received.

However, when invited to use these powers for love and for service, they were blinded by their own perfections and cried out with one voice, "We will not serve!" Immediately, all of their great powers turned in upon themselves. Their free choice began an eternal fire because their wills chose only themselves.

In that moment, hell began in the heart of each fallen angel. They hated themselves and each other and were bound together in this fire of hatred. Such are the flames of hell, which now spread so rapidly in human history and can be seen everywhere.

Do not say that the destructive fires of Syria, Iraq, ISIS, the Ukraine and Gaza are human fires. They are the fires of hell, flowing from the hearts of those who would turn the whole world into a hell. This is the mystery I am trying to reveal.

Comment
The world's destruction can only be understood and defeated
by those who believe in hell. Everyone else does not know what is going on!

September 24, 2014
5. Satan's Use of the Syrian Revolution

Hell's Power over Earth

Mary

The world is in total ignorance of these destructive powers that I am describing. It relegates these truths to its fiction novels and its movies. It moves in only one plane, as if reality were one-dimensional. It rejects the reality of heaven and the power of hell. Now, as hell feels empowered and able to break forth into the news, the world and its leaders have no answers. So, I must use these locutions to hammer home my basic message.

All the destructive events that now make the headlines, the wars, the executions and the extensive, massive human sufferings which follow, come from hell. They do not have a human source. Human beings, knowingly or unknowingly, are merely instruments of hell. The important conclusion is the following.

Your human intellects are so puny that you will never have a strategy to defeat these evils. They confound you. They twist you in circles. One year you go in one direction. A year later, you go in another. You arm your friends and they become your enemies. You do not even know who is who. You are not sure whom you should bomb and whom you should arm. You do not even know the names of all the groups or how they interact.

Whom should I blame? You have long ago cast aside your faith and heaven's help. You have built your own world and taught your children to be secular. Now you are bereft, like an unarmed soldier facing a deadly foe.

As the events continue, these locutions will grow in importance. Remember that they began with the Egyptian Revolution (January, 2011). That was my sign to the locutionist that these words had to go forth. That was the beginning, but it was the Syrian revolution that lit the fuse. I spoke a year ago about this (August 23 and 26, 2013). Now you can see all the evils that have followed.

I have not abandoned the world. These locutions are a proof of my care for my children.

O reader, do not think your prayers and sacrifices are small. They are important to me. Your love, especially, consoles me. Continue in your little devotions. My great gifts have not been released. Oh, when will the Holy Father consecrate Russia? I wait, but I also actively prepare for that moment.

Comment
The locutions grow deeper and become much more serious. A great war between heaven and hell is about to break forth upon the earth. The signs are becoming evident to all.

September 25, 2014
6. Hell's Nuclear Arsenal

Hell's Power over Earth

Mary

There are fires of hell which the world has not yet seen. Only the beginning fires have billowed forth. Hell began in the hearts of the fallen angels. They were created to love God but chose only to love themselves. This fire is an intense hatred for themselves.

They did not want God's presence, so they gathered together in their own hatred. What a kingdom! Highly intelligent and powerful creatures are inexorably linked together by the fires of hatred. No love and no friendships exist in hell. All are enemies.

From this caldron of unimaginable hatred comes forth the destruction and suffering on earth. The door was opened by man's own rebellion and a refusal to serve God. The effects can be seen by all, especially in the intense hatreds and violence of the Middle East. Hatred, suffering, destruction – these are the clear signs of hell's presence and power.

I teach all of this to underscore the total inability of mankind to put out these fires. Sometimes, human efforts multiply and spread the fires. Now, I come to the heart of my teaching – nuclear weapons. In all of these conflicts, conventional weapons have been used. Their power is great but still limited. Although Satan has not yet reached into his nuclear arsenal, the weapons are being made ready and soon they will find their way into the hands of those who will gladly use them.

At that moment, the world will come to a point which it has never reached, nuclear arms in the possession of hell itself. That is the combination which must be feared.

People will ask, "What are we to do?" Always I answer that human solutions do not exist but heaven will cast down another fire, a more powerful fire. The heavenly Father has already placed these fires in my Immaculate Heart. For almost a century, I have been speaking of these fires and all the blessings they contain. Over and over again, my central message has been about world peace. These fires must come forth. Yet who clamors to have them released? Especially in the Church, the great silence prevails. Changes must happen quickly. I do not want the annihilation of the nations.

Comment

Thank God that up to now, all of man's hatred has been expressed only in conventional weapons.

September 26, 2014
7. Seeking to Destroy Everyone

Hell's Power over Earth

Mary

Hell seeks to control everyone and every aspect of earth. Earth is a kingdom that it dearly covets. Earth is quite different from both heaven and hell. On earth everyone lives in time. There is a past, present and future. Earth has a history of events and God's plan for earth unfolds day by day. Hell sees its great opportunity. It can interfere, change, or even destroy that plan. For hell, earth is a place where it can get back at God and steal from him his own creatures. This is the reality I am trying to reveal.

Hell seeks to control everyone, every event and every aspect of earth. Hell is inexorable. It has no free will. It marches along a path it does not choose, a path of total hatred. As such, every person must be their target. Hell plots on the individual level, the national level and the international level. It plots in the heart of every person and in the gatherings of world leaders. Its plans are total. Every aspect of human life is analyzed. Every part of its plan fits together. Such is the kingdom of hell, about which man knows so little and is totally defenseless.

Have I made my case? Do you see now how important is the fire in my Immaculate Heart? Do you not want me as your companion on the journey? Is it not foolhardy for the Church to set me aside? I have made my point and revealed hell's secrets. Let this word go forth. I will now reveal heaven's secrets and the steps which the Father wants to happen.

Comment
Understanding the powers and extent of hell's
influence should lead us to seek heaven's help.

Heaven's Power upon Present Human History

September 27, 2014
1. The Activity of Heaven upon Earth

Heaven's Power upon Present Human History

Mary

As hell begins to manifest itself, the whole world can see the face of hell, a face filled with suffering, hatred, and destruction, a face where there is not a moment or a place for peace. Where is this road for peace? Certainly world leaders cannot find it. (Their own hearts are tainted and corrupted by selfish interests.) The generals cannot bring it about because the common person feels helpless, not knowing what will happen next.

Is there a road to peace? To answer that, I must explain heaven.

Heaven is too often considered just a place that people go to after death. Heaven is much more. Just as hell knows everything that happens on earth and intervenes everywhere to spread its hatred, so heaven is a kingdom that is active in human history, and is the very purpose of human creation. Every person is created for heaven. No one can say, "I refuse to exist forever. I will end my existence at my death." That decision has already been made for you. God created you and has decided that you will always exist. Heaven and hell both know this well.

So begin my teachings. The human person, immortal from the first moment of conception, standing between heaven and hell, coveted by both kingdoms, is the great prize in the war between the kingdoms of heaven and hell. What a joy to open your eyes to the mysteries of heaven.

Comment
Many do not see the tremendous powers of hell twisting human history.
Also many do not see how close and powerful is heaven.

September 28, 201
2. Comparing the Two Kingdoms
Heaven's Power upon Present Human History

Mary

Heaven can pour forth its powers and extinguish the fires of hell. Why, then, does hell seem to be more powerful than heaven? This is the question that needs answers. When heaven pours out its blessings, then the fires of hell will be extinguished. This is the first truth. Man is helpless against hell unless heaven comes to his aid.

If heaven is always pouring out its powers, why is man so helpless? Because he knows nothing about heaven. He has become the modern man of science, captivated by all that he has discovered. He is surrounded by his own technology without realizing that hell uses that technology for its own purposes. Man has set heaven aside. He no longer looks to heaven, does not understand its ways, does not receive its help, and has no defense against the powers of hell. Heaven always pours out its powers but man has lost his faith and cannot receive the blessings.

On earth, therefore, the kingdoms are not equal. Hell has the field all to itself. It has trained its followers, initiated them, taught them its ways and gladly shares with them all of its intelligence and all of its powers. Hell seems to be more powerful than heaven. Right now, every aspect of human life is succumbing to its influence.

This is why I speak because this destruction is not the full reality. Heaven is infinite. Hell is finite. Heaven has all power and can easily extinguish hell's fires. The two are not equal but both exist and man freely chooses. Free will is the one power which heaven always respects. Even if man chooses hell, God will honor his choice.

Comment

Heaven and hell are certainly not equal but if man chooses hell, heaven is powerless.

September 29, 2014

3. Heaven Embraces Earth

Heaven's Power upon Present Human History

Mary

Heaven wants to embrace earth and breathe life upon it. This happened in the beginning of creation. Then, the power of hell entered into history. Heaven embraced earth a second time when Jesus announced that the kingdom of heaven was at hand and manifested heaven's powers in his miracles and healings.

The greatest moments of heaven's powers happened when Jesus was raised from the dead, ascended into heaven and sent the Holy Spirit. At that moment, heaven had definitively embraced earth. As Jesus said, "I will be with you until the end of the world." The Father had fulfilled his promise of a woman and her offspring (Gen. 3:15). Satan controls the world but heaven has set up its city, the kingdom.

As the kingdom spread, God's breath came upon the world. The satanic had to retreat. Human life changed. Man was freed from the demonic. In many ways, the world began to look like the kingdom. There was happiness and peace. Human life flourished.

However, mankind forgot about the kingdom, rejected the faith, and established the goddess of reason upon the altar of his heart. The demonic saw its opportunity to regain its foothold and to re-establish its kingdom in great power.

All is evident now. The wars, the destruction, the fires, the executions, the savagery, the hatred against believers show that the demonic is emerging. Man is helpless, but heaven is ready to help.

Comment

Our Lady describes what is happening behind the scenes and is now evident to all.

September 30, 2014

4. The Three Places of Divine Fire

Heaven's Power upon Present Human History

Mary

The flames leap up but these are not the destructive fires of hell. They are heaven's flames that bring life. Two fires fight for earth, a fire of death and a fire of life. Which one does mankind choose? This determines the course of human history.

Currently, hell's fires are prominent and attracting many into its deadly flames. Heaven's fires seem hidden and powerless. I speak so all is changed and the divine flames can leap up.

Where is heaven's fire? It lies in many places and these fires are meant to help. The fires reside in the heart of every believer who has been baptized. At times, these baptismal fires do not burn at all because the person forfeited divine grace by serious sin. At other times, the fires burn only slightly, because the heart chooses so many worldly goals. First, I must stir into flames, O reader, the divine fire placed within you, the Holy Spirit of your Baptism. If these fires burn brightly, no darkness can overcome you.

The second fire lies in the Church and again is subject to human free will. At times, the Church has been ablaze with divine love. At other times, it has sunk in darkness and needed great saints to rescue it. Today's Church is at the crossroads, facing the greatest question in its history. Can the Church become so rooted in the divine fire that it will pour out light even in the great darkness that lies ahead? Today, the great questions are not within the Church but outside the Church. How effective will the Church be when the events begin? The light which it currently has is woefully weak compared to the growing darkness of hell.

So, I come to the third place of divine fire, my Immaculate Heart. This fire comes from the bosom of the Father and is Jesus Christ himself. Why is this fire in my heart? Because it must be close and easily available. It must flow out at the tiniest request and it must cover the whole earth.

That is what I mean when I say that the Church is at the crossroads. The future events will pour out tremendous darkness. The Church's light is weak. However, powerful divine fire lies in my Immaculate Heart. To seek it anywhere else will result only in failure.

Comment
The teaching is very clear and corresponds to the current world events.

October 1, 2014
5. The Church Confronts Hell's Powers
Heaven's Power upon Present Human History
Mary

The events move quickly. The threats grow greater. The urgency of the kingdom of heaven grows greater because the time frame leaps forward. Hell's strength multiplies and heaven is kept at bay. What must be done so the heavenly fire is released?

I must speak to the Church. O Church, you have no armies, no weapons, and no generals. Yet, with you and you alone, lie the fires of world peace. Yet, you do not understand and you do not believe. So I must stir you by my words.

O Church, you are the bride of my Son. You are the light of the world. You have a great destiny to fulfill in these years. The world has set you aside, as if you were an orphan. The world does not listen to your teachings and does not follow your ways. Therefore, it plunges into the kingdom of hell. Only you can save earth from becoming a hell. I place in you the saving of the world from the terrible events that have come so close to fulfillment.

I have revealed these events to many, especially the visionaries of Medjugorje. I have spoken of my plan almost 100 years ago at Fatima. What I am saying is not new or surprising. I am now using these locutions as my pulpit to the world.

The world is plunging into hell's darkness and only the Church can enter the center of that darkness and destroy it. The world is experiencing the fires of hell and only the Church can enter these fires and destroy them. Jesus' death on the cross was the great moment when he entered the center of hell's powers. There will also be a modern moment, when the Church, in the person of the Holy Father, deliberately accepts its role of entering into the center of hell's destruction. That moment must be prepared for by devotion to my Immaculate Heart. This is not a new message but greater details are revealed.

Comment
This is an extraordinary locution. The message has been given often,
but now with a new sharpness.

October 2, 2014
6. Let the Nightly News Preach to You
Heaven's Power upon Present Human History
Mary

The battle between heaven and hell goes on, waged every single moment. Some call this human history, saying that these moments are always happening. However, my message is quite different. The human race is not just at another moment of its history. This is a moment of an abyss, a lowering, a going down, a falling into a pit. Will the floor of the earth open up and mankind find no ground for his feet? Has hell plotted a destruction of the human race which no one can imagine?

Look at the world scene. Let it preach to you. If you don't believe my words, then believe the words of those who bring you the news. Let them be your preachers. Each night, do they describe a world formed by heaven or by hell? Do they describe solutions and breakthroughs that will solve these problems? Or is the message always more somber, and everyone waits for the next development. You are seeing the unfolding of hell's plan, right before your eyes.

Only by my word can you believe that heaven also has a plan, a plan that waits and waits because what I have revealed is set aside and the Church takes another road for peace. However, a day will come when I will raise up him whom I have prepared at the very center of my heart. He will not equivocate. He will know only one road. He is the one whom I have chosen to open fully the doors of my Immaculate Heart. Pray for him.

Comment
People might not believe our Lady but they
cannot deny what they see on the nightly news.

October 3, 2014
7. Preparing for the Night

Heaven's Power upon Present Human History

Mary

The night is coming. When this happens, where will any light exist? In that moment, I want to lift up my Church and place it on the lampstand. It will give a different light, a light which cannot be put out by hell.

I speak now of great mysteries which cannot be comprehended. Mankind will enter into a darkness that will come from every side. All the usual lights will be put out. At the same time, an emergency light prepared by heaven will come on, a light that the Father has placed in my Immaculate Heart. How effective that light will be depends on two things.

First, the light will be in the Church, and only in the Church. I do not mean just the physical church, but in all that the Church does in and for the world. I want the world to acknowledge its own darkness and to see the great gift offered only by the Church.

However, how powerful this light will be and whether it will extend from one end of the earth to the other, depends upon the Church itself. That is why I must lift up the person who fully understands this truth, namely, that a moment will come when all is darkness except for the light placed by the heavenly Father in my Immaculate

Heart. The Church must realize this and be fully committed to the reign of my Immaculate Heart or the light will not go forth fully and completely.

Secondly, the light will go forth to people's hearts. If their heart loves my Immaculate Heart, then the light will be full. If not, then a purifying must take place so the light is effective.

The Church will be the bestower of light, and you, reader, the receiver of this light. Neither can remain idle. Both must seek the light in my Immaculate Heart before the night begins.

Comment:

All of this is a mystery which Our Lady tries
to describe in simple language.

October 4, 2014
8. The Light That Will Always Shine

Heaven's Power upon Present Human History

Mary

As the events happen, people are beginning to see the new realities of a world in which hell has been set loose. What was unimaginable is happening before their very eyes – a rise in violence, a spreading of disease, and many restrictions to their life of freedom. These are the ways of hell. Life narrows. Happiness is curtailed and fresh burdens are imposed. The purpose is to place clouds that cover over the sun of God's love so that people lose faith.

That is why I must speak. No clouds can cover the sun of my words, for they pierce every darkness. O reader, in the time ahead you will need my words! They will be one of the few lights that continue to shine.

Always remember my teachings on heaven and hell. Ascribe all that is evil to hell so you never want to be part of its legions. Always trust heaven. I have revealed the great secret. All of heaven's blessings are stored in my Immaculate Heart. The door is always open. You can enter any moment and take from my heart whatever blessing you might need. Always remember that only one road leads to peace. Only in my Immaculate Heart can all the blessings be found so easily. This is the Father's will and the secret I spend so much time explaining.

Comment

Our Lady concludes this series with a heartening invitation.

❖

The Mysteries of Mary's Immaculate Heart

October 5, 2014
1. The Seal of the Immaculate

The Mysteries of Mary's Immaculate Heart

Mary

All do not believe my words. Others believe but shrink from putting them into practice. What good are words which find no hearts that practice them? They are like seeds which fall by the wayside, producing no fruit.

It is not just faith, but action that is needed. If you believe, then preach. If you hope, then spread the word. If you pray, then gather others to pray. My people must rise up.

I do not ask protests in the streets or confrontations with authorities. I ask gatherings of prayer, large and small. I ask that the message be received and go forth. I will multiply your efforts. All that you need is to have your heart sealed by my heart. You must carry the sign of the Immaculata. In this sign, you will conquer.

I am finally reaching the deep truths, the mystical truths that cannot be erased by hell. I promise to work great mysteries in the hearts of all who are dedicated to my Immaculate Heart. These mysteries cannot be destroyed by hell because hell cannot understand them. In these mysteries, everyone will persevere, be protected, walk in my light and attract others. This is how I will raise up my army, by sealing every heart in my Immaculate Conception.

Comment
Our Lady brings us to a new mystery, some mystical action
upon the hearts of all who believe in her.

.

October 6, 2014
2. Being Sealed with the Immaculate Conception

The Mysteries of Mary's Immaculate Heart

Mary

All can be sealed with my Immaculate Heart from the least to the greatest. We come now to the heart of the mystery. I have spoken so frequently of world events and my Immaculate Heart as the road to world peace. These events are out of control because the fires of my heart have not been released. But the great mystery of this age takes place within the heart and the new graces that God is giving to the human race.

The Book of Revelation speaks of the seal of God on the foreheads of the elect (Ch. 7). Now, I speak of another mystery, revealed for this age which so needs the love and protection of a mother. My help is not just words or guidance or prophecy. I want to bring about a special grace for the whole world. I call it the seal of my Immaculate Conception.

Would anyone doubt that if I were living in this present age that I would persevere in any trials that are ahead? I suffered the greatest agonies and never wavered. No matter what the soldiers did to my Son, my own heart never wavered. I now want to give this same gift to all the world, from the least to the greatest. All of God's powers were contained in the first grace of my Immaculate Conception and I want to place this grace in everyone's heart. I call this "being sealed with my Immaculate Conception."

Comment
Our Lady is revealing the great mysteries
contained in her Immaculate Heart.

October 7, 2014
3. Plunged into the Holy Spirit
The Mysteries of Mary's Immaculate Heart

Mary

The power of my Immaculate Conception must go forth in new ways and I must first explain this gift. From the very beginning, the Lord conceived me. I was always in his mind as the mother of His Son. When sin entered the world, I took on another role. I was the Woman, the Woman whose Son would crush Satan's head and the Woman Clothed with the Sun.

Yet, I myself was to be conceived like everyone else, as a descendent of sinful Adam. I would be tainted by original sin. In light of the great mystery of Jesus, this could not be. So, the Father himself had to intervene with the greatest grace. I was physically conceived like everyone else, but as my soul came forth from the Father's hand, he plunged me into the Holy Spirit (who would be my spouse).

Satan believed that by leading the first parents into sin, he gained power over all their children, the entire human race. By this Immaculate Conception, for the first time, he had no control over a creature. I was not his. I was plunged into the Holy Spirit. This is the mystery of the Immaculate Conception. This immaculate gift is

190

thedoor out of sin and darkness, a surprising escape over which Satan has no power.

The Immaculate Conception is everyone's door to escape Satan's darkness. With these words, I begin to reveal the great mystery, the only road to peace.

Comment
Our Lady reveals the hidden mysteries
which happened over 2000 years ago.

October 8, 2014

4. Plunged into the Immaculate Conception

The Mysteries of Mary's Immaculate Heart

Mary

The time has come to reveal the great mysteries placed in my heart from all eternity. These mysteries are linked to the darkness that now covers the world and can be seen by all. O reader, search into these mysteries for they are God's saving actions for the present moment.

I was sealed with the Immaculate Conception and plunged into the Holy Spirit at the first moment of my conception. Even in my mother's womb, I was filled with the greatest light. Love for God overwhelmed me and I frequently leapt for joy, just as John the Baptist leapt in Elizabeth's womb.

While I was in the womb, God was revealing his divine plan. All during my life, I saw this plan unfold, and as the gospels say, "I kept all these secrets in my heart." Then came the culmination. As I was about to give Jesus back to the Father, he entrusted the whole world to me. "Woman behold your son," he said (Jn. 19:26).

Suddenly, every person in the world was placed in my womb and I was asked to give birth into life eternal for all. "What can I do?" I thought. Then, I realized what had happened to Jesus. He was plunged into the mystery of the Immaculate Conception. This favor was the only way the Father could prepare me for being Jesus' mother. I realized that the Father had created me without sin, not just for Jesus, but for every person born into this world.

I speak of all these favors for you to know. I was conceived immaculate for you and I want to plunge you into my Immaculate Heart. These mysteries must be known to realize the Father's plan. While the world is plunged into darkness, all can be plunged into my Immaculate Conception.

Comment
Our Lady is revealing why her Immaculate Heart is
central to our salvation from all darkness.

October 9, 2014
5. Repeating the Gift of the Immaculate Conception

The Mysteries of Mary's Immaculate Heart

Mary

My protecting hand will be upon everyone who is sealed with my Immaculate Conception. The Father plunged me into the Holy Spirit before he sent me into my mother's womb. This seal prevented the Evil One from gaining any control over me. This immaculate seal exercised a constant power over me, touching my body, my senses and all the faculties of my soul. The daily events and decisions had a much different effect upon me. Let me explain.

I experienced life on earth like anyone else, the normal growth of my body, the cares, the sorrows and the daily joys. However, everything within me was perfect because I had been conceived without sin. Darkness, disorders, fears, unjust anger, moods and so many other inner turmoils that plagued everyone else, had no power over me. I was sealed with the Immaculate Conception. All know that I deeply loved Jesus and saw him nailed to a cross, a suffering which I experienced daily because Simeon had prophesied that my own heart would be pierced with a sword. Although not spared these sorrows, because of the immaculate seal I was able to persevere because I enjoyed an unbelievable inner peace.

This is my gift to the whole world. The events will come. They will affect the good and the bad. (These are events that need not have happened if only my words were obeyed) because mankind has made its decisions. However, those sealed with my Immaculate Conception will share fully in the inner peace and, more important, in my perseverance to the end.

Let me repeat. "In these trials, I will never, never abandon my children. That is why I am revealing these secrets kept hidden until now. I will pour out the powers of my Immaculate Conception. I will seal the whole world (if it believes and so desires). In this way, I will defeat the Evil One just as the heavenly Father did when he plunged me into the Holy Spirit." The gift is meant to be repeated according to the capacity of each person.

Comment
Our Lady reveals a great mystery,
our own sharing in her Immaculate Conception.

October 10, 2014
6. Behold Your Mother

The Mysteries of Mary's Immaculate Heart

Mary

On Calvary, when Jesus said to the Beloved Disciple, "Behold your mother," God's plan unfolded before my eyes. I felt that the whole world was placed in my heart which had been prepared by the Immaculate Conception. I understood all my privileges and why I was so lowly. I understood all the events of my own life and all the mysteries of Jesus' life. I saw all of history, the ages past and the centuries to come. I saw the long lines of human persons who would be born and die. I saw everything, just as I saw the great mystery of Jesus' conception when explained by the Angel Gabriel.

Would I accept the Beloved Disciple as my son? Would I accept the whole world as my children? Would I be willing to experience their sufferings and sorrows, as I did with Jesus? How difficult to explain that moment. I was to begin again. Start over. Be a mother to everyone until the end of time. I was prepared for this by the Immaculate Conception, except that these children would not be sinless as Jesus had been.

My Immaculate Conception was not to preserve their sinlessness, but to bestow it. This is the mystery being revealed in these latter times, the riches of the Immaculate Conception must pour out upon the world.

There are two rivers, the river of hell and the river of my Immaculate Conception. In which river will mankind bathe? Which river will pull him along? Look at the world events! All can see clearly, the river of hell pulls mankind into its suffering.

There is another river, a river of grace flowing from God's throne. This river, from the beginning, always flowed through my heart. This river is my Immaculate Conception and I want these waters to flow into your heart.

Comment
Our Lady reveals her inner secrets which are
so important for the whole world.

October 11, 2014
7. Why is Mary Rejected?

The Mysteries of Mary's Immaculate Heart

Mary

I want to cover the whole world in my Immaculate Conception. I want its power to enter every heart and to wipe away every sin. I want to bring about a new world by plunging it into the Holy Spirit. That happened to me at my conception and it can happen to everyone. This is the mystery I am trying to reveal.

Why am I set aside? Why am I rejected? Because this mystery of my Immaculate Conception is misunderstood. The mystery is not about me, but about the Father's gift of the Holy Spirit. The Immaculate Conception was the Father's first action in fulfilling his promise of sending a Redeemer. By extending the Immaculate Conception to the whole world, Jesus wants to do to you what the Father did to me. He wants to plunge you into the Holy Spirit. Did not Jesus come "to take away the sins of the world"? How will he accomplish this task? He will use me as his instrument, like a flaming torch that burns away sin with the most gentle touch.

How many images must I use? The message is clear. The mystery is now revealed. In this final age, the Father has moved me onto the world stage. What was hidden can be seen by all. At the very moment when the fires of hell lap up the world, the Father reveals the greatest fire. Through the mystery of my Immaculate Conception, God will send the Holy Spirit to cleanse the whole world.

Comment

This series of locutions is now complete.
The power of the Immaculate Conception is available to everyone.

The Viruses in the Human Blood Stream

October 12, 2014
1. Dishonesty in the Money Supply

The Viruses in the Human Blood Stream

Mary

While the world keeps its eyes on the passing goals, changes take place every day which only weigh down the human heart. These forces are hidden but easily revealed. They are a growing stream, like infections in the blood, which slowly destroy life. As I enumerate and describe these deadly viruses, I will also be revealing the great need for the gifts that I have promised.

The first deadly virus is the dishonesty in the money supply, a disease that began slowly but is now totally out of control, beyond the powers of even the richest of nations. The sickness grows each day. The fever rises. No one responds. The solutions are too complicated and would require sacrifices which no one wants to make.

This is not like other problems which seem so real. Economic sickness does not kidnap, kill, execute or drop bombs. It shows up in numbers, on accounting sheets, as if the problems were only theoretical. The economic disease is no more theoretical than the ebola virus. Every day it claims more victims, strangling man's ability to act freely and to release blessings in which all participate.

I will speak more to these issues.

Comment
The world is like the human body. It has its life which is sometimes
very healthy and, at times, very sick. Our Lady will reveal
the problems in our blood stream.

October 13, 2014
2. The Social Consequences of Lust
The Viruses in the Human Blood Stream

Mary

Hidden diseases must come to light, but often it is too late because the illness has spread and grown too strong. Therefore, I must reveal these sinful and evil powers that are sapping the strength of humanity. Later, all will see that I have correctly diagnosed these powerful forces that lie hidden in man's blood stream.

A spirit of impurity imprisons mankind. From this comes disorder of every kind. Man is absorbed with his sexual powers and enshrines them like a goddess upon the throne of his heart. The inner disorder is multiplied by all the external stimuli that have so multiplied. At first society tolerated this misuse of technology. Now it welcomes it and protects. Enslaved to his passions, man sacrifices himself to this power of lust.

This is my teaching. Many discount this power of lust in causing the problems of mankind. They claim that the problems of lust begin and end with the person. This is not true. Lust releases powers within a society which cause great disorders. As a culture becomes saturated with lust, this lack of control extends to every aspect. Discipline breaks down. Disorders of every kind are tolerated. No one is held responsible. The human person withdraws from taking responsibility. Pleasures of every kind become man's focus. Has this not happened? Look and see.

O reader, remove lust from your heart. Struggle against every sexual disorder. Do not grow discouraged. I will be with you in this daily battle. Do not give in. Set a high standard. Use the sacraments. Those who teach you a different road only lead you into greater darkness.

Comment
In assessing the many external problems, we often overlook sexual disorders

October 14, 2014
3. The Stubbornness of the Human Heart
The Viruses in the Human Blood Stream

Mary

By God's will, I enjoy the fullness of his power in helping others. This is the mystery which I am revealing. Deep within man's heart is a great obstacle which must be removed. Everyone, at the very center of their personality, carries the sin of stubbornness, a pride, a refusal to submit, even when someone is trying to help them.

This stubbornness is present from the beginning, from the very first "no" said by the child to his parents. With adulthood, this stubbornness grows imperceptibly, a false feeling of wanting to be independent and submit to no one.

Certainly, the person should not submit to evil and darkness, but here I am speaking of not submitting to love, to God's love. This problem lies at the center of the human race. God is love and man more easily submits to Satan's hatred than to God's entreaties.

So, the Father sends the Woman! Does not a woman easily enter a person's heart? She plots and plans. She waits for her opening. She prepares delicious food and carefully dresses to attract. She knows when to speak and when to keep silent. Suddenly, when no one else had been able to enter, she arrives at the very center of the heart.

O reader, I know your heart, your stubbornness and your fierce independence that, on so many occasions, have caused you to throw away God's invitations and have thwarted his plans for your life.

The heavenly Father sends the Woman, clothes her with the Sun and places all his powers within her. Learn of me. See my ways. What has eluded you for years will suddenly be in your heart – an overcoming of your fierce independence and a total submission to God's love for you. This will be the new day, the beginning of new life.

Comment
So many of us are unaware of our inner forces,
which put up a wall against God's love.

October 15, 2014
4. An Experience of Holiness

The Viruses in the Human Blood Stream

Mary

So many are unaware of this war which takes place within the human heart. The enemy gains a stronghold and then, total control, as a particular evil is allowed to expand. Many people take on the challenges of life, but few accept the demands of purifying their hearts. I will show you what is needed.

The first gift is a conversion experience. This grace comes from my Immaculate Heart. I do not begin at the borders, the margins. I pierce to the very center, the core. I bathe in light. I reveal. I tear away the veils. The person cannot escape my light. They cannot flee from it because the light embraces them.

Nothing else matters. They see what they never saw before. The kingdom of God has suddenly entered their heart. They do not know how it got there. Although they had tried to be faithful, they never expected such a gift. They need only to accept it, and pay the price needed to cooperate with their new call. They were lost but now are found. The gift demands everything, but they see this as a small price to pay.

I am placing before you two realities, the hidden stream of sinfulness that flows in every human heart and the great experience of holiness that comes from my heart. This experience is the mystery that I am revealing. This experience of holiness is the only salvation for mankind and it is readily available in my Immaculate Heart. I was conceived without sin and I want to share this gift with everyone.

Comment
Our Lady does not combat our sins by making great demands on us.
Instead, she calls us to receive her gift.

October 16, 2014
The Locutions – An Abiding Gift

The Viruses in the Human Blood Stream

Mary

How many years have passed since we began this little path of the locutions? So many events have happened since then, and so many new evils have appeared on the stage of human history.

All of this I spoke about clearly, especially the important role that the Syrian revolution would play in being the spawning grounds of new evils. I foresaw all of these evils and began to speak years ago so my voice did not just ring out after everything had happened.

Recall that I spoke of many future events. When President Obama was at his political height, I said that he would be plagued by scandal after scandal that would reduce his powers. I spoke of terrorist groups and their growing effectiveness. I spoke of the many young Muslims who would see terrorism as their only hope. I spoke of the growing economic disorders which no one could control.

These are the themes that lead me to my teaching today.

These are not passing evils which the human race has constantly encountered, overcome and moved on. These are defining evils which want to change the face of the earth forever.

These locutions also are not just a passing gift. They are the seal of my promise that I will not abandon the world. I will be with you as the world plunges into these events. The events will happen. They are chastisements from the heavenly Father, needed to purify the world.

However, they can be softened and some can be removed. Much more important, I can guide you and your family through these events. I will come wherever I am invoked. When large groups cry out to me day and night, I will visibly change the situation and shorten the trial, so all know that their heavenly mother has visited them.

Comment
People perceive the modern events as very serious.
Our Lady, by these locutions, is giving more than just knowledge.
She promises her presence and protection.

October 17, 2014
6. Enlightened by Darkness

The Viruses in the Human Blood Stream

Mary

When the time comes for all of these events to unfold (and they will unfold one by one over a period of a year and a half), I will have prepared everything. Currently, the world sees only the evil forces, mounting their armies. They do not see what I am doing, because it is behind the scenes. I am preparing hearts. Some already know that they are an important part of my plan, like the visionaries at Medjugorje. Others know that I will use them, but they are unknown to the world.

This is my message, "Do not be afraid." The extraordinary events of evil will be more than matched by the extraordinary outpouring of my love. This love is already pouring out, even though I have not been invoked. It is flowing, even though there have been no outward signs (and these, too, will be part of my plan).

Now, I can only speak and describe. I give words and promises. But a time will come when I will pour forth power and glory, gifts both interior and exterior, all that is needed. I speak now so your eyes are opened and you can see. This is my promise. As you see each moment that evil spreads, when you learn about the extending power of darkness, at that very same moment, I am pouring out the greatest helps into your heart.

Do not be blinded by the darkness (that is what usually happens), but let the darkness enlighten you. Whenever you learn of new darkness, let it preach to you, "Mary is giving me new graces and I must be more faithful."

Go to Church. Go to confession. Be cleansed of your sins. Let your fears be removed. In this way, the world's darkness will have no power over you. I can save the whole world, but only if it listens.

Comment

In these days, great fears abound and darkness is everywhere.
Our Lady's words scatter that darkness and bring light.

October 18, 2014

7. Mary's Path

The Viruses in the Human Blood Stream

Mary

What is the path through all of these events? Satan will believe that he has entrapped the whole world. I will provide a path for everyone which will be right at hand. I will visit every heart and enlighten every mind.

It will be a time of a great coming together because people will need one another. To the heads of families, I will give great wisdom.

To my priests, I will give great zeal and extraordinary self-sacrifice, and to the Church I will give great light.

This is the moment when the Church will become the light of the world and I will begin to fulfill my mission as the Woman Clothed with the Sun. A world cast into darkness will become a humbled world, a repentant world, and the only light will be the Church.

I speak now because this cannot happen overnight. Years of preparation are needed. My message is: "Begin now for much time has already been wasted. Do not wait for the darkness; let me clothe you in my light from this moment forward."

199

All must begin, priest and people, young and old. Gather for the rosary. This is where I will begin, because Catholics understand this devotion. As you gather for the rosary, I will send many messengers of light. You will learn from them, all the many new and powerful devotions that I have revealed. Slowly, you will move ahead. As a person drawn by a powerful stream, you will be pulled more and more into my Immaculate Heart which is the new Ark of Noah. You and your loved ones will be safe, no matter now much it rains. But you must begin now. Too many delay and are unprepared. Begin now. Begin now. Begin now.

Comment

Our Lady's messages are always filled with hope.

She tells us where to begin.

Gather with others for the rosary.

October 19, 2014

8. Mary's Heart Permanently Opened

The Viruses in the Human Blood Stream

Mary

When I open up my heart, the gifts will flow out abundantly, every gift that is needed for every person on the face of the earth. Who will open my heart? The Holy Father will bring this about. He is the one to whom I have given this call so that the Church is seen by all as the true fountain of salvation.

All of this will happen as the world plunges deeper and deeper into darkness. At the same time, I will place in my Church new sources of light. Many will discount these rivers of light because they seem so small. However, they are little streams prepared to receive the great ocean that will pour forth. Otherwise, no hearts would be ready.

How often must I repeat the message? A time will come when the world will need my intervention. My coming will be internal and external. The internal gifts will be offered to everyone, but if the person is not prepared, if they have no capacity to receive, then the ocean cannot fill them.

These locutions began years ago, long before any of these world events happened. They are a sign that I have foreseen and have prepared for this moment. My promises are true. When the Holy Father consecrates Russia to my Immaculate Heart, this will begin an uninterrupted flow of graces, unknown up to now, which will constantly flow. My heart will be permanently opened according to the new design of the Father's plan. Unforeseen and unimaginable blessings will pour out. At the very

200

moment of the greatest darkness, suddenly a road to peace will appear. All will know that my help came from heaven through the Catholic Church. This is the Father's plan.

Comment
Our Lady describes in greater detail the effects of Russia being consecrated.

October 20, 2014
9. Becoming a Traveler
The Viruses in the Human Blood Stream

Mary

Take little steps into the light and suddenly a road will appear. This will be my road for you. It awaits you. It is prepared for you and will lead you through the coming darkness. Do not wait because you will not find this road once the darkness comes.

For every person in the world, I have prepared a road of light. It is not far away. No need to travel to foreign lands. The road comes to you. It is at your doorstep, even within your own home and among your own family.

Let the world events preach to you. They can say it better than any preacher, but their message is only half the truth. They can say, "The darkness is coming," but they cannot speak of a road of light, because that is the message hidden in my heart.

Let me bring all of these teachings together for you. Begin right now. Look into your heart. Discover the faith and the practices of faith that you already have. What practices have you abandoned and set aside? Start with these. They are familiar. Be faithful to them each day. By doing this, you will set out and start on your journey. You will become a traveler. A traveler looks and searches. He is not at home. He is not content. He must find his way.

When you become a traveler, I will guide your steps. You will find fellow travelers who, like you, are searching. They are your road and you are their road. Join together in your searching. In this way, others can join with you and find their road. Do not separate. While you are together and helping one another, I can protect you.

Comment
Our Lady is very practical. Each person has some familiar devotions (often set aside).
They must take them up again. Soon, you will meet others who are also searching.
Join with them and help each other along the road.

The Modern Crises

October 21, 2014
1. The Middle East

The Modern Crises

Mary

In the past, I have spoken about terrorism, saying that terrorist groups were small and fragmented, but that they would grow and come together as a more powerful force. The timetable of their violence would jump ahead because of the American withdrawal and that the Syrian revolution would not end quickly (as the other revolutions did). That it would continue, and from Syria would come forth the destruction of stability in the Middle East. All of this is now before your eyes. It has taken place. The Middle East has become Satan's boiling pot.

Now, I must begin to speak again. The Middle East is the sorrow of my heart. In sorrow, I pour out my words. At this point, there is no human answer. What could have been prevented now exists. The fires have spread too far and too rapidly. The groups have become too strong, too widespread, and too well known in the Muslim world. Their growing fame is their strong point, constantly attracting young Muslims who finally see a cause that has power against the West. This touches the deepest parts of the young, who grew up in hopelessness. It fans emotions that lead to great sacrifice. The young are swept along by an illusion of a new world, not knowing that violence never ceases.

So, I will begin to teach, to instruct, to enlighten, so all the world can know the future of terrorism and the threats that it poses.

Comment
Our Lady returns to a theme that filled many of the earlier locutions.

October 22, 2014
2. The Dream of the Terrorists

The Modern Crises

Mary

I must speak quickly about this threat of terrorism. The Middle East is like a caldron that burns deeply and many people see the West as their enemies. Their eyes are always on the West. Their minds are filled with the grievances which they hold against the West and their hearts are filled with hatred.

As the wars go on and the violence destroys their own countries, the fires of hatred grow greater. Fires send off sparks and great fires send their sparks flying in every direction.

Although the West is beginning to grasp the seriousness of the threat, so much has happened, that the fires cannot be put out. Many have acted in hatred. They have joined together and have seen great destruction which, in their eyes, are good results.

The terrorists see themselves on a road, and this road leads westward to all the great cities of the world. They want those cities, first to terrorize, then to destabilize, and finally to conquer and own. They do not yet have this capability, but it will suddenly be theirs if more powerful weapons fall into their hands and if they can extend their organization.

Need I say more about this terrible threat whose desires have no limit? I am the Woman of Fatima and I have promised world peace through my Immaculate Heart. When will the whole Church heed my voice?

Comment

Our Lady looks ahead and sees the forces of
terrorism that have not yet unfolded.

October 22, 2014
3. The Ebola Crisis

The Modern Crises

Mary

I will speak of the Ebola crisis. This epidemic is caused by the breakdown of governments and the corruption that so plagues Africa. It arises from the poverty and the social conditions of the people. These should never have existed. They are conditions brought about by sinfulness and selfishness.

Who will break these long-standing practices, whereby those who come to power serve themselves? They turn all to their own benefit, and literally rape their people. Do not blame these evils upon the Almighty God. They are afflictions that inevitably happen when people are forced to live in poverty. God's blessing should have been flowing to these nations, but corrupt officials block progress and keep the people in a lowly condition. I will speak more to this topic.

There is a demonic hold upon Africa which must be broken, so Africa can fulfill its role in the family of nations. People always expect its great emergence because it is blessed by so many resources. This will never take place until Satan's hold over that continent is broken and the streams of grace flow freely.

I have begun my great work at Kibeho and the flames of my heart will go out from there.

Comment
Our Lady pinpoints the grave evils in Africa –
government corruption and Satanic powers.

October 23, 2014

4. Poverty – The Seedbed of Evil

The Modern Crises

Mary

All is separating, dividing and pulling apart because the rich have separated from the poor. I will not allow the rich to sit at a table filled with abundance while the poor are excluded.

So, where do the problems begin? With the disadvantaged, because they are wounded and hurt. They lie by the wayside and when the Good Samaritan does not come for them, they are easy prey for those who seek only evil.

They cannot overcome violence, nor the temptation to respond with violence. Their situation is an open door to those who would exploit them. Now, the harvest suddenly appears—terrorism in some areas, Ebola in others. Poverty is the seedbed and, for so long, the rich nations have exploited the poorer ones, using every means to sustain their own lifestyles and taking no account of the lifestyle of the poor nations. Look at all these seedbeds and realize that the world of evil has many fields that have not yet brought forth their harvest.

These seeds have been sown for centuries, and only now comes forth the full harvest. What can be done at this late date? What efforts can overcome evil that has so long been allowed to grow?

The answers are not easy. The road to world peace is not short, but if the world will just listen to me, at least it will find that road. Right now, all is confusion, and millions are spent on weapons that destroy, instead of addressing the poverty that enables the evil to flourish.

Comment
Satan stirs up the violence but the great injustices done to the poor nations
provide the seedbed of this destruction

October 24, 2014
5. The Ultimate Question People Ask

The Modern Crises

Mary

As all the problems break forth at once, the question arises, "What is this present age?" This is the ultimate question. Dare I give the answer? I must speak now, always with a message of hope. Let me begin this way.

I came to Fatima because I foresaw this present age. I came in the middle of what was called the Great War and promised that the war would end successfully. However, I saw on the horizon a second, greater war, which I said would happen if people did not heed my voice. I even promised Lucy that great sign which was seen and recorded by scientists.

My messages went beyond that Second World War and prophesied the destruction of nations. I must say clearly that this is the present age. The world has not yet reached that point and all that I have said can still be avoided, but the time is very short. I can no longer hold back my sorrow. I must continue to speak. The present problems will open out to newer and greater ones. All will unfold in Satan's plans unless the Woman Clothed with the Sun steps forward to touch earth. This is the remedy, the antidote chosen beforehand by the Heavenly Father.

Is this "present age" to be stolen from me? The heavenly Father had quite different plans. This was to be a glorious age, the Age of Mary, the age of peace, when Satan would be humbled and even conquered. Alas, this has not happened. However, the gift and the promise still exist.

Yes, this present age is the culmination of events, but I will be with you, releasing my powers whenever I am invited and, at some point, the fullness of the gift will pour forth.

Comment
*Our Lady's message is filled with travail and hope – as she addresses
the ultimate question, "What is the present age?"*

Personal Spiritual Growth

October 25, 2014
1. Having Your Own Locutions

Personal Spiritual Growth

Mary

In the midst of these problems, how do you find the way to peace? I will speak. Listen to my promptings. Where do I speak? In the quiet of your heart. I begin right now. Stop and listen. Do not fear if I chastise you. Some parts of your life might have to change. They are just obstacles that need to be swept away so you can see the road ahead.

I speak in these locutions but they are external words, general words of guidance for all the world. I promise to also speak to every heart. How do I speak? What words do I use? From reading the locutions, you know that I speak clearly and simply. I do not use big words but little words that even a child can understand.

You also know that I point out what needs to be changed, but always with words of encouragement. You know that my words are filled with promises and hope. I speak gently and invite, so no one is scared away. This is how I will speak to you in your own heart.

Can I not pour out the gift of locutions upon the whole world? I do not mean that I will give you great words that should be published. I will give you little words to guide you on your path. Once in a while, I will give you words for others, for your family or your friends. At times, I will want you to do a work for me. Then, I will speak more strongly in your heart, when you are better prepared.

How faithful you have been in reading these locutions. By doing so, you have learned to listen to my words spoken in your own heart. Be still. Pray. Go into your own heart. You will find me waiting there for you.

Comment
Our Lady, surprisingly, turns quickly from world events,
to invite us to personal prayer and spiritual growth.

October 26, 2014
2. Places and Groups Dedicated to Mary

Personal Spiritual Growth

Mary

How many Churches are dedicated to me. How many shrines and groups bear my name. This is where I will begin because it will be so clear that I am acting. Every place and every group that bears my name and has been placed under my care will be a place where my blessings will begin to pour forth.

I will pour out my gifts at these special places so faith will grow. People will know that I have not abandoned them in these difficult hours. So, let this word go forth. I will visit every place that bears my name. When people enter that Church or shrine, I will be there to meet them.

Let them bring their sorrows and their pains. I will console everyone. Tears will flow and peace will come. Hearts will be strengthened and the signs and wonders can take place. People will know that I have heard their prayers and listened to their sighs. Unexpected answers will be given. All of this is to stir up faith, to strengthen hearts and to give inner joy. As others learn that a place has become a great source of consolation, they, too, will come.

I do not point out one Church or shrine. The needs are too great. But the great shrines will grow even stronger because there my name has been constantly invoked. The crowds there will grow greater. I have planted this blessing on the very foundation of that Church or shrine. Those who named it had faith in me. Now, I want to release the hidden stream contained in that faith.

O reader, where is there a Church or shrine or group dedicated to me? Go there often and I will release this hidden stream into your life.

Comment

We need Mary's promises to stir our faith.
Whenever you are in a Church or at a shrine dedicated to her,
know that she will fulfill these promises.

October 27, 2014

3. Promises for Those Who Gather

Personal Spiritual Growth

Mary

All must gather. In the gathering I will manifest my presence and pour forth my gifts. Many will be converted. They will see what must be changed. I will call others to great works. All will be zealous for my name to be exalted.

In the gatherings, I will pour out great faith, an inner gift of peace filled with confidence, a belief that I am able to rescue all who trust in me. I will place many gifts within the person. These gifts will be oil for the lamps, which cannot be purchased at the last minute.

I will be with you. I will dwell in your hearts and pour out my strength, but these gifts must be received now. The strengthening is today and every day. The secret lies in the gatherings. Begin in the home. Gather for prayer. I will visit you. If groups of families are of one accord, then let them gather in larger numbers. I will raise up many and bless their efforts to gather even more people in public places. Here, too, I will be present.

This is my great promise. In this time of so many problems, I will bless, protect, guard and guide all who gather in my name. I will cover them with my mantle, protecting them in ways both hidden and seen. I will go with them wherever they go. I will guide their steps and keep them away from all that endangers them, in body or soul. These are my promises upon all who gather each day in my name.

Comment
Gatherings invite us. When we have another who shares
in our prayer, we have found a true friend.

October 28, 2014
4. Freeing from Drug Addictions

Personal Spiritual Growth

Mary

I open my heart and invite everyone to see flames of love which leap up within. These flames will purify any heart which decides to enter. Do not fear, the flames are gentle. The warmth that you feel will console you and free you. I am opening my heart in this new way because so many have become entangled in vices that have taken control. There is no other means available to bring about the cleansing.

I speak now to those addicted to drugs. Some are deeply involved in heroin. Others have become attached to prescription medications. Some believe that they need to use marijuana to relax. To all of these, I offer these flames of freedom.

As I remove the addiction, you will not panic. I will substitute a new confidence, a peace which fills you and assures you that you can live without these drugs. I will take you quickly, but step by step. I know your fears and the hold which the Evil One has upon you. I will break that hold. This will be the first gift. You will enjoy a newly discovered freedom.

Where will you find this gift? Go to a church or a shrine that is dedicated to me. That will give you a special faith that I am there. When you go there, think of only one thing, that your heavenly Mother waits for you. Come often. Stay even for just a few minutes. That is all I need to bring you into the flames in my heart. Use the title of that place to ask for these favors. The name is very important, chosen by Church authorities.

Comment
Personal spiritual growth always begins with freedom from evil powers.

October 29. 2014
5. New Chambers of Mary's Heart

Personal Spiritual Growth

Mary

The great mysteries unfold and the power contained in these flames of my love comes forth only when I enter into a person's life. I must now reveal the great mysteries, hidden for all the ages and made known in this special time.

I speak now to those who love me and serve me. I know your fidelity. I know your longing for me. But I say to you. You do not yet know me because so many mysteries that have been hidden will be hidden no more. As they come forth, you will see how small was the light that you previously had, like the light of the stars compared with the sun.

I will be everywhere. I will consume your thoughts and fill your affections. What you received up to now was little. What you knew about me was quite small. All will multiply – your knowledge, your faith, your love, your surrender. This will prepare you for the multiplication of my blessings and protections.

I declare a new day. Those who know me will understand that they did not know me. All of this will happen in the new light that I am casting upon the world. Do not judge as you judged in the past. Do not think as you thought before. The new light will open unseen vistas, new mysteries and deeper understandings.

I invite the whole world into chambers of my heart that, up to now, have been accessible only to the great saints. Read the books of all those saints who wrote about me. Their gifts will be your gifts.

Comment
In these days of great darkness, Our Lady opens new gifts.

October 30, 2014
6. Pouring Out the Great Gifts

Personal Spiritual Growth

Mary

There are too many delays. Too much time passes. The great gifts are meant to flow out of my heart and into the hearts of all who believe. Instead, believers are caught up in other pursuits. They do not judge correctly. They do not see the coming collapse, when so much of what they now seek and hope for will be taken away from them.

Never have Jesus' words been more important. "Do not seek what passes away. Lay up treasure in heaven." The world you see will pass away so quickly. What existed will suddenly no longer exist. What stood so firm will stand no more.

This is not the time for buying and selling but for receiving the great gifts from above. These are stored deeply in my heart and are readily available. If I spoke of great penances or of long labor, I would understand your hesitancy. But I speak of gifts, of receiving, of being filled and blessed. I speak of the important gifts that you will need so badly. I will list them.

I will give to all the gifts of prayer, a constant attraction to come into my presence, and to withdraw from the powers of the senses in order to enjoy the riches of the kingdom.

I will give you love for your family and forgiveness towards those who have hurt you. I will give you great hope. You will enjoy holy desires to accomplish everything. I will give you friends who will accompany you in the difficult times that lie ahead.

Finally, I will give you my presence, an experience that I am with you at all times and that you enjoy my special protection. These are the important gifts. Do not search for any others. If you empty your heart, I will gladly fill it to the brim. Do not wait. The time is very short. Receive these gifts today.

Comment

What an invitation! Who should not want to receive heavenly gifts?

Preparing for the Worldwide Events

October 31, 2014
1. The Path of Hope

Preparing for the Worldwide Events

Mary

I am the Mother of Holy Hope and anyone who enters my heart finds themselves filled with hope. They can give no reason for this hope because all the signs point to despair and ruin. Yet, this great feeling, that no matter what happens I will guide them through, permeates their being. They cannot account for this gift, nor even know how to bring it about, but they are clothed in a hope that overcomes all despair.

Right now, people place their hopes in all that they have stored up. They watch their financial investments very closely and keep an eye on their assets. They calculate their income and weigh it against their debts. This is the normal course of human hope. But when the financial markets collapse, when fortunes are wiped away, when currency is devalued, when the foundations of the American economy are shaken and topple, where will be their hope?

Because of these problems, I speak now and say, "Prepare!" Yes, steps must be taken, but what steps? Without divine hope, you take the wrong steps. Let me teach you what to do.

First, stop putting your trust in material wealth. Jesus says that it is easily stolen away. Go to a church dedicated to me. I will be waiting for you. Present to me all of your financial responsibilities and I will give you very simple wisdom. Slowly, your attitude toward material wealth will change. You will place more emphasis on love for others and strong personal relationships. You will see where you have neglected these important foundations of security.

You will see that you and your loved ones need a much deeper practice of your faith. I will rekindle the religious spirit that alone can truly bind a family. You will dedicate less time to storing up material wealth and more time in seeking first the kingdom of God. Only then, will you be walking my path of true hope.

Comment
The financial future is very questionable.
Our Lady provides the true secrets of security and hope.

November 1, 2014
2. The Weakness of the Economic System

Preparing for the Worldwide Events

Mary

Whatever is in my heart will be saved. Whatever is not in my heart will be lost. It will be like the days of Noah when only those in the ark did survive.

People will say that this is not fair. Why should they be swept away? But it is fair. God has spoken. His word goes forth. The word tells everyone to repent and to seek the kingdom of God. Yet, the world sets aside that word, having no interest in responding to Jesus' pleas. That is why I must speak out about this need to repent and to do so now.

O reader, in the following locutions, I will put before you every possible teaching, filled with images, with words of warnings and of encouragement. If you open your heart to these words, I will fill you with light to see what you can do to prepare for the future events. I speak these words because I foresee what is ahead, just as the heavenly Father instructed Noah because He foresaw the great flood.

Indeed, a great flood is coming that will cover the whole earth, not with water but with collapses, especially economic collapses that will trigger widespread breakdowns. These economic systems have been built on the shakiest of foundations. Many are quite aware that everything could topple, triggering world-wide events. I want to prepare you for these events just as the Father prepared Noah.

Comment
Our economic foundations have been weakened for decades.
No one knows the future.

November 2, 2014
3. Loss of Confidence

Preparing for the Worldwide Events

Mary

I will not hold back any of my sorrows, because I see the afflictions that will soon come upon the face of the world. Mankind plunges ahead, totally unaware of the path it has chosen.

For decades, countries have lived beyond their means with an ever-expanding use of credit. The money supply has increased to feed the appetites, but with no foundation in reality. All is based upon a false confidence that this will just continue and that life will not be interrupted. The system is weak, and as the money flows, leaks will appear. Nothing will be done and the leaks will be papered over – yes, papered over by false money, guaranteed by absolutely nothing.

All of this can only go on for a limited time. Inevitably, somewhere the gigantic leak happens, and the false confidence in the economic system is destroyed. As the system collapses, everything comes to a halt, and efforts to revive the economy are of no avail.

Many see this scenario on the horizon, but they have no answers because governments cannot respond politically to what is needed. This is the present road of mankind and no one can tell when or where the collapse will take place.

The collapse will inevitably come, but if a person, a family, a community, even a nation accepts my gifts, they will survive. It is not the wealthy who will survive, nor those who hold power. Only the man of faith, the family of faith, the community or nation of faith will make the long-term commitment needed to ride out the storm.

Comment
Our Lady continues to speak of the difficulties present in our economic system.

November 3, 2014
4. The Steps to Collapse

Preparing for the Worldwide Events

Mary

The events will begin with a jolt, a partial collapse from economic difficulties in one part of the world. All will view this with alarm but no one will see this as the beginning of a series of events.

In the beginning, there will be enough resources to paper over the damage so that confidence is restored. Many, however, will see this as a sign to move their assets. This will hasten the events as other parts of the economic structure are exposed as weak and unstable. The economic world is volatile, based so much on trust and confidence in the system itself. As these weaknesses are exposed, the confidence will slowly evaporate and even the strongest structures will come under assault.

The world has built an economic system which will not stand the test of its sins, of its margins of profit, of its false foundation, and of the burden it has put upon the poor nations. Fairness and equity have long since been discarded. Systems have been built around conference tables, making decisions that favor those who sit at those tables.

Now comes the time of reckoning. The bills are long overdue. The economic system cannot continue. It does not need God's chastising hand. It will collapse from its own frailty.

A time of a complete reassessment will begin. Many will focus on economics. Few will focus on a change of heart, of repentance, of a return to God and religious practice. I speak now for those who will listen to my voice. These days are precious. Do not waste them. Return now to God. Reorder your day. Pray from your heart. I will help you with extraordinary graces. Much will be prepared. New beginnings. Deeper peace. Fresh faith and hope. Deeper love for your family. All must share my new gifts. Do not wait. Do not wait.

Comment
In spite of the darkened future, Our Lady always speaks of action and hope.

November 4, 2014
5. We Will Begin Again

Preparing for the Worldwide Events

Mary

When all the events culminate and the economic systems are in ruins, man will see what he has brought about. Almighty God created the universe, but mankind constructed his economies. When mankind sees what has happened, he will remember the former glory when he bought and sold and traded with great glee. Man will say, "Let us rebuild." What fools! You know only how to rebuild a system that has collapsed. You know only how to build on the backs of the poor. You know only how to rebuild for your own advantage. But I have stripped you and exposed you to public view. Your sins are evident to all.

Repentance must set in, accompanied by a turning to God. "We will rebuild" is the wrong approach. You must say, "We will worship God and he will help us." The economic collapse will allow the religious spirit to be released upon the world. Many will be in despair, not knowing what they must do. However, those whom I have trained, who read these words and put them into practice will survive these events because their lives are built on faith and not on the "almighty" dollar. Such will be the state of the world after the economic collapse.

For many, it will be too late. Long ago they set aside their faith, and will be unable to find any inner strength to survive these events. Others will be confused, not knowing what to do. They will cling to their families and loved ones to survive. But others will discover new powers in their Catholic faith. They will find others who also are returned to faith.

We will begin again. This is my promise. We will not seek to rebuild. We will seek rather to begin again. Even in the midst of destruction, I will give new life. I promise, "We will begin again," and the religious spirit will once more call America back to life.

Comment
Our Lady continues to describe the economic collapse and its aftermath.

November 5, 2014
6. The Next President
Preparing for the Worldwide Events

Mary

The washing, the cleansing, the purifying, and the stripping away come only with great pain and hardship. All of this is needed for an economic system that is built on poor foundations. The market forces will be violent and unforgiving. No one will be able to chart the correct course. How important is the choice of the next president. So, let me speak to this choice that lies two years ahead.

The problem with America lies not primarily in its economy, but in its morality and loss of faith. Its economy runs like a wild horse, with a government paying no attention to the realities. However, this is just a symptom of an America run wild, with no restraints upon its desires and instincts, and little relationship to Almighty God. The economic collapse is tied directly to its secularism. Moving away from God has deceived America into moving away from economic restraints.

Everything is coming to a head and nothing can prevent the economic collapse. So, who will lead America through these troubled times? That will be the task of the next president. How important is this choice. The next president will need the greatest skills and the trust of everyone, on both sides of the aisle. The person must be a believer, with a heart rooted deeply in faith, and a life that is exemplary. The next president must do what is right and make the difficult decisions. The American people must not look at superficial qualities, like oratorical skills. They must look to the heart of the candidates, to their truth and their goodness, because the next president must inspire a country that will be going through devastating times.

Comment
With the mid-term elections completed, America turns to the 2016 elections. Our Lady prophesies extraordinary difficulties and the need for a president with great integrity.

❖

The Year Ahead

November 6, 2014
1. The Four Difficulties of the Coming Year

The Year Ahead

Mary

The year ahead will be filled with difficulties and dangers. Difficulties will come from events. Dangers will involve human decisions. The difficulties cannot be avoided. They will happen. The dangers will come about from the wrong human responses.

I speak now about this year to come for many reasons. I am not appealing to man's curiosity to know future events. I speak to console my children and to give them direction. I speak now of this coming year from a distant perspective. As this year goes on, I will speak more particularly. In this way, your minds are somewhat prepared and can better understand. Let us begin.

Many explosive forces lie right beneath the surface of world events. They are difficulties waiting to burst forth. In the coming year some, but not all, of these difficulties will surface. They will cause many difficulties and some aspects of human life will be changed forever.

More dangerous, however, will be the world's response to these difficulties. People will want to regain what they formerly had. World leaders will feel pressured to find quick solutions when really none exist. I will outline specific areas of these difficulties and decisions.

Putin will continue his aggressive strikes to gain lands and to destabilize Europe. The West has no wisdom or capability to encircle him and keep him contained.

Muslim terrorists will grow much stronger. The West has been disengaged from the fight and, as the threat grows, will grow even weaker in its resolve.

The biggest difficulties lie in the economies, which are too bloated, and long ago have cut themselves off from reality. All is pretend. Trillions of dollars are just shifted around, a paper network that feeds upon itself.

The Ebola crisis will not be solved. Thousands will die. This is the effect of widespread poverty inflicted upon the people by corrupt African governments and worldwide economic policies.

Comment
Our Lady outlines these four difficulties in the coming year.
In doing so, she shows that she will be offering her help.

November 7, 2014
2. The Downward Spiral

The Year Ahead

Mary

The events will rush in from every side, far beyond the capacity of the world to respond. A cycle will be created, one event feeding the other and leading to the next in a downward spiral.

The world will have no firm footing. Anxiety will be everywhere. Man will look to his own strengths and find them greatly wanting. They will then reevaluate all of their leaders. A sobering process will set in.

Into this setting, I will raise up people of integrity, whose hearts seek the good of the people and who walk in truth. A complete shift in thinking will occur and those who brought about these conditions will be in disgrace. Their foolishness will be unveiled for all to see.

But the response to these problems must go far deeper than choosing new leaders. America must return to the religious spirit which it has set aside for so long. There will be important religious leaders who can lead millions back to faith.

These events will bring about the time for a great decision, because America will be at the crossroads. Those who choose the path of faith will find comfort and hope, even in the greatest trials. Those who seek secular solutions will experience only despair.

Prepare. Prepare. Prepare for this coming year. Do not delay. Make every effort to reclaim and to deepen your religious practices. I will give you surprising success and new helps.

Comment
Even in speaking about events that are out of control,
Our Lady shows a path of hope.

November 8, 2014
3. Hope amid the Implosion

The Year Ahead

Mary

As gaping holes open up and the shortages of resources become evident, great fears will grip so many. They will realize that irrevocable changes have taken place which have no solutions. The sinful decisions that have been made for decades, the wasteful spending, the false money supply, and the credit that expanded beyond

217

control have finally hit their limit, an inevitable outcome of the present policies.

There will be an implosion. When gigantic waves hit a wall, they turn back upon themselves. Instead of expanding, everything will contract. How far this will happen, no one will know. Only time and the market forces will determine the final outcome.

All will be swept up in these financial collapses, from the richest financier to the poorest citizen. That is the nature of an economy. It is a system that embraces all.

Why do I speak when there is such an inevitability, when the forces move ahead with no restraint? My goal is the salvation of souls, that all arrive in their heavenly home. Satan will use all of these disasters to cast the world into darkness and despair. I have constantly taught that Satan causes sufferings. He uses sufferings to cast a darkness. He uses the darkness to get souls into despair. He uses despair so people end up in his hands and not in mine.

So, I speak to give hope. Where there is hope, there is light. Where there is light, the sufferings are less. When the sufferings are less, people can find their way to heaven. There is so much more to say. I will continue to speak during this year as the events come closer.

Comment
Our Lady always gives hope.

November 9, 2014
4. Satan's End Game

The Year Ahead

Mary

The gaps continue to widen and the economic structures grow weaker daily. There are also the gigantic costs of waging wars and the destruction of nations and societies. The problems are not limited to one place or to one area of society.

Satan's plan has been manifold. He has placed his dynamite everywhere, in the hearts of his chosen leaders like Putin, in the hearts of the Muslim radicals, in the hearts of politicians making self-serving decisions, and in the hearts of all who have been caught up in selfish lifestyles. His dynamite is planted everywhere, in the wars, the killing of the unborn, and the total turning away from religious practices, which have prepared for his end game.

That is the word that I have held back until now – the endgame. The world is entering the era of Satan's endgame, the goal he has had, not for just one century but for twenty centuries, ever since Jesus defeated him on Calvary and the gospel went forth. After that, he suffered many defeats. The word of God spread. Believers were baptized. Satan was renounced. Cultures were formed, especially in the Middle East and the West. Missionaries went forth to Latin America and to Africa. The waters of Baptism were putting out the fires of hell. Satan was being cast out.

So, he developed a new strategy. He could not put out the light of Jesus' resurrection but he could cover it over. So, he began, especially with the French Revolution and installing the goddess of reason in a church dedicated to me. Then, he sowed the seeds of hatred, leading to two world wars. He brought the world into the atomic age, the electronic age, the worldwide, global economy. All of these were established on poor foundations, easily able to bring about worldwide chaos and destruction. How many times I have already saved the world, as in the Cuban missile crisis.

Now, I use these little locutions to speak. In the face of all of these sources of destruction, I promise to do all in my power to save the world. However, the time is not just short, Satan has begun the events leading to his endgame strategy. The Church must be aware. The Holy Father must awaken to this new reality. More important, you, the reader, must run to me with total hope in your heart. I will save whoever comes to me.

Comment
Our Lady helps us to look down the road that the world is traveling.

November 10, 2014
5. Babylon Is Fallen

The Year Ahead

Mary

Walls are built to protect cities and systems. Walls were also built to protect banks and economies. These were the rules which governed the financial markets. These walls have been destroyed, not by God, but by man himself by decisions made secretly and unknown to many.

Voices were raised in warning but were not heeded. Year after year, the broken walls allowed enemies to enter who consumed the wealth of nations. Yes, the wealth of entire nations has been stolen. These nations are worse than bankrupt. They are flooded in debt. Do not blame God for these problems. Man has violated every law of God, the laws that demand honesty and true accounting.

Long ago, you removed your walls. The enemies are not at the gates. They are within your city, too numerous for you to dispel or overcome. These enemies will consume you. You will no longer own your own cities. Others will claim

219

them. America, you have sold yourself into the slavery of debt. You are owned by others who soon will come to claim what is truly theirs. Then, your shame shall be seen. You will be like the fallen Babylon. Merchants will grieve over you. Those who sold you their goods will also despair. You were their richest customer but now your economy is in shambles.

Can I save you? Are there not ten just men in your midst? I will save, but only those who follow me, the Woman Clothed with the Sun.

Comment
Our Lady alludes to the fall of Babylon in Revelation, Chapter 18,
and the saving of Lot's family in Genesis, Chapter 19. Read those texts.

November 11, 2014
6. Israel and Iran

The Year Ahead

Mary

Where do all these events lead? I must again speak of Israel, the forgotten nation in the Middle East conflicts. Satan has his eyes on Jerusalem. Jerusalem is his prize. There he was defeated and cast out. God's blood still abides in that city and it has never lost its place in my heart.

The fires that ravage the Middle East are really aimed at Israel and its destruction. Satan has never lost sight of that goal. Other world leaders have set Israel aside and have jeopardized its existence. They have even signed treaties with Iran, which has pledged to destroy Israel.

World leaders walk in such darkness that Satan easily plans his steps. They do not grasp what is of true value. So, I must speak. Israel sees itself abandoned. Its enemies are protected. Its friends are absorbed with other goals. It stands alone. Better than any other nation, Israel knows the dangers that imperil its existence. It sees that it cannot wait. Others will not act in its defense, so it will act on its own. It cannot allow the tide to continue to flow in. It cannot allow these events to take their course, because their course is the destruction of Israel.

In Israel's eyes, everything is clear. Its enemies are strong and near. Its friends show no interest and are powerless to put out the Middle East fires. So, it must act in its own defense. It cannot allow a nuclear Iran.

Comment
Our Lady says that Israel will take whatever steps are needed
to prevent Iran from getting nuclear arms.

November 12, 2014
7. The Two Floods

The Year Ahead

Mary

Once the walls break down, who can stop the floods? Who can even predict where the waters will go? Do they not take on their own life, set free to flow anywhere? Such will be the flow of events once the walls are pierced, the weak and tottering walls that many know cannot hold back the floods of events.

There will be many floods, all converging and aiding one another in their destructive paths. The convergence is deliberate, the design of the Evil One who has plotted out this moment for centuries.

He believes that his plans are foolproof. He has arranged the people whom he needs as leaders. He has stirred up the hearts of millions who are ready to respond to his signal. He has weakened all the resources that can be used against him. He has led Western nations into financial debt. He has weakened the resolve of millions by their sinful lifestyles. He has slain millions of children in the wombs of their mothers.

Is this not a true picture? Who will argue against me? Who will defend the opposite positions? Will not all of these forces continue? Who will reverse the tide? This is my surprise, the promise which flows from the deepest regions of my Immaculate Heart.

To Satan, his plans seem perfect, flawless and inevitable. But even he knows that the Woman is his enemy and that she stands on the sidelines, still not invoked or invited to come full into the battle.

This is my promise. As the events begin (and remember there will be a series of events) an opening will be created. Voices will be raised. "Why has Russia not been consecrated as Our Lady has asked?" Other events, within the Church, will coincide. Finally, the consecration of Russia will take place. A surprising flood will be released. There will then be two floods, good and evil, one destroying and the other saving.

Comment
Our Lady describes the first flood, which we can all see.
She promises a second flood of her blessings when Russia has been consecrated.

To Faithful Catholics

November 13, 2013
1. Overcoming the Darkness

To Faithful Catholics

Mary

These events will come forth because human history moves on, bringing forth what has been imbedded in its past. I have tried to describe those forces that have been placed in the stream, waiting beneath the surface and ready to come forth. Now, I must move on to my Church and to describe its life. I will speak of what is hidden and often overlooked.

Many lay people take their Baptism very seriously. They offer their help at the parishes, attend its services and keep their hearts loyal. They are faithful Catholics and even though there have been many scandals, they do not allow them to shake their faith.

They have received a Catholic heritage and they want to pass this on to their children and grandchildren. They have never given up the dreams placed in their hearts from the beginning. They have always believed in the Church. Even when the scandals came, they held on in the darkness and continued to serve and to believe.

Their numbers are much larger than the public perception. These Catholic will be my foundation. In so many ways, they have come through the darkness. They have believed when the darkness of events covered over their churches. Now, I am ready to use them. To these I will speak now.

Comment
So many Catholics remained faithful during the scandals.
Now Our Lady will prepare them for what is ahead.

November 14, 2014
2. New Gifts for Faithful People

To Faithful Catholics

Mary

How flourishing my Church was, so many vocations and so many faithful laity. All were gathered around me and my name was on their lips. Now, the flourishing harvest of vocations has become just a handful and many laity have walked away from their faith. This is what catches the eyes of most.

But, look! How many are still in the fields, laboring to bring forth good fruit. How many still cherish the sacraments and the Catholic devotions. Even among the young, the gift of faith flourishes in many hearts. This is where I will begin. They need only a light, a signal of hope, a direction, a new voice, clear and true, to inspire their hearts. This is why I speak.

To you who labor in the fields, who have always sought to preserve the faith in your homes and in your parishes, I know your travail. I know your sadness that many do not respond, even the members of your family. I know the darkness that you have been through, not just the personal darkness, but your dismay at all that has happened to a once glorious Church. Do not say that the Church is in ruins and decay. Within the Church is much hidden life, many people doing all that they can to preserve and pass on the ancient faith that is always new.

To you, I will speak. Read these words carefully. They will be your guide. I know the labor of your hearts and all the efforts you have made. None of them is lost, even when your words and your deeds seemingly had no effect.

Now, I call you in a different direction. Before you continue on, come into my heart. Find the new gifts that await you. Should not you, who have been faithful to my Church, be the first ones to discover the new gifts of my heart?

Comment
Our Lady accurately describes many Catholics who have been faithful to the Church, but saddened. She knows their efforts and will open to them, first of all, the gifts of her heart.

November 15, 2014
3. The Beginning Gifts

To Faithful Catholics

Mary

With the many new blessings flowing from my heart should not these faithful Catholics be the first ones to know and to receive? They already attend Mass and call upon my name. They have not abandoned their religious practices, even though others have walked away. They are confused by all that is happening in the world, but the light of faith and practice still burns within their hearts. They will be the first group to receive, the first ones to experience the outpouring of my heart. To them, I speak now.

When I come to you, when I offer you my new gifts, open wide your hearts. I am preparing you. You need these new gifts. They will begin with an invitation, an opportunity to attend a gathering, to read a book, or to join a group. Do not set this invitation aside. It is an invitation to a new way of life, to join with others on the road.

Others will not yet have this opportunity. These, too, I will prepare by special private graces. Everything that bears my name – the churches, the books, the traditional devotions will gain a hold upon you. You will find new attractions. Whatever carries my name will draw you, without any personal effort, into its power.

These are the beginning gifts. For those who accept these invitations, greater, more powerful and more lasting gifts await. All is needed to prepare for the darkness.

Comment
Our Lady is speaking first to devout Catholics,
saying that new graces await them.

November 16, 2014
4. Light for Devout Catholics

To Faithful Catholics

Mary

When all of the events begin, devout Catholics are the ones who will be bathed in my light. I must speak about this light. When darkness comes and the usual lights go out, emergency lights come on to provide safety. They do not give the fullness of light but they are sufficient to protect and sustain life.

Such are my special lights which flow from my heart and which I want to give to all. However, devout Catholics who have held fast to their faith in the midst of all that has happened will be the first to receive. Then, the graces will go forth to others. None of my lights are limited, but devout Catholics are better prepared to receive than others.

I speak now so that as these lights go forth, devout Catholics do not miss their opportunity. You must not think, "I have enough light. I am not walking in darkness." Certainly, you are not in darkness, but the darkness will come, and then you desperately need the light that I am now offering to you. How does this new light come? I will teach you.

Be attentive. Be sensitive to devotions, new and old, that would lead you to me. I will place new attractions in your hearts. Those who were always devoted to me will find a hunger and thirst for my devotions. Those who never experienced any particular attraction will realize that a new flame has been put in their heart.

Realize what I am doing. I am taking your faith, which still burns within you, and

I am giving you fresh oil for your lamps. In this way, you will have the new light that will not go out in the darkness.

<u>Comment</u>

Our Lady will give light for all. Devout Catholics are just better prepared to receive.

November 17, 2014

5. Entering Mary's Heart

To Faithful Catholics

<u>Mary</u>

The life that I will offer to these Catholics is so new that many will find it difficult to believe. They will ask, "How can this be?" Then they will see for themselves that I am pouring forth a special fire which offers helps that have never been given before.

All of these new graces are so needed because of the new problems that will suddenly arise on the earth, for which there will be no apparent solutions. My response will be taking place within the hearts of those who receive.

A new power will be released from my heart to their hearts. All will know that I have embraced them and drawn them into my heart where they are safe, even though the external turmoil increases.

I have spoken before of this invitation. My heart is like Noah's ark, but this time, the numbers are not limited. All can enter. There is plenty of space for the whole world. I must begin to teach everyone how they can enter. No one must delay. The door will remain open until the last minute, but the earlier you enter, the deeper will be the protection.

My heart has many doors, accommodated to everyone's situation and way of life. All will be able to enter.

<u>Comment</u>

Before the events begin, we must enter Mary's heart.
She will tell us what to do.

November 18, 2014

6. Preparing for Mary's Fire

To Faithful Catholics

<u>Mary</u>

I must make these new gifts, which are easily available and tell the whole world how they are received.

They are inner gifts, received into a heart that has been purified and is seeking my

225

help. The first gift begins as a new stirring, like a lonely but attractive voice that says, "Come with me. Come in this new direction. Leave behind what is familiar and be drawn into a life that feeds your spirit."

This voice will invite you to leave behind everything that soils your heart and to be generous in the things of God. The voice will point out much that must be changed. Be generous. Do not resist. All of this is the needed purifying action of the Holy Spirit.

The voice will lead you into a new style of life, with new priorities. The old will be set aside, even those attractions that were not sinful but still claimed your heart. The goal is to set you free so your spirit can respond and receive.

The voice will lead you into new waters, gentle and peaceful. You will find rest and a new kind of happiness, a contentment with what you have and a spirit of thanksgiving to God for all that he saved you from.

At this point, you are ready for the fire that comes from my heart and which I want to pour forth over the whole world. It is so easy. As your spirit seeks heavenly graces, ask specifically for my fire to be given and you will receive it. Ask time and again, "O Mary, please give me your fire." My heart will break open and the fire will pour forth.

Comment
Our Lady outlines the easy steps of being purified and of receiving her fire.

November 19, 2014
7. Preparing for the Consecration of Russia
To Faithful Catholics

Mary

The fullness of my gifts will only flow as mankind falls deeper and deeper into darkness. This will happen as the events, coordinated by Satan, unfold. At that time, a hopelessness and feeling of inevitability will come upon the human race. As Satan cleverly unfolds one part at a time, people will realize what has happened. The important events of the past led to these troubles. Mankind will see itself as cornered, with its back to the wall.

Only after these events begin, will the Church realize the great power that has been given at Fatima. At last, the Holy Father will consecrate Russia, together with all of the bishops. New lights and new hope will be released, the deepest gifts of my Immaculate Heart.

The world will not return to the way it was. Some parts will have already collapsed and many places will have been destroyed, but new life will be offered to all. This is why I must speak and explain my gifts so all can receive. Right now, I am pouring out preparatory gifts, new attractions to greater devotion. They must be received so each soul is more ready for the great gifts that will pour out after Russia is consecrated.

Comment

Our Lady explains very clearly that special graces are being given now.
These come to each one by having special devotion to her.

The Sorrows of Mary

November 20, 2014
1. Satan's Smoke in the Vatican

The Sorrows of Mary

Mary

My sorrows. These are what I must begin to share again. Sorrows lie at the center of my soul. I am the Mother of Sorrows, a role that I accepted from the beginning and which Simeon prophesied in the temple. The temple became my place of sorrows. I was wounded by Jesus' words when I found him in the temple.

My greatest sorrows are reserved for my Church, the bride of my Son. The fires of Satan have burned brightly within the Church, even in its highest offices. This smoke arises today from those who hold back the fullness of my graces.

I must teach the world. The Catholic Church is the bride of Jesus. It is his Mystical Body and enjoys the fullness of his truths and his powers. Nothing is lacking in its gifts, as it faithfully proclaims the gospel and joyfully celebrates the mysteries. I have kept it faithful for 2000 years, beginning with my work among the apostles and disciples. From the Beloved Disciple at Ephesus there were messages to the churches and the heavenly liturgies were revealed to all. The Catholic Church is deepest within me. It lies at the center of my heart and I cherish deeply the role and the power given to the Holy Father. These are the very gifts that I want to use as a light to the whole world. I will accomplish this as the events of darkness begin.

However, I must speak so the whole world and especially the Holy Father understands. Satan's smoke has reached the highest levels of the Vatican. His deceptions fill the Vatican and so many whom he has planted there. Would this not be his plan, to enter the very stronghold of the Church? This is my greatest sorrow. To overcome this, I must make alternate plans so my Church is exalted.

Comment

Our Lady speaks honestly of Satan's influence in the Vatican
that holds back the Church's full light.

November 21, 2014

2. Seeking Total Surrender

The Sorrows of Mary

Mary

Time is slipping away. The light is dimming and the darkness is growing. All of this I see so clearly and try to warn the world. Every day, there are new sorrows and no answers are found. Mankind is surrounded by evil. Satan wants a moment when the world will surrender to him and make him king. Earth will become his new kingdom. Cast out from heaven, he will at last claim what heaven so desires, an earth taken up into God's glory. God prizes earth and covets mankind which he created for his glory. Satan will so rejoice, seeking to replace Jesus as the king of earth.

Many have already surrendered. They have given themselves, heart and soul, to Satan. He has already tasted of their blood and filled them with his evils. He multiplies their numbers, equips them with powers, enlightens them with his own intelligence and sends them out to conquer the whole world for his kingdom. He is not satisfied with all the victories, big and small, which have claimed so many. He will be satisfied only with total surrender, where no vestige of light or hope remains.

Is this not the deepest sorrow of my heart? Not just to see what has already happened but also to see all that Satan plans and hopes to accomplish. So many events lie ahead. So many traps of darkness. So many places where literally the earth will open up to swallow its victims.

Every day, the number that I can save grows less and less. Once Satan grasps a soul, he quickly brings it deeper into his darkness, so the soul does not know how to respond to my light.

So, I visit the earth. I go to the homes and places where my name is invoked. I especially use these locutions. I always whisper words of encouragement: "Stay strong. Abide in the light. Let no darkness enter your heart or your home. Do not fear what is happening." To those who invoke me, I will give the strength never to surrender and even to help others not to surrender.

Comment
Our Lady reveals Satan's goal which is total surrender.
She, however, never abandons anyone who calls on her.

November 22, 2014
3. The Sacred Moment of Worldly Emptiness

The Sorrows of Mary

Mary

I see all that will come about. These events are still hidden from human eyes but soon all will be seen clearly. Human life will be changed. Many will lose hope. Severe changes will result, one after another. Hearts will be dismayed. Many will despair. Life will not be the same.

How I hate to speak those words, how much better to promise a bright and glorious future. However, that is not the road which man has chosen. He is free. He makes his daily decisions. He decides the road and the direction.

Soon, he will come to the end of the road, with seemingly nowhere to go. Many options will have been ripped from his hands. The greatness of his systems will be gone. Even what he considered his lifelines will be jeopardized and, in some instances, will no longer function. Enough will remain for people to survive, but at a much lower level than now. Such will be the reduced state of the human race.

The effects will be felt everywhere and all will admit that human life has been severely changed. That will be the moment of my coming, when the very powers of the world are muted. When the voice of the world is silenced. When men no longer listen to the sweet tunes of profitable music. When so much has been taken away from human hearts.

What a sacred moment. A door is ajar. Hearts are empty. This is when I can come and say, "Come here. Walk this way. I will save you." Blessed are those who have prepared for those times. They will see the new road.

Comment
Our Lady will use the events to speak to our hearts.

November 23, 2014
4. Gathering with Others

The Sorrows of Mary

Mary

All is not hopeless, but the road of hope will be seen only by a divine light given to groups dedicated to me. This I want to explain very deeply.

When a person receives my light, they see the need for others. They cannot walk alone. There must be others. Where are the people who believe in my messages and gather to fulfill my requests? Everywhere I have appeared, I have urged people to gather and to help one another. But the groups come and go. Many start with a burst of enthusiasm and then allow their zeal to cool.

In the year ahead, you will need a great light of hope which you can only receive if you are bonded to others in communal prayer, where all search for the road of light. If you are faithful to this regular gathering, even if it is just within your home, I will assure you of the light needed for hope. How often I have spoken of the coming darkness. A certitude grows within you that it will certainly take place. I want you also to be certain of my light in the darkness, which I can only give you if you gather as often as possible with others.

Gathering with others is the secret that I want to reveal. Personal prayer is important but my special gifts are given when people gather, when they commit themselves to join their hearts. If, when the darkness comes, you remain with others, I will constantly pour out my light and you will find the road of hope.

Comment
Our Lady reveals the way to the road of hope – to gather for prayer with others.

November 24, 2014
5. The Three Stages

The Sorrows of Mary

Mary

I am taking the Church into my own hands, just as a mother lifts into her arms a child who is endangered. I will do this in many ways. First, new devotions must spread quickly so people become more attentive. A fresh awareness must come over the Church, a widespread sense that all must return to my Immaculate Heart.

This will prepare for the next stage when the great difficulties begin, which I call "the events." People will begin to search. For many with faith, this will be a religious search and the new awareness will lead them to search for me.

Finally, there is the third stage, when by the Holy Father's consecration of Russia, I will come completely onto the world stage, offering to mankind the full gifts of my Immaculate Heart.

Then, the war will break out. Until now, there have been only "surrenders." There has been no Army of Mary because I have been kept out of the limelight. All of that will end. I will come onto the scene. All will see my actions in every part of the world. Great new devotions will spring up and be embraced by millions. It will be like a massive tsunami, but one that brings life not death.

My advice for now is, "Prepare." Take up once again the familiar devotions. I will impart to everyone a very simple trust in me and a new sense of my presence watching over each one. Let us begin to walk this road of hope.

Comment

Our Lady outlines the three stages – an awareness, events that lead us to turn to her, and her interventions after Russia is consecrated.

November 25, 2014

6. Mary's Promises to Beginners

The Sorrows of Mary

Mary

When the events begin, it will be too late. Many will find themselves unable to respond because they are bereft of any faith in supernatural help. They will not know the ways of God or how he can save them. They know only natural powers and human resources, which will totally fail them in these events. So, I must explain my help.

I am present to every person in the world. To each one, I offer my help. I do not limit my presence or my saving power. Some are keenly aware of this. They always experience my help and turn to me in every need. They also live according to the gospel teachings and are faithful to the Church. They understand my promises because they are already experiencing my presence.

Now I speak to others. Through these locutions they are beginning to grasp the need for my help. They also see my promise and my new gifts that will be needed to face the future events which will severely change the whole world.

To these I say, "You have beginning faith. Your hearts are filled with beginning light. You sense something new. Your mind has been plunged into all my promises. You see a new road which you want to walk. This road is true. The invitation is so vital. Follow these new hopes. Commit yourself to my ways. I am awakening you while there is still time. Follow these holy desires. Soon, you, too, will realize that I am always present, always helping and always leading. You have found the door to my Immaculate Heart. Enter quickly and remain there. You will be safe."

231

November 26, 2014
7. Evils Not Yet Seen

The Sorrows of Mary

Mary

Time moves on and events take control. Mankind loses power and looks on helplessly, as forces that he has released take their own path. Such is the state of the world. By so many decisions, mankind has released forces that are shaping his destiny and forming his systems. Even those who understand what is happening, have no power to control the events.

Yet, the events that I am speaking of are still hidden. They are not the same as those which fill today's headlines. They are forces imbedded in the human structures whose time has not yet come. Satan knows well the destructive powers which he long ago planted in human life, through the selfish decisions of those whose hearts he controlled.

Now, he waits for the right moment when these destructive powers will best be used. These are the sorrows of my heart which I see so clearly, future evils not yet brought forth.

My response is to visit people. I visit those with great powers so they make decisions. I visit those who hold authority in the Church, so they might be enlightened. I visit you, O reader, and I offer you special graces. Listen to what I am saying within you. Do not put off until tomorrow what you must do today. How important are the inner stirrings of your heart. Listen. Receive. Act. Tell others. Nothing is too little. I will bless every prayer and every effort.

Comment
Our Lady reveals that many future evils are not even seen.
She actively visits everyone to prepare.

The Treasures in Mary's Heart

November 27, 2014
1. Treasures Placed by Jesus

The Treasures in Mary's Heart

Mary

I want to reveal to the whole world the treasures which Jesus has placed in my heart. He began to place these riches from the first moment of my Immaculate Conception. He poured out infinite treasures during the nine months that he lived in my womb. However, it was during his mortal life that he gave me the greatest gifts.

First, I saw his tiny face and hands. Later, I heard his words, which revealed so much of his own thoughts and desires. Finally, I saw him preach and heal. Then, there was the journey to Jerusalem and his death on the cross. Every moment, his riches multiplied within me.

After his resurrection, he appeared to me and imparted his risen glory. Later, Jesus sent his Spirit on Pentecost. The Spirit abided with me all the days of my life, finally assuming me, body and soul, into heaven, where I was clothed with the sun.

I have stored up all of these riches, like a mother saving for her children. I reveal them so you can receive. We will take time. I will go slowly and explain each treasure. You are not just to listen. You must make the efforts needed to receive.

Comment
If we receive Our Lady's treasures, we will remain faithful to God's will.

November 28, 2014
2. The Heavenly Father's Decision

The Treasures in Mary's Heart

Mary

No one understands all the gifts which Jesus has placed in my Immaculate Heart. They wait there, always ready to be given away. They are the only means of man's salvation because all of Jesus' graces must pass through my hands.

The Heavenly Father has decreed a Marian Age. This began when I revealed the miraculous medal to St. Catherine Labouré (1831). Soon afterward, Pope Pius IX declared the dogma of my Immaculate Conception (1854). All was prepared for the great apparitions of Fatima (1917). The Marian Age was fully launched.

Very soon, the 100th anniversary of Fatima will take place. What has happened? Has the peace that I brought taken place? Not at all. The fires of war burn everywhere and future destruction will be greater. The heavenly Father has not released the gifts of Jesus in my heart. They lie there unopened, set aside, and not seen as important.

Instead, human beings, within and outside the Church, put forth their human solutions, which fail time and again. When they call upon heaven's help, they do not listen to the Father's answer, "I have already placed all that you need in the Immaculate Heart. I will not change my plan. Go there and find all that you need."

That is my message, also, and I will speak of these gifts, revealing all that the Father has done.

Comment

God has been very consistent. He has decreed this Marian Age
and he has no intention of changing his mind. We are the ones who must listen.

November 29, 2014
3. Waking Up!

The Treasures in Mary's Heart

Mary

My gifts do not come in any order. They pour out. Whatever is needed is given immediately. Others are held back until the person is able to receive. All is according to the Father's desire.

All must know about these gifts. They are essential for the time ahead. There will be ordinary gifts to fulfill daily duties and extraordinary gifts to face the events. Do not waste any time. You must receive now, according to my instructions.

First, you must believe. Faith comes from hearing, so I must speak. You have entered a new moment of human history. The war between Satan and the Woman Clothed with the Sun has begun. The first shots have already been fired. He has launched his offensive, but very few are aware. Others buy and sell as if nothing is happening and the world will just continue on.

We must prepare by only one means. I equip my soldiers with the most extraordinary powers to repulse Satan's attacks and to weave a wall of protection around their families and communities. What is now in place is woefully inadequate. It is outdated and ineffective. Besides, few are really interested.

So, the first gift that I pour out is an awakening. People must wake up to the new realities. Satan has chosen this time in history to launch his offensive. The heavenly Father has prepared for this moment and has placed every gift in my Immaculate

Heart. I wake you up to these realities so you do not despair at the events and so that you daily seek my gifts.

Comment

Yesterday was Black Friday, when millions did a lot of buying and selling.
People are often slow to realize that things have changed.

November 30, 2014
4. A New Life of Purity

The Treasures in Mary's Heart

Mary

The winds will blow and the rains will come, but those whose hearts are filled with my gifts will survive the great events. They will enjoy a strength and a perseverance. Nothing, absolutely nothing, that Satan hurls against them will destroy their resolve to be faithful. So, let me begin to list those powers which I am already pouring out.

Satan attacks through lust. He twists the powerful sexual drive, meant to enhance marital love, and sends it in every possible direction. Lust is a mighty river that frequently overflows its banks and destroys.

O reader, I know your own struggles with lust and I offer you the great gift of purity. Accept my gift. Ask for the continence needed for your state in life. In this way, true love will be released within you. Darkness and shame will have no power over you. The chains of lust will fall to the ground, and you will easily walk away from their grasp.

I offer you a new life, where you can rejoice in a freedom that you have never understood because lust has so limited your steps and blinded your eyes.

Come. I will lead you into a world of purity, where true love flourishes and all relationships are kept sacred. When purified of your lusts, you will enjoy peace. The former days will give way to a new glory. No one will need to teach you God's road. You will see it for yourself.

Comment

Our Lady does not condemn. She just offers a new freedom
which allows the person to respond to true love, both human and divine.

December 1, 2014
5. Extraordinary Unshakeable Faith

The Treasures in Mary's Heart

Mary

Not everyone will understand what is happening when these events begin. Many will not see any hope. Others will curse and even blaspheme. It will be the special person who will be able to see a road that leads to peace.

Hidden deeply in my heart is light, special light for the days of darkness. I will not reserve this light for special people. Everyone who now reads this locution is ready for the light. First, I must explain.

The first effect from this light is to know that I am present. This is the moment of my visitation, my coming to you just as I came to Elizabeth. I am not alone. I carry Jesus within me. Without my saying a word of explanation, Elizabeth knew the mystery: "Who am I that the mother of my Lord should come to me?"

In this great light, you, too, will know that I have come to you. I, the mother of Jesus, have come to you. You will have total faith. Nothing will shake that complete confidence. Even in the middle of the events you will stand firm, living one day at a time and having no fear of tomorrow (which is always useless). I will give this extraordinary, unshakeable faith to everyone who welcomes me as Elizabeth did.

Comment
The world's lack of faith limits Our Lady's gifts.
So, she gives them individually, to each person.

December 2, 2014
6. Believing before Seeing

The Treasures in Mary's Heart

Mary

I want to pour out my gifts like a mighty river, but why waste these waters if hearts are not ready to receive? Before everything else, I must pour out the gift of faith. O reader, how I want to stir up your faith, deepen your faith, activate your faith, so you can receive. Let us begin.

You see for yourself the problems which the world faces, unsolvable problems for a world that has few resources to respond. These problems will grow. They will multiply. They will interconnect and will evolve into greater problems which will seem totally resistant to any solution.

The Church is on the sidelines. While the world moves along its own road, the Church is a voice crying in the wilderness. Her voice is not heard in the marketplace and she brings no great power to the world stage. Will this state of affairs continue, to the total detriment of the world?

Here is where I pour out new faith. True faith is to see with supernatural eyes what cannot be seen and to believe with supernatural faith what does not yet exist.

Faith is the only way that God enters the world. Jesus became a man because I believed what I did not yet see (that the Holy Spirit would make me God's mother). I need the Holy Father and all the bishops and all the Church to see that I will come upon the world stage only when they believe. Otherwise, I sit on the sidelines and the world races to its own destruction. I want to do a new thing but I need people to believe before they see my actions.

Comment
We must believe that Our Lady will act in ways in which she has never acted before.

December 3, 2014
7. Clothing You with Light

The Treasures in Mary's Heart

Mary

Because the works of evil, the great designs of the Evil One, will increase, and because world leaders do not know to turn to me for help, I must protect those who do believe. Later, after Russia is consecrated to me and the Holy Father has turned all the eyes of the world upon my saving role, I can act in universal and visible ways. For now, I can act freely only in the hearts of those who believe. Why should I wait? Why should I leave those who believe shorn of protection?

Like a mother clothing her children for a walk in the snow, so I will clothe my children. The first piece of clothing is light. Each person will understand. They will see the ways of evil which are at the door and are everywhere. In my light, they will turn away from evil. Even more, they will remove these causes of evil from themselves and their children.

This light will also show them the road. This path is not easy to discover. Years ago, when the culture was filled with light, the roads to light were many and easy to follow. Now, they are few, hard to find, and not easy to walk. This is my promise. If you ask, I will give you the needed inner light. You will become acutely aware of the ever-expanding darkness. You will say, "I must seek the road of light." You will search. You will find others. You will also find new paths of light. Do not hesitate. Begin immediately. The inner light and the paths which you find are my gifts.

Comment
Our Lady's great lights for the whole world are delayed
but her lights for you, personally, are available now.

December 4, 2014
8. Enlightened Confidence

The Treasures in Mary's Heart

Mary

When the world comes to the edge of the cliff, what happens then? Some continue to move on and plunge to their destruction. Others are filled with panic and are paralyzed with fear. Some, having been prepared by these locutions, will say, "Mary has always spoken about this moment. She has prepared us well. We are not to fear. We must act according to her word."

How will I describe this great gift that flows from my heart right now? It is not a gift that you should receive when the world comes to the edge of the cliff. It must be received beforehand, like the oil needed for the lamps to meet the Bridegroom.

I will call this gift "enlightened confidence" because it contains two powers. The person is filled with light. They know what to do, even in the greatest darkness. They also experience no panic or anxiety. They are confident that I have prepared them and will guide them.

How do your receive this enlightened confidence? Slowly, daily. By many moments spent in my presence. By the Eucharist. By little sacrifices. By trusting me more. By choosing my ways. By removing yourself from every aspect of the world's darkness. By fidelity. By loving your family. By reading about me. By helping the poor. By living with truth. Especially, by hearing my voice speaking in your heart.

Come. We will learn together. Light brings new confidence and confidence brings greater light. They go together, like your right foot and your left foot. One step at a time, we walk this road of enlightened confidence.

Comment
What an important gift. So needed in the coming darkness.

December 5, 2014
9. Destroying Your Kingdom

The Treasures in Mary's Heart

Mary

Remain with these teachings that I have given to you. Each one contains my gifts. You will need all of these because the darkness will come from many useless solutions. This darkness will be Satanic and only the Woman can defeat him. By these teachings, I wrap you in my mantle of protection and guide you. Let me speak of both Satan's darkness and of my light.

Not since the death of my Son, Jesus, has Satan had such a control over the world. Step by step, he has plotted this moment. At times, his plans were delayed because someone, like Pope John Paul II, rose up to push back the darkness. Yet, his darkness has never been fully overcome, just pushed back and delayed. He has not been slain or bound up. He still roams the world seeking the ruin of souls. This is what lies behind all the current problems.

No one, not even the Holy Father, can destroy Satan's kingdom and rout the enemy. The Father had given that power only to me, as his first-born daughter and the mother of his Son. This is the great mystery, whose many parts I have been revealing. Keep all of this in mind. Never forget my words. They will be the only real light in the coming darkness.

Comment
Only Our Lady, wielding Jesus' power, can destroy the Evil One.

The Future, Unforeseen Events

December 6, 2014
1. The Crisis of 2015

The Future, Unforeseen Events

Mary

These words must be recorded now so all the world will know that I have issued the gravest warnings. The words must go forth, published openly, "written on the walls" so to speak, so that when they come true, all must say that I had been a true mother and did not hold back my wisdom.

This is the year of the events. Many, many dangers are present. They are already in the headlines, but I am speaking of new events, surprising events which no one foresees. This is already happening in the racial divide that is now appearing in America, when all thought that the issues had been resolved by the Civil Rights legislation. That is only the beginning of new events. These forces are already embedded in human history, forces that will divide and separate, forces that will break forth in great destruction.

The greatest events will be the collapse of the economic structures. This will lead to even more enormous problems. There will be rivalries among nations, breakups of friendly cooperation that has been in place for years. The causes of these divisions will vary but when you see various nations pulling away from each other, when you see relationships being strained and even broken, then you know that I have told you ahead of time.

All of these divisions come from the Evil One. The divisions are not the final steps, but they prepare for greater problems. When nations are together in peace, they can overcome and work out difficult situations. When they are separated by divisions, they cannot adequately respond to new crises, those which they did not foresee.

Comment
In the past, Our Lady has spoken of the Arab revolutions, the problems of Syria, Russia, Ukraine and ISIS. These are now seen by all. They are evident. She now begins to speak of what cannot be seen.

December 7, 2014
2. Russia Destabilizing the European Economy
The Future, Unforeseen Events

Mary

I plunge you into the great mysteries and reveal all that is possible because I can no longer hold these events in my heart. Like a sorrowing mother, I must speak to relieve the burdens.

Russia will continue to persecute my people in the Ukraine. The sanctions will not turn Putin back. Even though they inflict great wounds, he will absorb the punishment, like a fighter who will not give up,

Russia will become like Syria, a constant source of disruption. However, something even deeper is happening. Just as the Syrian revolution has destabilized the Middle East because it has perdured for many years, so will Russia become to Europe. Russia had become an important part of the European economy. President Obama insists upon economic sanctions and refuses to aid the Ukraine militarily. He is weakening the European economies. This is the long-term fallout from the sanctions, which will have many repercussions as other problems come forth this year.

All of this is not foreseen, but I see Satan's plan all too clearly. He hides his real goals and gets nations to walk along his paths. This year it will be step by step, one event at a time with each event linked closely to what has happened and will happen.

Man's intellect is no match for his. Human solutions are like paper walls placed in his fires. Only the Woman Clothed with the Sun knows the true path to peace and I am trying to enlighten the world.

Comment

Without heaven's light, human solutions only play into Satan's hands.

December 8, 2014

3. The First Decisions of Human History

The Future, Unforeseen Events

Mary

I enter into these coming events with the sorrow of a mother. My one goal is to protect my children. First, I must have their attention to instruct them. Second, I must show them the path to safety and peace. Third, I must act in history, forming the events and shaping them. This is what I want to explain – the forces present in human history and how I intervene.

The heavenly Father created the world and the human person. With that decision, human history began. Time had already existed but there had never been a human history, a history of free, intelligent brings living on earth. Earth was not God's first creation. Angels already existed and the angelic decision of "yes" or "no" had already been made.

As human history opens, the first parents are beloved by God. They will be the source of all other human beings that will come forth. This is not true of angels, for each comes totally and directly from God's hand.

Imagine the importance of this first man and woman, the font of all human life. Their decisions were so important. They had the ability to pass on spiritual life, the riches placed in their own hearts. But this did not happen. Satan stole these riches. They surrendered them so easily. These were the first decisions of human history.

Comment

Our Lady wants us to understand the forces of human history.

December 9, 2014

4. The Shattered Dream

The Future, Unforeseen Events

Mary

Once sin entered the world, the Father's plan was shattered into a million pieces. All that he dreamed and all the blessings he wanted to bestow had been lost. How would he restore the gift? He chose a woman. She would be the new Eve, the mother of the living (Gen. 3:15). This was the Father's plan from the beginning. What I am teaching is based upon the ancient promise which is now coming into reality before your very eyes.

Yes, before your very eyes! You will see these events and understand where they come from. They are manifestations of sins which have been buried within human history for centuries. Now is the time for them to come forth. They come forth so they can be purged, like a human body suffering from a great fever.

Who will guide poor humanity through these manifestations? I am the physician, a mother bending over her sick child, at once comforting and healing, planning each step until the illness is purged.

Remember my words and you will understand this coming year. I will be at the bedside of mankind until he is well again. Blessed are those who see, who believe, and who know to seek my comfort.

Comment
With all of man's sins, there must be a purging.
Our Lady promises her help in these events.

December 10, 2014
5. Satan's Traps

The Future, Unforeseen Events

Mary

"I must tell my children. I must warn my children. I must protect my children." These are a mother's thoughts when she learns of dangers. They are my feelings that lead me to pour out these words.

World leaders do not act in faith. People, also, do not allow faith to illumine their decisions. All is done from the human intellect, which casts a very shallow light. It sees only the surface and never penetrates. It cannot perceive the forces buried in human hearts nor can it confront evil. Decisions which arise from expediency cause a thousand missteps and lead into Satan's traps.

All will become so evident, like an army which has been cornered because of the foolishness of its generals. Day by day, the trap is set and the world, enticed by false goals, eagerly enters. A moment will come when the trap is closed and the world will see itself captured by forces that are suddenly and surprisingly released. All is clear to my vision – the time, the moment, the places, the causes and the results.

Like a mother, all I can say is, "Stay close to me. The forces are too complex for me to give you directions. But if you stay with me, I will keep you safe. Now is not the time to wander. Do not set aside the graces I give you today." The time is short and there is so little opposition to slow down Satan's timetable. He waits only because he sees greater opportunities if he does not rush ahead. Do not be fooled by the delay. He wants to entrap the whole world and is merely waiting until he has greater control over a few important centers of power.

Comment
Our Lady warns us. People often judge a delay as if it will never take place.

December 11, 2014
6. Always Saying "Tomorrow"
The Future, Unforeseen Events

Mary

From all of these events, a great gift will come forth. Mankind will be humbled because the foolishness that seemed like wisdom will be exposed. As each of the events happen, people will ask, "Why did we build our house on sand?" and "Why did we not walk in truth?" Debts are postponed as if tomorrow does not come. Yet, tomorrow is quickly becoming today, and the future is becoming now.

This is today's theme. The economic system has been built on a million tomorrows. Everything will get paid tomorrow and the burden of debt grows. Prosperity reigns because no one pays for it. All is postponed. Credit flows like the flood of an overflowing ocean.

How long until the crash? It is constantly postponed by measures that will only multiply the problems when they come. "Not on my watch," say the political leaders, so they pass the debt on to future generations, who are ill-prepared for any acts of saving money.

Now, I must speak from my heart. The debts grow, not just in one country but in many at once. They all accumulate. The weight quickly becomes too much to bear. The breakthrough happens, small at first. However, so many economies are weak and all are interconnected, that the small beginnings lead to unforeseeable results. Suddenly comes the collapse, which no one could have foreseen and for which there are only a few inadequate answers.

Mankind will go on from there, constantly trying to solve its problems by the light of reason, believing that faith has nothing to do with economics. Yet, it is the lack of faith in God's ways that has led mankind on these roads in the first place.

At this time, I will still be on the sidelines. Other events will have to occur before I will be fully invoked by the Church. Yet, that day of consecrating Russia to my Immaculate Heart will take place, although it will be late.

Comment
Without making decisions in the light of faith, man inevitably builds false systems.

December 12, 2014
7. New Light for the Darkness

The Future, Unforeseen Events

Mary

Mankind must be washed, cleansed and purified. Otherwise, he cannot receive the great graces that are stored in my Immaculate Heart. If mankind turns to me, a way will open up for this purification to occur quickly and even with a great joy. Do I not know the ways of good and evil? Has not the heavenly Father filled me with wisdom? Am I not trying to pour out this light upon all?

I will not allow anyone who turns to me to be lost. When the events begin, I will gather them into the secret recesses of my heart. They will find others also gathered there and together, they will persevere.

So much will change. The mighty and the strong will find great difficulty in coping, but the little ones will enjoy my protection. Let these words be embedded in your hearts, "Our mother, filled with wisdom, can guide us through the darkness."

So much is hidden from your eyes. That is why you need a heavenly mother to guide your steps. In the events that lie ahead, many who are powerful and rich will not know what to do. But, the little ones whom I guide will walk in the greatest light.

All that I ask of you is to walk in truth. In your life right now are pockets of darkness, the little lies that allow you to make selfish decisions. Are you ready for the full light? Can you walk in perfect light? Of course you can because I will lead you. When the events begin, you will be guided by this new light which I give you today.

Comment
Our Lady promises light and asks us to reject any darkness in our lives.

December 13, 2014
8. These Words Prepare You

The Future, Unforeseen Events

Mary

When the events take place, people will see that my words are true. They will have great faith and prepared hearts. Right now, you have no need for the special words. The purpose of speaking now is to prepare you to have faith so you will believe my future words. Right now, your lives continue on as usual and you do not need my special words, which I reserve for the darkness.

These events have no exact timetable because they do not come from God. They result from evil embedded into human history and into human hearts, which can freely choose. If people choose prayer and repentance, the effects will be less and will come later. If people choose selfish goals and sins, the effects will be greater and come sooner. The events will reflect the sins of mankind. God will not cause them.

By these little locutions, I have prepared all who believe. A series of events will occur that will change much of human life. By telling you ahead of time, I give you faith so that, in the middle of the events, you will believe my daily words and I can lead you. Peace. Always peace. The Lord is near.

Comment
Our Lady sums up these teachings and explains that God does not cause evil.

The Torch of Faith

December 14, 2014
1. Retrieving Abandoned Lights

The Torch of Faith

Mary

I would bathe the world in quite different events. History does not have just one road, a path that leads only into darkness. That was the only road before Jesus came. Now, a new path lies before mankind.

Unfortunately, that path has been concealed and covered over. People have set aside their light of faith. It lies abandoned by the wayside. They have been captured by all that is new, all the promises of a world built upon science.

I have picked up all these abandoned lights of faith. They are not lost forever. I have saved them in my heart, waiting for the moment when the events of darkness shatter the false illusions which have captured so many.

That moment will come. The great illusions that science can produce a heaven on earth without the help of faith will be broken. Many will submit totally to despair. Others will seek their lost torch of faith. They will find it kept safely in my heart.

Why not seek it now? Why wait until the dangers encircle the earth? That is what I will explain now. O reader, I offer to you a new torch of faith. I will place it quickly in your heart. You will cherish it and will never abandon it again. Hold on to this light and it will never go out. You will need it for the darkness.

Comment
Our Lady invites us to a different path
which can be seen only by the torch of faith.

December 15, 2014
2. What God Did for Our Lady

The Torch of Faith

Mary

I want to reveal every secret in my heart. Only in this way, will the world enjoy enough light to overcome the darkness. I will begin with all that God did for me.

I am joined to God's Son, more than any mother to any child. This union comes from both nature and grace. I am joined by maternal love, the greatest love any mother has for a child. I am also joined to Jesus by my Immaculate Conception. From the very first instant of my existence, Jesus flooded me with his Holy Spirit. Not one inch, not one hair's breadth separated us. No other creature is so intimately joined to Jesus. The Father gave to Jesus' humanity (which he received from me) all the divine powers. Jesus shared with me every possible gift. "I will use you as my instrument," said Jesus.

Can the Father do this? Can He bring a woman so close to himself through the humanity that the Spirit formed in her, that He makes her an instrument of all his graces? Who dares to say that God cannot do this while at the same time allowing me to be a creature, infinitely below Him? Once this is understood, I can reveal all my secrets.

Comment
Our Lady sets the stage for great inner revelations.

December 16, 2014
3. The Heavenly Fire's Powers

The Torch of Faith

Mary

There are two fires. You see the fires of hell, which lead mankind to wars and destruction. Still hidden are my fires of heaven. Fire should be fought with fire, but until now the fires of heaven burn only in my heart. How I long to pour out these fires upon the whole earth.

This heavenly fire has three gifts. What can this heavenly fire do? Love is its greatest gift and will be so much needed when the events begin. In those days, people must love one another and care for one another. People will experience gigantic losses and will need a support that no government can provide. Only love from others will supply their needs.

This fire also gives light. So much will be different. The former wisdom will not suffice. New lights, new directions, and new initiatives will be needed that can only come from my fire.

Finally, my fire will protect. This is the most important. As Satan unleashes these events, one by one, the usual walls that protect society will crumble. Satan will be like an enemy attacking a city which he can enter easily. I will surround every person who calls on me, with my fire of protection. Although the walls collapse I will keep them safe, individually and collectively, privately and especially as they gather.

Comment
Our Lady reveals the three special powers of her fire.

December 17, 2014
4. Putin Is Dangerous

The Torch of Faith

Mary

I open up all my heart to the whole world. I hold back none of my vision nor any of my secrets because the time is so short.

For years, I have been appearing to chosen souls, revealing to the world through them the teachings needed for the future trials. These are well known and I invite the reader to study my revelations, especially at Fatima. You will see that in these present locutions, I am not saying anything new. The warnings have been on the table for decades. Yet, so many have not heeded my words.

The Fatima warnings spoke of future events and now, almost 100 years later, they have not yet happened. My words now are that the time is very short. The events are on the horizon. Although they have not yet happened, the events are beginning to come to the surface. Putin is at the center of some of these events. He himself has no set plan. He is totally guided by the Evil One who is always using him to disrupt. Putin is dangerous because he has so many resources at his disposal and because he is willing to risk everything to regain Russia's former stature.

<u>Comment</u>

Our Lady reveals two secrets –
that the events she has spoken of at Fatima are close
and that some of these events are linked to Putin.

December 18, 2014

5. Stop Limiting Our Lady's Power

The Torch of Faith

<u>Mary</u>

Stop limiting my love. Stop limiting my power. Stop limiting my presence! I speak so you throw off these limits to your faith. The heavenly Father has placed every gift in my heart. Do not be surprised at this. Did He not place His only Son in my womb? Did He not overshadow me with His Holy Spirit? Now, He has given me a command to be with the world in a new way. This is easy to explain.

The Word, the eternal Son of the Father, was always with the world. Through Him, all things were (Jn. 1:13). But in the fullness of time, the Word became flesh. This was according to the Father's will. The Son was told to be with the world in a new way.

Now, at this time and at this moment in world history, the Father has commanded me to come to the world in a new way, so He can reveal treasures that He has hidden in my Immaculate Heart and to release new powers that have never been given before.

All of this is the Father's plan to aid the world as it enters a time of great tribulations. I speak these words now as promises waiting to be fulfilled. The time is now but the gifts must wait until people stop limiting my love, my power and my presence.

All will break through, like fresh streams, surprising everyone. When this happens, you must believe. You must go and drink from those new streams. Otherwise, the Father's great gifts will be wasted.

<u>Comment</u>

Our Lady explains well how God always has new ideas of how to intervene.
The intervention is effective only if people believe
and take advantage of the new streams.

December 19, 2014
6. The World's Communication Systems

The Torch of Faith

Mary

There are no limits and there are no walls – all have access to the unlimited riches of my heart. Why hold back? Why try to save for the future when the future is now? Satan is ready to put everything on the table, to release all the evil he has stored up for 2000 years. Why, then, should I do less? Why should I hold back my gifts? This is the moment. All comes to a flashpoint. Suddenly and without warning. A breakthrough here. Another there. Suddenly, many at once, all interconnected, all planned by a great intellect that is totally saturated in evil.

Why, then, should I hold back? Why would I not give every power and every protection to my children? This will surprise Satan. He does not know these gifts which are hidden in my heart. He has never faced them before. They will puzzle and confuse him. They will blunt his powers. In spite of the destruction, people will not despair. They will not give up.

I am speaking very clearly. The world has built very sophisticated and complicated systems which can easily be rendered powerless. The world now depends on those systems, like a sick person dependent on machines to sustain his life. What if these systems are rendered powerless? What will result? Widespread confusion, turmoil and despair. That is why I reveal these new gifts. My children will be protected, but only in my Immaculate Heart. Go there and stay there. Let the churches be open for my people to come. Let the priests, religious and lay ministers be there to pray with them. I will be there. How much I want my priests and people to gather! This is not the time to scatter. I have spoken clearly enough for now. As the events get closer, my words will become sharper and more pointed.

Comment
Our Lady is obviously speaking about confusion and disruption
that will be caused by failure in the worldwide systems of communication.

December 20, 2014
7. The Moment of the Great Battle

The Torch of Faith

Mary

The army of darkness gathers on the horizon. However, the daylight has not yet arrived and they cannot be seen. This allows the forces of evil to spread out according to their plan. They take strategic positions so that when the attacks begin there will be no escape. They will capture and control. Their goal is to inflict sufferings upon mankind, so that despair and helplessness seize the hearts of all. In this way, their victory will be more complete. They know what they wish to accomplish. They want to cut mankind off from the Creator and to cast everyone into disbelief. They are not interested in capturing material earth but in claiming immortal souls.

They want to destroy man's spirit and cut him off from his life-giving relationship to Jesus and the power of the resurrection. Once that occurs, he will have successfully overcome the defeat he suffered when Jesus died on the cross. How he has waited for this moment! Through all the ages, he has planned this. Anyone believing that these are normal times and normal problems, is deceived. This is the moment of the great battle, when Satan uses his entire army. The battle will be fierce. The struggle an immense one. The victory great; but only with my help can anyone be saved.

Comment
Wake up! Future events will not just be the usual problems.
A spiritual war will break out with grave consequences for human history.

Time and Eternity

December 21, 2014
1. Today Vanishing into Tomorrow

Time and Eternity

Mary

Human life takes place within time. One moment opens out into the next in an endless series. No one can stop this process because God has created time. Man, therefore, is helpless. He can record time and assign a date to today, but he cannot stop today from vanishing and giving way to tomorrow.

A person who appreciates the passing nature of earth and the short moment of every life can grasp what I am saying. A world which lives by faith understands that no one can hold on to today. No one can build a permanent earthly city.

A world without faith is foolish and spends all of its time trying to build permanency upon the shifting sands of time. Satan uses this foolishness to build his cities and gather his armies. He has brought human history to this point where humanity has left behind the light of eternity and has chosen the darkness of time.

How many false beliefs flow from this foolishness, as if time heals all wounds, or that problems will be solved in due time, or that time is a cycle in which darkness is always followed by light and problems always have solutions.

My message is clear. Time is not an inevitable cycle. Time is a story, with man's free will playing an important role. Time is a road and man has chosen the road of darkness. The light does not come automatically, like day following night. At this present time, humanity is walking a road that is so dark, it will lead to permanent and disastrous changes to earth. I cannot and will not allow that to happen, but man must stop thinking about the passing goals of time and begin to seek the changeless riches of eternity. To act otherwise is complete and total foolishness. The greatest fools are the rich and the powerful.

Comment
Man's thinking is totally confused when he takes no account
that everything on earth passes away.

December 22, 2014
2. Manifesting Her Presence

Time and Eternity

Mary

All history is in my hands. I know the movements of every heart and of every event. I see all that has happened and all that will happen. Nothing is determined. Events are shaped by human decisions. This was God's plan from the beginning.

I am not a passive spectator, who merely watches the drama unfold. I am the Woman Clothed with the Sun who has power to intervene. I am part of human history. I was born into the world and lived in the world as everyone else.

My role now is more extensive and, in the Father's plan, I must assume greater and greater responsibilities for the safety and protection of humanity. I have been announcing this plan for years, but now it its taking place, right before your eyes.

As one event leads to another, as one problem begets greater ones, you can see the importance of my coming on the scene, of making myself known, of lifting up my special son and of manifesting my presence all over the world.

Right now, I am only interested in you, the reader. I have led you to these locutions and I want to give you extraordinary blessings. Others, who do not know me, will receive later. You will receive now. You do not understand everything but you want to receive. You have read all of my promises. You have studied my ways. Most important, you believe. Why should I delay? You are prepared to receive.

Close your eyes. I am with you. Experience my presence. Do not move. Stay still until the gift is complete. Repeat this often. Each time, I will act more deeply within you.

Comment
Our Lady does not wait. You, O reader, are ready to receive.
Do so, again and again.

December 23, 2014
3. The Year 2015

Time and Eternity

Mary

See what springs forth, surprising waters which no one can imagine. These waters are still hidden and can only be explained when they come to light and are seen by all. I do not hold back my words but speak as clearly as possible.

2014 has been a year of turmoil, of the appearance of many evils. However, life has continued on. The struggles are confined to certain areas of the world or to certain parts of society. The protecting walls built by man to assure a normal life have remained in place. There have been no breakthroughs.

2015 will be quite different. Even in the first six months of the year, new and different events will break through. However, not to the extent that life is totally disrupted. It will seem like these problems have been adequately responded to so that normal life can continue, even though limited.

In the Fall, however, the great problems will break forth and all will see that human life has seriously changed. This will be the mood as the year comes to an end.

All of these events will serve a purpose. They will awaken the Church that it needs my help, and those voices which have been declaring that the messages of Fatima must be studied more closely will be given a greater hearing.

Comment
2015 will awaken the world to the importance of Fatima.

December 24, 2014
4. One Hundred Years of Fatima

Time and Eternity

252

Mary

When the waters burst forth, who will tell them where to go? They will have a mind of their own, going where Satan has plotted for so long. They will be released at different times and different places. Such will be the coming year of 2015.

I will plot out this year for you. In the early months, new flood waters will break through. There will be human responses that seemingly work for a time, limiting the effects. It is only in the latter months of the year that the great floods come, and continue for the first half of 2016.

By July 2016, the world will see what has happened. On July 13, 2016 will begin the one-hundredth year of my speaking about the consecration of Russia. How important will be that year, leading up to the one-hundredth anniversary of my appearing at Fatima (2017).

As these flood waters rise, let the voice of Fatima grow louder in your ears. What other voice should you listen to?

Comment
To speak and not to be heeded for 100 years is being very patient.

December 25, 2014
5. The Spurned Gift of Fatima

Time and Eternity

Mary

As the days and the months stretch forth, the mysteries will be seen by all. In the next few years, leading up to the 100th anniversary of Fatima, all will be revealed. The mysteries of evil buried within human history and human hearts will slowly come to the surface.

In the beginning, many will see these events in the old perspective. However, as they continue to surface, the eyes of many will be opened, especially the eyes of the Church and of the Holy Father. It is no coincidence that these events will occur as the anniversary approaches.

Should not this 100th anniversary (1917-2017) be a great time of rejoicing, a time when the Fatima gift is poured out in its fullness? That was my plan. This entire century was meant to be 100 years of blessings, all leading up to the anniversary. A blessing that has been rejected becomes an accusation. A gift spurned becomes a great issue.

If the Church and the world had only listened, if they had fully welcomed the Fatima gift, there would have been no World War II, no atomic bomb, no arms race, no Cold War. Russia would have been converted. A great period of peace would have begun and the whole world would know that the 100th anniversary would become a time of the greatest blessings.

Now, the anniversary looms on the horizon as an unfulfilled promise, rejected by those who should have had faith. What will I do? What will happen in these next 2 ½ years? This is not settled. However, the quicker the Church fully responds to Fatima, and as devotion to the Woman Clothed with the Sun multiplies, the blessings will come. Otherwise, Fatima remains a gift that is still rejected.

Comment
Our Lady gives a clear timetable, an explanation of the causes
of twentieth century destruction and a path to peace.

December 26, 2014
6. New Powers Flooding Forth

Time and Eternity

Mary

Some powers that shake the existing order have already been released. These prepare the way. They occupy and distract mankind who then cannot see the greater difficulties which lie ahead. Currently, the world focuses upon the external threats of terrorism and Russia, while totally ignoring the internal problems of morality, abortion (which kills far more than all the terrorists), and spending.

2015 will see not just the continuation and expansion of the 2014 problems, but new powers that break forth. These are more internal to economic systems and the daily life, new leaks and new breakdowns in society, new divisions among people. Governments will be exhausted, unable to adequately respond. The 2014 strains upon their resources will have weakened their ability.

All will stretch and stretch until the resources cannot stretch any more. At that moment, comes the breakthrough, the flooding where no one suspected, for who can foresee the path of a flood?

What voices will be raised to give light? Who will be able to guide the world on these dark hours? In this very darkness, my light will shine. Do not wait. Time spent in devotion prepares the soil. The effects in coming together in my name are indispensable.

Comment
Our Lady does not speak of external causes
but internal difficulties built into our systems.

December 27, 2014
7. The New Year

Time and Eternity

Mary

How many events will flow forth this coming year. They will be linked, one to another. Yet, at the same time, they will flow from the free choices of humanity. This is the great mystery. Time opens out. Day follows day. Time gives each person a chance to decide, one decision after another.

Some persons, however, hold great power and their decisions affect millions. Also, ideas, such as terrorism, dominate many hearts at once so that thousands act in unison. Systems have been built and nations work within these systems.

Human life is complex and each day it depends upon many factors for its very existence. Whole nations can be wiped out and grave crises suddenly arise. This is the picture of life upon earth. Time moves on and the world is subjected to many forces that bring about change.

A new year is about to begin. As far as time is concerned, 2014 will flow quite unnoticed into 2015. The early days of the New Year will flow as if it were 2014, but not for long. 2015 will be much different. There will not be continuity, but a breaking off. There will not be a smooth flow, but troubled waters. There will be war in places that are now enjoying peace, and instability in nations that seemed to be strong.

A shaking will take place, followed by a settling. Then a second shaking that will be more serious. By the end of the year, life will be much different. Even as 2016 opens, the full battle between Satan and the Woman will not have been fought.

Comment
Our Lady tries to prepare us for the next few years that lie ahead.

December 28, 2014
8. The Blessings of the 100th Anniversary

Time and Eternity

Mary

As the new year begins, the events will happen slowly. Most importantly, people will not recognize their importance or how these events prepare the way for others. The events will be new and surprising sources of unrest and breakdowns.

Even as it becomes evident that this new reality will not pass quickly, people will still not grasp the importance of this year. Only toward the end of the year will the events take place that will seriously change the existing structures. Even in these cases, people will not see clearly. They will believe that the change is temporary and can be rolled back.

Only as the year ends, will people see the decisiveness of these events. Even here, their full force will not have been released, for there will be the years leading up to the 100th anniversary of Fatima.

I continually see these coming years in the light of that anniversary. A while ago, the world focused on 2000 and the new millennium. Human life moved into the new millennium without any serious change. The 100th anniversary of Fatima will be quite different because I will not abandon my children or my Church.

Comment

*Our Lady speaks of new difficulties that are ahead
as well as the special blessings of Fatima in 2017.*

December 29, 2014
9. Opening the Fatima Gift

Time and Eternity

Mary

In the beginning, many will be confused, wondering why many opportunities have been cut off. This is the first stage. Then, they will see that the wounds to society are even deeper and that life itself is endangered. This will be the progression of events in the next few years leading up to the 100 years of Fatima revelations.

Mankind need not walk that path. Another is available, a true path to peace, the path of Fatima. All must read the story of the three children, of the appearances and of my requests. There is also the great promise, "In the end, my Immaculate Heart will triumph." It will be late, but Russia will be consecrated.

Do not wait. Consecrate yourself and your family. Read. Learn. Live the Fatima message. Fatima is God's gift, the short cut, the easy way. Fatima is filled with my love and my tenderness. I visited the earth to protect you. I spoke so you might listen. I gave signs so you would believe. I did all of this for you. Please, open my Fatima gift.

Comment

The Church must fully open the Fatima gift but you can open your gift immediately.

December 30, 2014
10. A Summary of Teaching

Time and Eternity

Mary

I have raised up these locutions and in these few years, many have seen their value. This was to prepare their hearts and show them that my words will guide them. Filled with this light, they know much about human history. I have clearly taught the following:

1. Human history is a battle for souls and cannot be understood merely by reason.
2. This battle is between light and darkness. The great victory of Jesus took place on the cross.
3. For 2000 years, Satan has regrouped his forces and has put his plan in place through human beings who cooperate with him.
4. I foresaw that this battle would come to its greatest moments, so I appeared at Fatima to defeat Satan.
5. This defeat has obviously not happened because the responses to my requests were not lived out, causing the world to be plunged into a greater war and then constant conflicts.
6. Mankind is now entering a very dangerous time. The 100th anniversary of Fatima is a signal moment. Keep your eyes on that date. It can still be a moment of great victory.
7. I will continue to speak each day in the coming year. I will not hold back my words. My people need to know the secrets of my heart and its desires.

Now, I must take you on a new path, a road of strength and fortitude, a road of firmness and fidelity.

Comment
Our Lady sums up her recent teachings.

Dec 31, 2014

11. Russia Will Be Consecrated in 2016

Time and Eternity

Mary

The decisions are made. The story of this year is written. The book is closed, only to open quickly. Time does not stop, not for a single moment, like an unending stream. Mankind lives one moment at a time, able to see the past and experience the present, but incapable of seeing what lies ahead in 2015.

This year will be filled with wrong roads and terrible decisions, all because man's heart is so separated from God's will. A rude awakening awaits. Severe jolts of great warnings. Who will heed the message? Who will even know the message? That is why I speak. What good are chastisements unless accompanied by a message that shows the way to mercy?

The chastisements will come, inflicted by man himself, who holds great destructive powers in his grasp. Some of these will be warning blasts which signal deeper troubles ahead. In the long series of these events, there will always be my clear voice, showing the way. During 2015, my voice will grow much stronger. The urgency of my message will be seen. However, Russia will not be consecrated to my Immaculate Heart. Even so, as these events occur, a great stirring will begin in the Church, which will prepare for Russia's consecration in 2016.

Comment
Our Lady has often spoken about Russia's consecration,
but this is the first time she has given any date.

Made in the USA
Middletown, DE
14 August 2015